Summary of Contents

BUILD MOBILE WEBSITES AND APPS FOR SMART DEVICES

BY EARLE CASTLEDINE
MYLES EFTOS
MAX WHEELER

Build Mobile Websites and Apps for Smart Devices

by Earle Castledine, Myles Eftos, and Max Wheeler

Program Director: Lisa Lang
Technical Editor: Louis Simoneau
Expert Reviewer: Peter-Paul Koch
Printing History:
First Edition: June 2011

Indexer: Michele Combs
Editor: Kelly Steele
Cover Design: Alex Walker

Notice of Rights

Notice of Liability

Trademark Notice

Published by SitePoint Pty. Ltd.

48 Cambridge Street, Collingwood
VIC 3066 Australia
Web: www.sitepoint.com
Email: business@sitepoint.com

ISBN 978-0-9870908-4-3
Printed and bound in the United States of America

About Earle Castledine

Sporting a Masters in Information Technology and a lifetime of experience on the Web of Hard Knocks, Earle Castledine (aka Mr Speaker) holds an interest in everything computery. Raised in the wild by various 8-bit home computers, he settled in the Internet during the mid-nineties and has been working there ever since.

He is currently contributing towards JavaScript's world domination plans, creating Mobile Web Applications, developing snazzy frameworks, and drinking *vin rouge* with some super-smart guys at Zenexity in Paris.

As co-creator of the client-side opus TurnTubelist (http://www.turntubelist.com/), as well as countless web-based experiments, Earle recognizes the Internet not as a lubricant for social change, but as a vehicle for unleashing frivolous ECMAScript gadgets and interesting time-wasting technologies.

About Myles Eftos

Myles Eftos is a Perth-based web developer who feels just as at home building INNER JOINS as calculating the specificity of CSS selectors. He has worked in all the major web languages, his weapon of choice being Ruby on Rails—although he's found himself doing more front-end development in JavaScript, HTML, and CSS.

Under the moniker of MadPilot Productions (http://www.madpilot.com.au), he has worked on a number of applications such as 88 Miles (http://www.88miles.net). This also includes apps for the iPhone and iPad using PhoneGap, such as the popular Counter Culture (http://www.counterculturapp.com).

He is rather excited that JavaScript is finally receiving the kudos it deserves as a serious language.

About Max Wheeler

An interaction designer, Max Wheeler believes interactive media should function as beautifully as it looks. Currently residing in Canberra, Australia, he works with Icelab (http://icelab.com.au/), a media-agnostic design agency filled with nice, well-caffeinated people. Aside from client work, Icelab's projects include the community-oriented Decaf Sucks and real estate startup RentMonkey.

When Max is not designing or building for the Web, he takes photographs, travels the world, plays Ultimate frisbee for Australia, and drinks twice the daily recommended intake of espresso. On occasion, he's been known to drop in at Web Directions South to speak about building mobile web applications.

About the Expert Reviewer

Peter-Paul Koch is a mobile platform strategist, consultant, and trainer in Amsterdam, the Netherlands. ppk (as he is universally known on the Web) specializes in HTML, CSS, JavaScript, and browser compatibility. He has earned international renown with his browser-compatibility research, and publications such as http://www.quirksmode.org/blog. A frequent speaker at conferences, ppk founded Fronteers—the Dutch association of front-end professionals—and advises browser vendors on their implementation of web standards. In 2009, ppk shifted from desktop browsers and sites to the mobile web, and discovered that mobile devices are in more need of description than their desktop counterparts. He has set himself to the task.

About SitePoint

SitePoint specializes in publishing fun, practical, and easy-to-understand content for web professionals. Visit http://www.sitepoint.com/ to access our blogs, books, newsletters, articles, and community forums.

For Amy

—Earle

For Giovanna

—Myles

For Lexi and Frank

—Max

Table of Contents

Preface

It's the year 1995, and you're waiting for an email to download to your state-of-the-art 486 personal computer. Hundreds of megabytes of storage, 16 megabytes of memory, and 256 glorious colors on screen. Suddenly, there's a flash of light in the corner of the room, and You—from the future—appear in a time machine. Future You emerges from the mist, and slowly hands you a slick, handheld device. Your eyes widen as you gaze upon the high-resolution display panel. *This* is your internet now: always on, always with you. High-bandwidth, beautifully smooth animations, stunning visual effects. No `<blink>` tags.

The Web (or at least, our experience of it) has been slowly but steadily evolving and improving since it hit mainstream consciousness late last century. However, the last few years have seen a revolutionary shift in how we consume—and produce—information: the mobile web. It's more than a "smaller," portable web—it's a fundamental change in how people interact with each other and with your products. Mobile device ubiquity, combined with the openness of the Web, have sparked the imaginations of both consumers and inventors.

The benefits of the old Web are still with us. We can buy tickets or pay bills … only now we can do it on the train, or in the bathroom! But even more interesting are the new possibilities opening up to us. When we combine today's hardware with the funky new HTML5 APIs (and some good ol' fashion web know-how), we can start to mash up the Internet with our real lives—merging the Web with our immediate surroundings, having relevant data in the palm of our hand when we need it most, and being able to contribute responses and feedback instantly.

Throughout this book, we'll learn how to make the transition from a clunky old website (you know we still love you!) to a shiny, sexy, mobile site. We will then look at the fine art of *app-ifying* our sites to behave like a mobile application, by integrating some of the fantastic HTML5 APIs that are becoming available to us: geolocation, local storage, accelerometers, and more. And finally, we take our web applications head to head with the big guys: bridging the gap between the open Web and the seductive (and potentially lucrative) world of the native application.

At the end of the book, you'll not only have the skills to create mobile web applications—you'll have become part of the most exciting and important development in computing since the Internet itself: the mobile web. A field filled with futuristic geolocatable, gyroscope-enabled gadgets that get cooler every day—a field where the best ideas and most innovative applications are still in the future … it's just up to us to invent them!

Who Should Read This Book

This book is aimed at web developers who want to learn how to build sites and apps that take advantage of the functionality available in the latest generation of mobile devices, including smartphones and tablets. You should already have intermediate knowledge of HTML, CSS, and JavaScript, as we won't be spending any time covering the basics of those topics; instead, we'll be focusing on what's relevant for the mobile context. It will include some HTML5 and CSS3, but don't worry if you're unfamiliar with these new standards—anything we use that's either new or uncommon will be explained in greater detail.

What's in This Book

This book features eight chapters and one appendix. Most chapters follow on from each other, so you're more likely to benefit from reading them in sequence. Feel free to skip sections, though, if you only need a refresher on a particular topic.

Chapter 1: *Introduction to Mobile Web Design*
We'll start by covering what designing for mobile devices means. You'll be guided through the process of designing and building a mobile web application, including what needs to be considered when producing for a mobile context. Although we'll focus primarily on designing for smartphones, much of the advice provided can apply to any form of mobile device.

Chapter 2: *Design for Mobile*
Naturally, we want to deliver the best content and experience to our users, but what's key for mobile applications is the *context* in which users will access that information. In this chapter, we'll address how this influences our role as web developers and designers, and what changes we need to make.

Chapter 3: *Markup for Mobile*
In this chapter, we'll focus on the HTML5 and CSS3 features we'll employ to create mobile web apps using standards-based web development techniques. A page with well-structured HTML and clean markup will display and be usable on any device, be it desktop or mobile.

Chapter 4: *Mobile Web Apps*
This is where we make our mobile website more interactive by turning it into an application to sell in the app marketplaces. We'll recreate native behaviors in a web setting, being mindful of our limitations whilst playing up to our strengths—transforming our websites into apps that are fun to use.

Chapter 5: *Using Device Features from Web Apps*
The rise of the smartphone has brought with it all sorts of advanced features—the functionality of which you'd expect could only be served by the native app. Luckily for us, the speedy implementation by mobile browsers of emerging standards has meant that web apps are gaining ground in functionality. This chapter will explore how we can make the most of event-based APIs interacting with the new hardware.

Chapter 6: *Polishing Up Our App*
: Now that we've done the groundwork, it's time to apply some spit and polish to our app. In this chapter, we'll explore what's available to help us manage inconsistencies between web and native applications, in order to refine and produce a scintillating app for the marketplace.

Chapter 7: *Introducing PhoneGap*
: In this chapter, we'll address how to convert our web app into a native app that can run on several platforms with the help of the PhoneGap framework. We'll look at installing all the required software to develop for iOS, Android, BlackBerry, and webOS, as well as PhoneGap itself.

Chapter 8: *Making Our Application Native*
: In the final chapter, we unleash our web app into the native environment. We'll cover what's involved in customizing our app for each of the main platforms, as well as some necessary tweaks to iron out any inefficiencies that might stop us from gaining marketplace approval. Finally, we'll look at simulators as we detail the all-important testing process.

Appendix A: *Running a Server for Testing*
: Testing sites on mobile devices can be a little trickier than testing on desktop browsers. In this short appendix, we'll look at a few simple web servers you can use to deliver pages to your phone from your development machine.

Where to Find Help

SitePoint has a thriving community of web designers and developers ready and waiting to help you out if you run into trouble. We also maintain a list of known errata for the book, which you can consult for the latest updates.

The SitePoint Forums

The SitePoint Forums[1] are discussion forums where you can ask questions about anything related to web development. You may, of course, answer questions too. That's how a forum site works—some people ask, some people answer, and most people do a bit of both. Sharing your knowledge benefits others and strengthens the community. A lot of interesting and experienced web designers and developers hang out there. It's a good way to learn new stuff, have questions answered in a hurry, and generally have a blast.

The Book's Website

Located at http://sitepoint.com/books/mobile1/, the website that supports this book will give you access to the following facilities:

[1] http://www.sitepoint.com/forums/

The Code Archive

As you progress through this book, you'll note a number of references to the code archive. This is a downloadable ZIP archive that contains every line of example source code printed in this book. If you want to cheat (or save yourself from carpal tunnel syndrome), go ahead and download the archive.[2]

Updates and Errata

No book is perfect, and we expect that watchful readers will be able to spot at least one or two mistakes before the end of this one. The Errata page[3] on the book's website will always have the latest information about known typographical and code errors.

The SitePoint Newsletters

In addition to books like this one, SitePoint publishes free email newsletters, such as the *SitePoint Tech Times*, *SitePoint Tribune*, and *SitePoint Design View*, to name a few. In them, you'll read about the latest news, product releases, trends, tips, and techniques for all aspects of web development. Sign up to one or more SitePoint newsletters at http://www.sitepoint.com/newsletter/.

The SitePoint Podcast

Join the SitePoint Podcast team for news, interviews, opinion, and fresh thinking for web developers and designers. We discuss the latest web industry topics, present guest speakers, and interview some of the best minds in the industry. You can catch up on the latest and previous podcasts at http://www.sitepoint.com/podcast/, or subscribe via iTunes.

Your Feedback

If you're unable to find an answer through the forums, or if you wish to contact us for any other reason, the best place to write is `books@sitepoint.com`. We have a well-staffed email support system set up to track your inquiries, and if our support team members can't answer your question, they'll send it straight to us. Suggestions for improvements, as well as notices of any mistakes you may find, are especially welcome.

---

[2] http://www.sitepoint.com/books/mobile1/code.php

[3] http://www.sitepoint.com/books/mobile1/errata.php

Acknowledgments

Earle Castledine

I'd like to thank to Max and Lily (you guys are very far away but you still helped a lot), Amelia Carlin for suffering through it all again, Maxime Dantec for teaching me all your sneaky HTML5 and CSS3 secrets, and the SitePoint gang.

Thanks to Douglas Crockford for teaching everyone that JavaScript is fantastic, and Brendan Eich for keeping it that way.

Myles Eftos

Thanks to Earle, and to the ace people at SitePoint for giving me the opportunity to tick off writing a book from my bucket list (Louis and Lisa!). Thanks to John and Maxine at Web Directions for allowing me to speak about PhoneGap off the back of a small HTML-based app, which fired off this crazy adventure.

Thanks also to my group of ragtag, fun-loving nerds who have inspired me, challenged me, and taught me. Without you guys, I wouldn't be having as much fun on the Web as I am right now.

And finally, to my beautiful girlfriend, for putting up with the late nights and early mornings that allowed this (and all my other crazy ideas) to come to fruition. I couldn't do it without your support and immeasurable understanding.

Max Wheeler

Thanks to the great people at SitePoint for both giving me the opportunity to help write this book, and putting up with me along the way. In particular, recognition must be given to our long-suffering technical editor, Louis Simoneau, and program director, Lisa Lang, who kept me in line. Credit too for Peter-Paul Koch, who took the time to pass his eyes over each chapter and correct any momentary lapses of concentration. Many thanks to my co-authors, without whom this book would be far less interesting and informative, I'm sure. Props to Tim Lucas for his not-so-gentle prodding, and to my colleagues at Icelab for allowing me the time to write this tome. To the countless numbers of designers and developers who are willing to share their experiences (and their code) for others to learn from and build upon, thank you. This sort of publication isn't possible without the contributions from those who take the time to chronicle the lessons they've learned along the way.

Thanks to my family for their encouragement—most of all to Lexi, for keeping me alive and relatively sane throughout this process. She deserves much credit for feeding my hopelessly sleep-deprived body while simultaneously resisting the urge to kill me.

Conventions Used in This Book

You'll notice that we've used certain typographic and layout styles throughout the book to signify different types of information. Look out for the following items:

Code Samples

Code in this book will be displayed using a fixed-width font, like so:

```
<h1>A Perfect Summer's Day</h1>
<p>It was a lovely day for a walk in the park. The birds
were singing and the kids were all back at school.</p>
```

If the code is to be found in the book's code archive, the name of the file will appear at the top of the program listing, like this:

example.css

```
.footer {
  background-color: #CCC;
  border-top: 1px solid #333;
}
```

If only part of the file is displayed, this is indicated by the word *excerpt*:

example.css *(excerpt)*

```
  border-top: 1px solid #333;
```

If additional code is to be inserted into an existing example, the new code will be displayed in bold:

```
function animate() {
  new_variable = "Hello";
}
```

Where existing code is required for context, rather than repeat all the code, a vertical ellipsis will be displayed:

```
function animate() {
  ⋮
  return new_variable;
}
```

Some lines of code are intended to be entered on one line, but we've had to wrap them because of page constraints. A ➥ indicates a line break that exists for formatting purposes only, and should be ignored:

```
URL.open("http://www.sitepoint.com/blogs/2007/05/28/user-style-she
➥ets-come-of-age/");
```

Tips, Notes, and Warnings

Hey, You!

Tips will give you helpful little pointers.

Ahem, Excuse Me …

Notes are useful asides that are related—but not critical—to the topic at hand. Think of them as extra tidbits of information.

Make Sure You Always …

… pay attention to these important points.

Watch Out!

Warnings will highlight any gotchas that are likely to trip you up along the way.

Chapter 1

Introduction to Mobile Web Design

Are you ready to step into the next big arena of web design? *Build Mobile Websites and Apps for Smart Devices*, as the name suggests, is all about designing for mobile devices. It's about designing for the future. This book will guide you through the process of designing and building a mobile web application from scratch. We'll take a look at what you should consider when designing in a mobile context—building the base of our application using web standards, and layering interaction on top of that base. Ultimately, we'll have our application up and running in a native wrapper so that it can be downloaded from the various app marketplaces. This book will focus on building for phone-sized devices, though many of the concepts and techniques can be applied to other mobile devices and contexts, such as tablets or netbooks.

From a technical perspective, we're going to be talking about the same technologies we're used to building with; HTML, CSS, and JavaScript are going to form the basis for (almost) everything we cover. So you will need a basic understanding of those technologies at the very least.

What does it mean?

First of all, let us make sure we are on the same page. You may well ask, "What do you mean by *mobile*?" The answer is: many things. On the surface, building for the mobile web may appear to be not all that different from building for any other web application or site; we're simply optimizing for viewing on mobile devices. Dig a little deeper, though, and there's a lot more we need to think about.

Discussions about the mobile web tend to focus on the devices and their capabilities—things like the latest iPhone, the newest Android phone, or this week in webOS. It's a rapidly changing landscape and thus an exciting time for web development, so it's easy to get caught up in discussions of the technical requirements and solutions for targeting mobile devices. But this misses the great opportunity we have with mobile design, because, ultimately, it's about people, not devices. The definition Barbara Ballard gives in her book, *Designing the Mobile User Experience*, is right on the money:[1]

> Fundamentally, "mobile" refers to the user, and not the device or the application.

People, not things. Mobility is more than just freedom from the confines of our desks. It's a different context, a distinct user experience. Strangely enough, people use mobile apps *when they're mobile*, and it's this anywhere-and-everywhere convenience of mobile design that makes mobile applications incredibly useful, yet so hard to design. We need to think hard about who we're targeting and what they want or require. Our focus has to be on having our application shine in that context. And while, for much of this book, we'll be focusing on the technical implementation, we'll be keeping Ballard's definition at the forefront of our decision-making.

Why does it matter?

Estimates put the combined number of smartphones and other browser-equipped phones at around 1.82 billion by 2013, compared to 1.78 billion PCs.[2] Reliable stats on mobile browser usage are notoriously difficult to find, but regardless of the source, the trend is clear. According to StatCounter, the mobile share of overall web browsing is currently sitting at 4.36%, and while that figure may seem small, bear in mind that's a whopping 430% increase over the last two years. And this is just the very beginning of mobile browsing. We're never going to spend less time on our phones and other mobile devices than we do now. Inevitably, more powerful mobile devices and ubiquitous internet access will become the norm. And the context in which those devices are used will change rapidly. The likelihood of our potential customers being on mobile devices is higher and higher. We ignore the mobile web at our peril.

The Natives Are Restless

The inevitable decision when designing for the mobile space is the choice between building a native application or a web application. Let's first define both of those terms. A **web application** is one that's accessed on the Web via the device's browser—a website that offers app-like functionality, in other words. A so-called **native application** is built specifically for a given platform—Android or iOS, for example—and is installed on the device much like a desktop application. These are

---

[1] Hoboken: Wiley, 2007

[2] http://www.gartner.com/it/page.jsp?id=1278413

generally made available to consumers via a platform-specific app marketplace. Most famous among these is Apple's App Store for the iPhone and iPad.

Let's now take a look at the pros and cons of native apps and web apps. As a general rule, native apps offer a superior experience when compared to web applications; the difference is even more pronounced on slower devices. Native applications are built, optimized, and, most importantly, compiled specifically for the device and platform they're running on. On iOS, this means they're written in Objective-C, and on Android, in Java. In contrast, web applications are interpreted; that is, they have to be read and understood on the fly by the browser's rendering and JavaScript engines. For iOS, Android, BlackBerry, Symbian, and webOS, the browser engine of choice is the open source WebKit project—the same engine that powers Safari and Chrome. For Windows Phone 7, the engine is currently a version of Internet Explorer 7, though Microsoft have announced plans to change that to the rendering engine inside Internet Explorer 9. This extra layer between our code and the device means that web applications will never perform as well as native apps, and that's problematic if we're building an app that requires high-resolution 3D graphics or a lot of number crunching. However, if we're building something simpler, a web app will do the job just fine. There will still be a difference in performance, but we will be able to provide a good user experience nonetheless.

The need for web applications to be interpreted by an engine also means we're bound to that engine's limitations. Where native applications can access the full stack of methods exposed by the operating system, web applications can only talk to the operating system through the browser engine. This means we're limited to the APIs that are made available by the browser. In iOS, for example, native applications have access to a whole set of functionality that's unavailable through Mobile Safari; for example, push notifications, the camera, the microphone, and the user's contacts. This means we could never build a web application that allowed users to upload photos to a service like Flickr or Facebook. It's simply not possible. That said, there are a range of device functions that are exposed through the browser: the Geolocation API lets us find out where our users are (if they permit us); the DeviceOrientation API gives us access to the gyroscope and accelerometer data; and with the Web Storage API we can save data between browsing sessions. Throw in HTML5 audio and video, gestures through browser touch events, CSS transitions and transforms, and 3D graphics using WebGL, and we can see that the gulf in functionality is narrowing. But it's likely that there'll always be something—usually the latest and greatest feature—that we're unable to use.

So, if we agree that native apps are the ideal, why are we talking about building web apps at all?

The Problem with Going Native

One issue with building a native application is market fragmentation. Because they are platform-specific, it begs the question: what platforms do we target? Should our application be in Apple's App Store first, or the Android Marketplace? What about BlackBerry or Windows Phone 7? Keep in mind that for each platform we want to support, our app will have to be rewritten. In an ideal world, we'd build a native application for all those platforms and more, but in the real world, our resources are limited; so we're forced to choose which platforms—or more accurately, which users—will miss out. Building a web application, however, means that as long as those devices come fitted with a web browser, we can build a single application from a single codebase that services all those platforms and more. The issue of fragmentation applies to browsers, hence web applications as well, but this is a familiar problem to web designers, and the differences are usually minor.

Another issue is the speed of development. As web professionals, we have a wealth of experience in building and managing web applications. Learning a whole new set of development tools, or hiring a person with those skills, takes time, effort, and money. We need a reason to justify that hassle and expense, rather than just simply betting on the skills we already have. The counter argument is that such reasons are predicated on what is best for our business, not what is best for our users, and that's a fair point. It's a delicate balancing act. We're trading user experience for familiarity, development speed, and platform flexibility. Of course, we want to make the best possible application for our users whatever their preferred platform, but an app that gets built offers a far greater user experience than one that never sees the light of day.

In recent times, some high profile companies have weighed up this equation and then put their efforts behind the Web. 37signals, purveyor of various web-based productivity applications, including Basecamp and Highrise, eschewed the native app path in releasing Basecamp mobile:

> Eventually we came to the conclusion that we should stick with what we're good at: web apps. We know the technologies well, we have a great development environment and workflow, we can control the release cycle, and everyone at 37signals can do the work.
>
> [...] we work in HTML/CSS/JS every day and have been for years. Gains we make on the desktop can make it into mobile, and gains we make in mobile can make it back to the desktop. It's the right circle for us.[3]

For the team at 37signals, dedicating money and resources was not the issue. They simply decided that building a web application provides a better experience for more users, and that building it using technologies they're familiar with gives them better control over the application in its entirety. Netflix came to a similar conclusion. Its application for the PlayStation 3 is written entirely in web technologies, enabling its developers to test and iterate the application continuously so that the best result is achieved for users:

> Our core mandate is to relentlessly experiment with the technologies, features and experiences we deliver to our members. We test every new idea, so we can measure the impact we're having on our customers. [...]

---

[3] Jason Fried on *Signal vs. Noise*, 1st February, 2001 [http://37signals.com/svn/posts/2761-launch-basecamp-mobile]

> That's where HTML5 comes in. The technology is delivered from Netflix servers every time you launch our application. This means we can constantly update, test, and improve the experience we offer. We've already run several experiments on the PS3, for example, and we're working hard on more as I write this. Our customers don't have to go through a manual process to install new software every time we make a change, it "just happens."[4]

Even Facebook, a company with more than a modicum of engineering resources (having produced the number one iPhone app of *all time*), finds it difficult to manage the platform fragmentation and is embracing web standards as the future of their mobile strategy.[5]

Mobile web apps offer several advantages over native apps, and though they face some design, development, and deployment challenges, they're a powerful cross-platform solution that's both scalable and affordable.

APIs enable

Despite 37signals's decision to stay away from native app development internally, there are no less than ten native clients for its Basecamp web application currently for sale in Apple's App Store. The comprehensive API it makes available means that third-party developers have been able to build native applications on top of Basecamp, while still allowing 37signals to control the level of interaction allowed with users' data. A well-constructed API means that your users can build your apps for you, some that you might not have expected.

Start at the Beginning

"We *need* an iPhone app." Yes, you might, but a native application for the various platforms isn't the be-all and end-all. There has to be more behind our decision than "but everyone else has one." We need to consider whether building a mobile application—whatever the technology—is the right decision for us and our users. If you have a coffee chain with 1,000 locations nationwide, perhaps a mobile application that helps your customers find your nearest store is a great idea. But if you represent the neighborhood's hipster bicycle-shop-*cum*-café-bar, perhaps a simpler alternative is more fitting.

Do people need what we're offering? Why would people want to use our application while they're mobile? Where will they use it? What are the outcomes for us as a business?

A great way to get answers to those questions is to examine information that's readily available to you. Look at your current website statistics: how many visitors are viewing it on their mobiles?

---

[4] John Ciancutti, *The Netflix "Tech" Blog*, 3rd December, 2010 [http://techblog.netflix.com/2010/12/why-we-choose-html5-for-user.html]

[5] http://networkeffect.allthingsd.com/20110125/facebook-sets-mobile-sights-on-html5/

What devices are they using? Which content are they looking at? Such data can provide an insight into what people are seeking in a mobile context. Of course, the data will be influenced by the constraints of your current website, so any conclusions you glean should only form part of your decision process.

What if you have no data to be mined? Well, you could always try talking to your users; there's no harm in asking people what they want. In simple terms, it's probably whatever you're selling, as quickly as possible. If you're a florist, they want flowers—*now*. Own a café? They want coffee, *now*. Whatever your product or service, if you can create an application that meets those demands, it will be tremendously gratifying for your users (and will make you money).

The App Store Effect

The success of Apple's App Store can't be ignored: there's an undeniable marketing advantage to having an app that appears in such a popular forum, and having your icon in the middle of a user's home screen gives your app exposure in a way that a bookmark does not. In addition, the path to monetization is very clear: the various application marketplaces bring customers, and those customers bring money. We're going to build a mobile web application, but that doesn't mean we have to miss out on a potentially lucrative outlet for our product. This is where a web-native hybrid app can come in. But we're getting ahead of ourselves—all this and more will be covered in Chapter 7.

An App is not Enough

The biggest argument for making a mobile application using web technologies is that we're going to have to do at least some of that work anyway. Users, rightfully, will expect the website we already have to work on their mobile devices. No assumptions should be made about a user's device or its capabilities—an underlying principle of the Web at large—because inevitably those assumptions will be wrong. A native app is not the solution to that problem.

We've identified that mobile design is about context, but it's also about speed. We're aiming to give our users what they want, as fast as possible. Having a fantastic native application is good only if users already have it installed. Asking our users to go to an app marketplace to download a separate application—usually a large, upfront hit—can be too much to expect if they're already on the go and relying on mobile internet coverage. Providing a version of our site to mobile users is going to be important regardless of whether or not we have a native application. So what do we do?

Option One: Nada

Doing nothing is seriously one option, and shouldn't be dismissed. The new breed of smartphones make it incredibly easy to navigate around a large and complex page. The home page from *The New York Times*, for example, contains an enormous amount of information across a range of topics. If we take a look under the hood, though, we can see that this volume of information comes at a price;

to download the front page of http://nytimes.com/ takes up almost 1MB of data, as Figure 1.1 reveals using Chrome's Web Inspector tool.

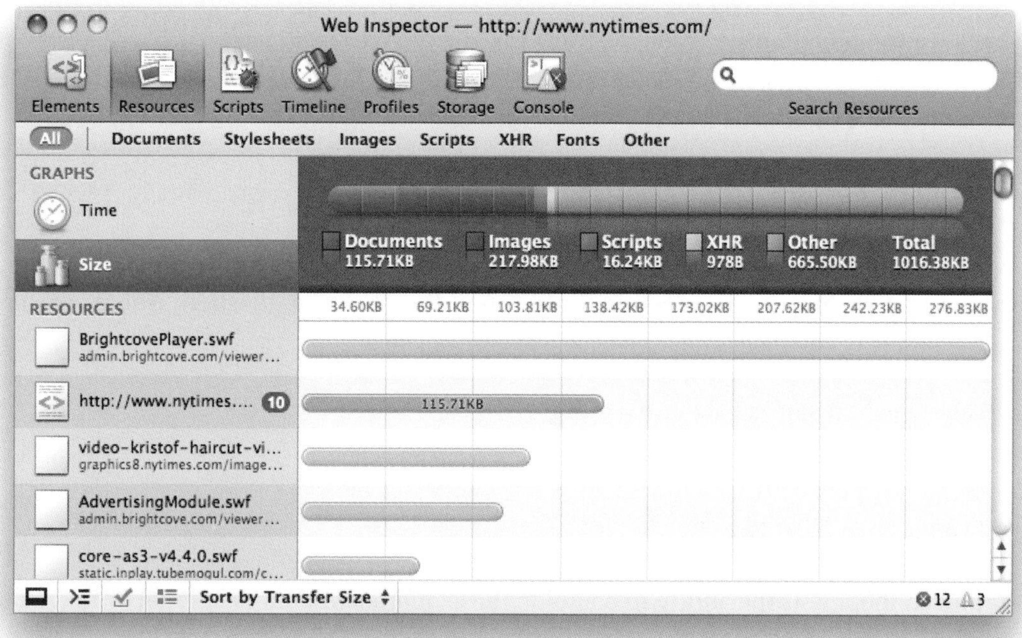

Figure 1.1. Chrome's Web Inspector reveals the true cost of full-featured pages

Sure, 3G coverage is fairly decent these days, but we're still asking our users to wait a good four to five seconds before they can interact with our site. This isn't terribly mobile- or user-friendly. If we do choose the path of least resistance, it's imperative that we build our site using well-structured and meaningful markup. Adhering to all the conventional best-practices for desktop web design will bear even greater fruit when it comes to mobile. Lightweight, CSS-based layouts, content-out design, and a focus on accessibility and usability matter even more when screen size, attention, and bandwidth are limited.

Option Two: Transform and Move Out

Responsive design to the rescue! Well, sort of. If you somehow missed the seminal article from Ethan Marcotte on this topic, we'd strongly recommended that you take the time to read it.[6] The phrase **responsive web design** refers to the art of using CSS media queries, fluid grid layouts, and fluid images to respond to the resolution of the user's device (or browser window) and adapting your design to provide the best layout for any given resolution.

---

[6] http://www.alistapart.com/articles/responsive-web-design/

It's a beautifully simple technique—if a little mind-bending at times—and worth looking into. Media queries are an extension of the familiar media-type attributes we've long used to deliver print stylesheets to our HTML pages. The difference is that instead of only allowing a singular context for those CSS rules, we can query (hence the name) the physical characteristics of our user's device. This means we can deliver different stylesheets (or bits of stylesheets) to only the devices that fit the criteria we specify. In the example below, we're saying, "Only load the **mobile.css** file if the viewport is at most 480px wide":

```
<link rel="stylesheet" type="text/css" media="screen and (max-width: 480px)"
➥href="mobile.css" />
```

Of course, we're not limited to inspecting the width of the device in question. Among the many supported features in the media queries spec, we can ask about:

- width and height (as in the above example)
- screen resolution
- orientation
- aspect ratio

The real power, though, is the ability to combine these queries into more complex rules. Want to serve some styles to a high-resolution device in landscape orientation? No problem:

```
<link rel="stylesheet" type="text/css" media="screen and
➥(min-resolution: 300dpi) and (orientation: landscape)"
➥href="mobile.css" />
```

That's fine and dandy, right? We can use this approach to serve a great mobile site, a great desktop site, and everything in between, from the same codebase.

Alas, that's not quite the case. The responsive design approach has limitations. In a sense it's a bit like putting lipstick on a pig. Reformatting the layout can make our content more palatable on a mobile device, but it's still only window dressing. There's an argument to be made that responsive design is actually worse than doing nothing, because you're forcing your users to download resources they may never be able to see. Fortunately, some of these problems can be mitigated with some careful planning.

First and foremost: *build for mobile first*. Whereas the the inclination is to use media queries as a means to add a bit of extra love to a near-complete desktop site, what we should be doing is the exact opposite. Start from a base of simplicity and layer the complexity on top for a more powerful desktop experience:

```
<link rel="stylesheet"
➥ media="screen and (min-width: 939px)" href="desktop.css" />
```

It's a concept we're quite familiar with: progressive enhancement. There's no way for us to avoid sending the same HTML to each device; however, if we're careful about how we construct our pages and serve our stylesheets, we can ensure an optimal experience for mobile users—providing the content they're most likely to want up front. We're minimizing the overhead without atrophying the desktop experience.

Option Three: Forever Alone

A more common option is to build a completely separate website for mobile users. Such a site can usually be found on an m. or mobile. subdomain (or both). Choosing this method means we can craft an experience that's focused solely on the needs of our users when they're out and about. Perfect.

Well, almost. There are some downsides to this approach. Having a separate mobile site usually means relying on some form of user agent detection to decide which device receives which edition of our site. For example, "serve the mobile site to users on iPhones, serve the desktop version to Firefox users" and so on. While great in theory, this sort of user agent sniffing (detecting the user's browser based on the information it provides about itself in requests to our server) is notoriously unreliable; the user agent string can be easily changed in many browsers (and often is to specifically get around this technique). Even if we were to make our mobile. site correctly detect the current crop of mobile browsers, we can cause unintended problems for users of devices we don't know about yet. It's a question of choice: do we want to force our users down the route we've chosen?

The solution is dead simple: allow them to choose their own path by providing a link to our standard site on the mobile version (and vice versa). Then, respect that decision. There's nothing wrong with encouraging our users to start at our mobile site, but we shouldn't restrict them from accessing everything they could normally access.

Facebook is a good example of the right behavior, addressing the reasons you may want to allow your users to switch between the standard site and the mobile site. It offers two mobile sites: touch.facebook.com to cater for mobile users on touch-enabled smartphones, and m.facebook.com for users of non-touch devices. Both sites let you perform all the normal tasks and interactions that you'd expect Facebook to offer: you can read and respond to messages, post status updates, and view the wall of activity that's at the heart of the site. Still, we can't do *everything* that the standard desktop site lets us do—upload photographs or edit our profile, for example. If we absolutely have to perform a task that's only possible on the standard site (or works better on the standard site), both of Facebook's mobile editions provide a handy link in their footer to switch versions. The key is to always allow your users easy access to the full-featured site—don't wall them off from any functionality. Separate, don't segregate.

A Note on Frameworks

When doing research into building web applications for mobile devices, you'll no doubt come across projects that purport to provide cross-platform development frameworks for mobile. The most prominent of these are Sencha Touch[7] and the jQuery Mobile[8] projects. We'll skip delving into the specifics of their implementation, but they're worth taking a quick look at in order to decide whether or not they suit our purposes.

Both these frameworks are essentially JavaScript frameworks. In the case of Sencha Touch, the applications built with it are entirely reliant on our users' devices having a good JavaScript engine. We already know this is not always the case. View an application built in Sencha Touch without JavaScript and we get an empty shell that doesn't do anything. JQuery Mobile, meanwhile, chooses the more user-friendly approach of progressive enhancement; its applications are built in plain HTML, and their app-like behavior is layered on top. This is another trade-off—as you might be starting to grasp, the mobile world has a lot of those! Sencha Touch uses the all-JavaScript method because it means better performance—by virtue of building application logic in JavaScript rather than on top of the DOM. Regardless of their different approaches, the point to remember about these frameworks is that they both implement a whole host of features that replicate behavior and functionality present in native apps. So if you don't use all those features, you're including overhead that you have no need for.

This brings us to one of the design considerations when building a mobile web application: the **uncanny valley**. The uncanny valley is a theory that claims that the more lifelike a humanoid robot is, the more likely its appearance will cause revulsion in human beings. This idea can be applied to interfaces, so we should be aware of it when we start to look at the design (and behavior) of our application.

If it looks like a duck, quacks like a duck, and yet isn't a duck, how are our users supposed to treat it? By replicating the look and feel of a native application, mobile application frameworks set certain expectations—expectations that are, by definition, impossible to meet. The answer is simple: embrace the limitations. There's no need to pretend that we are outside the scope of the normal browser interface. Mobile isn't a curse; it's an opportunity to make an active decision about how we present ourselves. The mobile version of twitter.com doesn't attempt to behave like any of the native Twitter applications. It does what it's supposed to do: give you most of the information you want as quickly as possible.

---

[7] http://www.sencha.com/products/touch/

[8] http://jquerymobile.com/

Rolling Up Our Sleeves

All this discussion is wonderful, but isn't this supposed to be a book about, you know, *building* mobile web applications? Well, that it is; and while it's important to understand why we've chosen a particular strategy, it's much more fun to actually create something. So, what are we building? As luck would have it, we've been approached by a potential client to build a mobile version of their popular StarTrackr website. StarTrackr is a celebrity-spotting site that lets users log when and where they've seen a celebrity "out in the wild," and it's a perfect example of a task that's suited to the mobile web.[9] Let's review our options: we can do nothing (not sure our client will like that), craft a mobile-first responsive design, or create a separate (but related) mobile version of our site. It's a question of what we want—or rather what our client wants—to achieve. For StarTrackr, the client wants the user to be able to:

- see nearby spots (a location where a celebrity has been seen) and the various celebrity sightings at that spot
- find their favorite celebrities and see their recent sightings
- add a new sighting

If we look at that set of functionality, we can see we're talking about building a *web application*, not just a website. In simplistic terms, web applications are for performing tasks; websites are for consuming information. It's important to understand the distinction and how the techniques we've talked about are more appropriate to one or the other. We can do a lot with window dressing, but if our intention is to create a compelling and contextual experience for our users—and it is—we'll want to make the leap to a separate mobile application.

So let's get to it.

[9] Alas, StarTrackr is made up, so before you get too excited, you'll have to find an alternative means for your celebrity-spotting needs.

Chapter 2

Design for Mobile

Before we leap into designing our application, we'll look at some fundamental things to consider when crafting an interface for a mobile-centric app. It's easy to jump headfirst into creating the look and feel for an application. That's the fun part, right? The problem is that design doesn't start with Photoshop. First and foremost, it's about communication. Design is the process of organizing the information we want to present so that its structure is meaningful and instantly understandable. It's about controlling the navigation and flow of our application in a way that is clear, minimizes uncertainty, and feels efficient. As Jeffrey Zeldman, father of standards-based design, says in his seminal article "Style versus design":[1]

> Design communicates on every level. It tells you where you are, cues you to what you can do, and facilitates the doing.

We're looking to craft an interface that is functional, an interface our users can, well, *use*. We should be aiming to create an experience, or rather getting out of the way and letting our users create their own experience. The interface is simply the medium through which we enable it to happen.

For any website or web application we build, our goal should be to deliver the most appropriate content and experience to our users. What's crucial for for mobile applications is the *context*—the when and where—in which they'll be using that information. On our standard website, our users are quite likely sitting at a desk in front of a monitor with a keyboard and mouse at hand. Conversely, visitors who are browsing on a mobile device could be waiting in line, catching a train, lying on

[1] http://www.adobe.com/designcenter/dialogbox/stylevsdesign/

their couch, walking down the street, or perhaps even sitting on the toilet; and what's more, their screen is likely to be no larger than a few hundred pixels with a tiny (or onscreen) keyboard.

We need to think about how people use their mobile devices. More than the situations they're in, or the actions they're trying to achieve, consider how our users might physically be using their devices. How do they hold their phones? Are they using touch-enabled interfaces, or other input methods?

In general, we're going to adopt the same principles and thought processes that we'd normally apply to the Web—it's just that the issues are accentuated in the mobile space. The screen is smaller, input can be awkward, network connectivity is possibly slower and less reliable, and our users might be more distracted. We need to work harder than ever to maintain their attention and lead them to what they want (or what we want them) to do.

Build a Better Mouse

Many, if not most, of the new breed of mobile devices use touch as their main input method. While many of the principles we usually apply to interface design are the same, there are some shifts in mindset required.

Our fingers are remarkably dexterous, but they lack the same level of precision of a mouse. With some care, we can use a mouse to pinpoint a single pixel on an interface—but try touching a single pixel with your finger. The Apple Human Interface Guidelines for iOS specify a recommended hit target no smaller than 44×44px;[2] about 2,000 times bigger than our single pixel. Does this mean interfaces that rely on touch as their input method are a step backwards? Of course not. Touch as a mode of interaction is about removing the layer between us and our interfaces. What we lose in accuracy, we gain in having a better understanding of the interactions, because the experience is now tactile, and hence, more intuitive.

Interfaces that fail to accommodate the touch paradigm do so not because of any inherent failing of the input method, but because the designers have jammed too much onto a screen, or made buttons too small for fingers to easily tap. This is exacerbated by the inherent problem of touch as an input method: the very act of trying to touch an interface element obscures that element from our view. In addition, our users need to be able to understand and use our interface in a whole range of distracting contexts. There's a delicate balance between trying to fit as much information as possible into the smaller physical space of a mobile screen, and offering targets that are big enough for clumsy fingers to touch.

We should also never forget our users *without* touch screens! They're customers too, and their input method is likely to be extremely unfriendly. Older feature phones (and some smartphones) use

---

[2] http://developer.apple.com/library/ios/#documentation/userexperience/conceptual/mobilehig/UEBestPractices/UEBestPractices.html#//apple_ref/doc/uid/TP40006556-CH20-SW20

four-way navigation (often called a D-pad) as their primary input method, forcing users to scroll past several elements in our interface to reach the button they want. BlackBerry's browser uses a tiny trackball or scroll wheel to navigate the interface; hence, wherever possible, it's worth aiming to limit the number of elements on the screen.

Above all, it means simple interfaces. Simple means easy to understand, which leads to easy to use.

Simplicity is a feature, and while complexity is not necessarily a vice, we need to keep some perspective. As invested as we might be in the depths of functionality of our application, the behavior of our users is not likely to match our interest. Our users are likely to spend mere seconds or minutes in our application—if we can convince them to visit at all.

- What do they want?
- What do they expect?
- What do we want them to do?

We can't assume that users have the time (or the inclination) to figure out how our application works.

Hover Me

Designing for touch devices requires a shift in our thinking. Many of the techniques we've been used to employing no longer work, or at least don't quite work as we'd like. The most obvious of these is hover:

> Elements that rely only on `mousemove`, `mouseover`, `mouseout`, or the CSS pseudo-class `:hover` may not always behave as expected on a touch-screen device such as iPad or iPhone.
>
> —From Apple's "Preparing Your Web Content for iPad" guide[3]

Hovering as an interaction model permeates the Web. We're used to our mouse movements triggering changes to a page on hover: different colors or states for links, revealing drop-down navigation, and showing actionable items, to name a few. And as designers, we've readily embraced the possibilities that the hover state gives us. Most touch-based operating systems will do some work behind the scenes to try to ensure the interface deals with hover states in a non-catastrophic way, but we are going to have to start changing our habits. For example, in lieu of a hover state, consider:

- making buttons and hyperlinks obvious
- having content that doesn't rely on `:hover`; for example, increasing contrast on text
- avoiding drop-down menus without clear visual cues

---

[3] http://developer.apple.com/library/safari/#technotes/tn2010/tn2262/index.html

We might lose a little flair, but we'll gain clarity of interface.

Small Screens

There's no escaping that designing for mobile means designing for small screens. Mobile devices have displays that are significantly smaller—both in terms of physical size and resolution—than their desktop counterparts. This is an opportunity to be embraced.

Still, finding the right balance between information and interface to display on a small screen is a tricky problem. Too much detail and our interface will become cluttered and confusing. Too little and our users will have to work to find the information they need. This doesn't necessarily mean reducing content; it means reducing clutter.

In other words, don't be afraid of making an interface information-rich. A carefully designed interface can hold a wealth of information and communicate it effectively. Hiding information behind interaction may be the path of least resistance, but it's not necessarily the path we should take. People use their mobile devices to complete tasks or seek out information: they want to find out when the movie is playing, when the next train will arrive, or where the nearest café is. They would prefer not to spend hours exploring a sparse and delicately balanced interface. We want to give as much information as we can to our users without overwhelming them.

Cognitive Load

Simplifying the interface is really about reducing the cognitive burden we're placing on our users. This is essentially the overriding principle behind Fitts's Law.[4] For the uninitiated, Fitts's Law is a model of interaction that's become a fundamental when understanding user interface design. It states that the time to acquire a target—like say, moving a mouse over a button—is a function of the distance to and the size of the target. Simply put, the larger an item is and the closer it is to your cursor, the easier it is to click on.

A classic example of adapting to this principle is the menu bar in Mac OS X. It's a small target that's usually a fair distance from where your cursor normally sits; yet this is counterbalanced by placing the menu against the top of the screen, preventing users from overshooting the target. Being on the edge effectively gives the menu bar infinite height, resulting in fewer errors by the users, who reach their targets faster. For a touch screen, however, Fitt's Law has to be applied differently: our users aren't tied to the position of their mouse, so the origin of their movements is simply the default position of their fingers or thumbs. That position varies a lot on the device and its orientation; for example, with a mobile device, you might use the index finger of one hand or the thumbs of both hands.

Here's an example of this issue in a real application. Infinity Blade is an immensely popular game for iOS. It's available on both the iPhone and iPad, and uses the same interface for both devices.

---

[4] http://en.wikipedia.org/wiki/Fitts's_law

The game is played with the device in landscape mode, and the controls are anchored to the bottom of the screen (where your thumbs are), as you can see in Figure 2.1. On the iPhone, the "cast-spell" button is in the middle of the screen, within reach of either thumb. Yet this feature is less effective when found in the larger form of the iPad. The "cast-spell" button is still in the middle of the screen, but no longer within reach of our default hand position.

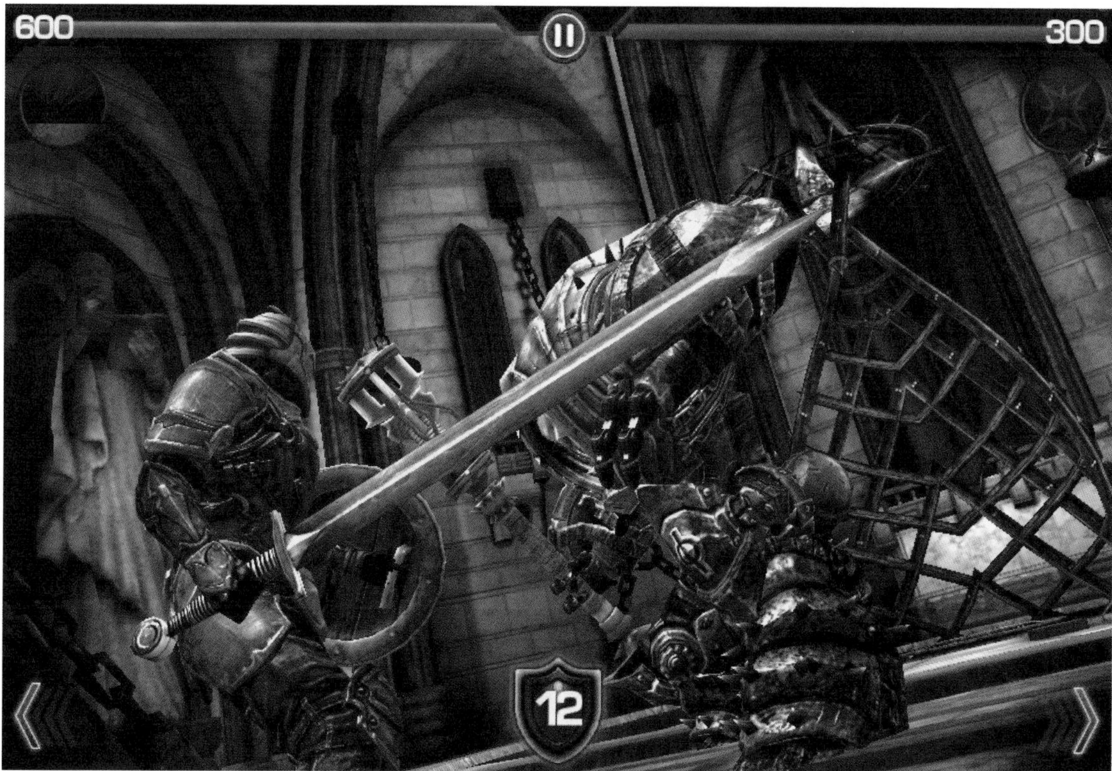

Figure 2.1. Infinity Blade on the iPhone

This is just one example, but it should serve to illustrate the importance of considering how your interface will be used on a real device. You need to think beyond "point-and-click"!

Standing on the Shoulders of Giants

A big part of the success of the iPhone, and the iOS ecosystem as a whole, has been Apple's focus on both the aesthetic and the experience of the platform and its applications. Apple did an enormous amount of work establishing the most common application design models while ensuring flexibility for their developers and consistency for their users. While our goal isn't to build an application that attempts to mimic the exact experience of using a native application, there's still plenty to be learned from examining the structure and design patterns used in mobile operating systems. Understanding the interfaces our users expect is important; it allows us to decide when it's worth trying to meet those expectations, and when to go in another direction.

Let's take a look at a few mobile design patterns we might find useful in our application.

The Carousel

Imagine some playing cards placed side by side in the screen, where users can flick between each "card" by sliding over the screen to the left or to the right.

The prototypical example of the carousel pattern on iOS is Apple's Weather app, seen in Figure 2.2. The Weather app assigns each city to a single card. One glance shows all the weather information we need for our city of choice without the distraction of what's happening elsewhere.

Figure 2.2. The carousel pattern in the flesh in Apple's Weather app

WebOS also uses the carousel pattern for switching between applications. Apps that use this pattern are normally information-rich but interaction-poor.

The carousel is the simplest pattern we'll look at—it usually consists of a single type of content organized in a linear set. What's nice about the carousel is that it's simple (which is good, remember?). The interface is minimal and the data structure is incredibly easy to understand. It also offers an implicit hierarchy of importance: the first items are the easiest to access, and are usually of the most interest to our users. The flip side to this structure is that there's no way to move between views more than one card away.

The Good

- It's simple to use.
- It utilizes a whole screen to show content.
- It requires a natural gesture for navigation.

The Bad

- It relies on gestures—the user has to swipe from card to card, which can be less intuitive than pressing buttons or menu items.
- All the information for a given page has to fit on the screen at the same time, otherwise the structure breaks down.
- Each page needs to be conceptually the same.
- Users have to progress through the sequence; they can't skip ahead.

Tab Bar

The tab bar pattern can be seen everywhere in iOS, Android, and webOS. For web designers and developers, tabs aren't exactly a new idea. We've been using them to establish hierarchy and group content into sections for many years. Conceptually, tabs in mobile applications are identical to those in desktop websites; the main difference is that the tab bar usually has a fixed position in mobile applications, and so always appears on the screen. It's interesting to note that on iOS, the tab bar component appears at the bottom of the page (near your thumbs), whereas on Android, the convention is to have the tab bar at the top of the screen (leading into the content).

The tab bar is useful for quickly establishing the structure of an application. It lets users move easily between the broad sections of an application, and also acts as an anchor point—the various selected states of the tab bar also signify where in an application the user currently is. As Figure 2.3 shows, the Twitter app for Android uses a tab bar to let users move between various modes of another user's profile.

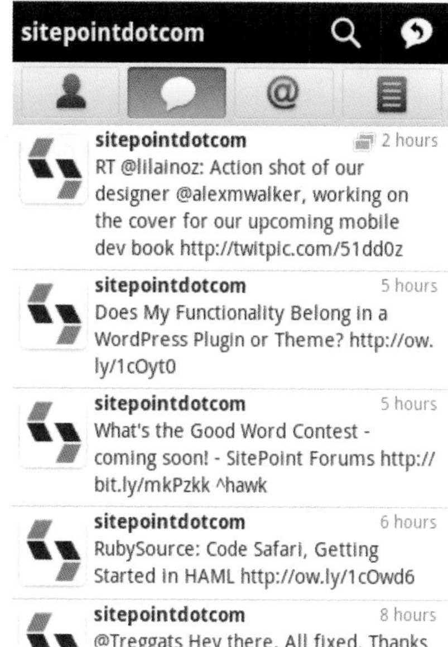

Figure 2.3. The tab bar in use in the Twitter app

Good

- It provides a familiar navigation for users.
- It allows easy switching between modes, views, or tasks.
- It indicates the current state/location of the app.

Bad

- Its hierarchy is flat—there's no easy way to have nested subpages.
- It always appears on the screen, taking up valuable real estate.
- It only handles up to five navigation items effectively, and is clunky beyond that.

Lists

Lists are the most commonly used design pattern for mobile applications. The list as an interface model is fairly self-explanatory: content is displayed in a vertical list, allowing users to scroll through the options. In iOS, they can be seen everywhere, featuring in all but the simplest of utility applications. While basic, they're also incredibly flexible. Lists can be used for presenting actionable options; acting as an index for a long list of content; and, most importantly, as a navigation hierarchy that lets users work their way down a tree structure.

It's as a navigation model that lists are most powerful. There are really no limits to the depths of navigational hierarchy that lists can accommodate and so, for applications with a structure more than one level deep, the list is almost universally turned to.

This pattern maps perfectly to the framework we're used to dealing with online. The list structure is a tree that can lead anywhere, and often it's used to let users drill down from an index of items to a detailed view of a single item. This is known as the **master/detail pattern**, a model that's used in desktop and mobile applications all the time. Just about every email application ever made uses this pattern of interaction, letting us quickly skim through the available items and then focus on a single one. We'll return to this idea a little later on.

For example, News.com.au uses the list pattern, allowing users to skim the headlines before moving into whichever story catches their interest, as you can see in Figure 2.4.

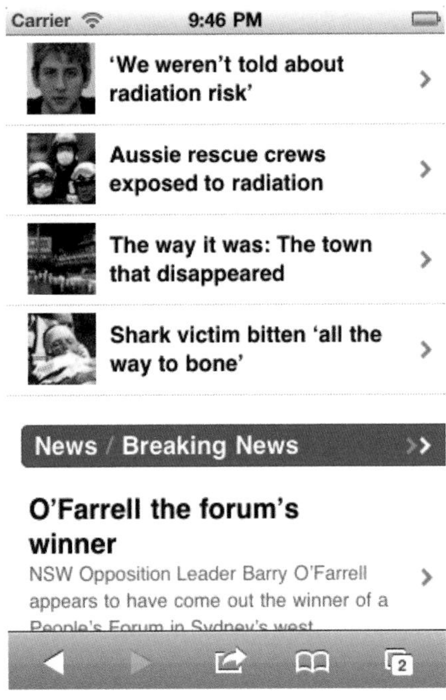

Figure 2.4. Lists are commonly used by news apps

The main limitation of lists is that as soon as a user moves down the tree, they lose the ability to move to any items on the levels above in one simple step. From four levels down, they would have to retrace back three levels to return to the top level—not ideal. To overcome this deficiency, the list structure is often combined with the tab bar pattern to create a strong, structured navigation with depth and flexibility.

Good

- It's flexible enough to handle lots of data.
- It's familiar and easy to understand.

Bad

- It's inherently hierarchical.
- Users need to return to the beginning to change paths.

Summary

Remember, these patterns offer a suggested structure—we don't *have* to use them. Familiarity and consistency can lend a design authority, but you can still break the mold. There are a myriad of examples of applications out there that eschew UI conventions to create delightful, intuitive, and unique interfaces for their users; by the same token, there are many apps that move away from these simple patterns without good reason and end up confusing and frustrating users.

We should always consider how breaking convention might enhance or detract from our app's primary task. If we're unable to design a better alternative to the conventional pattern, we probably shouldn't do it.

Putting It Into Practice

We've looked at some of the broader considerations when designing for mobile, so now let's address the business of our application. First, we need a plan. Our client has given us some high-level user scenarios, which we will need to examine in more detail to figure out what each means for our application. It's crucial to decide precisely which features we intend to deliver, and to whom. Only after we've figured that out can we ensure the look and feel of our app actually enables the task we'd like it to. So how do we go about that?

Thinking Big

In order to form the perfect feature set, we need to consider all the features our users *might* want. If we don't examine everything we might want to include, we're almost certainly going to miss some ideas that might make or break our app. Never mind if the list is long; it's better to start with grand possibilities and narrow our scope later. StarTrackr is a celebrity-spotting application, so our comprehensive feature list might include:

- Find sightings by location
- Find sightings by celebrity
- Sort celebrities by genre
- Search for a particular celebrity
- Find locations nearby that celebrities have been sighted at by address
- Find locations nearby that celebrities have been sighted at by GPS
- Favorite/follow a celebrity
- Favorite/follow a location
- Be notified when a particular celebrity is sighted
- Be notified when a particular location has a celebrity sighting
- View recent sightings
- Add a celebrity sighting
- Add a photograph of a celebrity sighting
- Add a video of a celebrity sighting

Putting Together a User Profile

As we talked about earlier, users are the most important consideration in the planning of our application. Who are they? What do we know about them? What are they doing? What do they want? What are the most important features to them? Why would they want to use our application? When are they going to use our app? What are they likely and unlikely to have an interest in? Such questions aren't always easy to answer, but if users are interested in the general concept for StarTrackr, we can probably make a few assumptions about them. We know they:

- like celebrities
- have an interest in celebrity gossip
- are more likely to be female than male
- are more likely to be younger than older (say, 14 to 25)
- are probably located near some celebrity hot spots, such as Hollywood or London

In the real world, our client would usually provide us with information on who their current users are and how they use the site. For our purposes, we'll make an educated guess: our typical user is a young woman who lives in a large city and enjoys celebrity gossip.

Deciding on a Core Feature Set

Start simple. Great mobile applications focus primarily on the tasks their users want to accomplish. In truth, we should be doing this with all our projects—mobile or not—but it's even more important with mobile web applications. It can be tempting to include more features in our application, thinking it will make it better. This isn't always so—in fact, it's hardly ever the case when talking about mobile design.

We have a list of features that we could include, and we have an idea of who our users are and what they're after. Next, we need to pare down our feature set to the most essential elements. This may seem easy enough, but deciding which features to leave out can be quite a challenge. Think about the minimum viable product: which features are essential for our application to be of any use at all. If we're brutal about whittling our list of functionality down to the basics, we can focus on three main features:

- Find sightings by location
- Find sightings by celebrity
- Add a celebrity sighting

And, secondary to that:

- Add a photograph of a celebrity sighting

For a first iteration at least, this gives us everything we need: celebrities are tied to locations, and we have the ability to filter through either of those data types—plus our users can add their own sightings while on the go. It's useful to look at this information and condense it into a single mission statement for our application; we can then return to it throughout the development to ensure we stay on track. For our app, this might be: "An app that lets people find and add sightings of their favorite celebrities."

Sketches

In any project, but particularly when we're designing for a form with which we're unfamiliar, sketching and **wireframing** is a great way to gain a sense of how the flow and overall structure of the app will work. What exactly is a wireframe, you ask? It's a low-fidelity visual representation of the layout of our application. We can use it to represent the basic page layout and navigational model of our app.

Since wireframes are considerably quicker to make than a fully fledged mockup, we can spend some time early on prototyping a range of approaches—testing our interface ideas and rejecting them promptly when they're not working. Once you start the design process, it's easy to get caught up in the small details: perfecting that shade of blue, or achieving just the right balance of type. At this early stage, sketches can provide a sense of the user experience as a whole, allowing us to spot potential usability problems before we commit too much time to building the interface.

How you build your wireframes is really a matter of personal preference. There are a whole host of tools out there that make the process very easy. Here are a few of the more popular options:

Pencil and paper

Sometimes the simplest tools are the best. There's something wonderful about the process of physically sketching a layout. It removes the distraction of the tools and lets us focus on the task at hand. The downside to hand-drawn wireframes is that when we want to iterate our design, we'll have to redraw each layout.

Balsamiq, http://www.balsamiq.com/products/mockups
Balsamiq is a simple wireframing application with a range of common interface elements. It's an Adobe Air application that runs on Windows, Mac, and Linux, and has a hand-drawn look that's designed to keep you focused on the structure rather than the appearance of your mockups.

Mockingbird, https://gomockingbird.com/
An online tool, Mockingbird lets you build and share your wireframes in-browser. It has a similar sketchy style to Balsamiq.

Omnigraffle, http://www.omnigroup.com/products/omnigraffle/
Omnigraffle is a Mac-only application that, among its many features, is a fully featured wireframing tool. The real benefit of Omnigraffle is the range of interface stencils that are available for free. Check out Graffletopia[5] for all your wireframing stencil needs, including many mobile-specific templates for various platforms.

For our purposes, OmniGraffle will do the job just fine. Let's have a look at some sketches for StarTrackr. Because there are a bunch of stencils available out there for iOS wireframes, we're going to use the chrome from an iPhone as the frame for our sketches—but our interface will look the same on any platform.

First, we'll need to set up the correct dimensions and place some of the default elements in there. You can see our starting point in Figure 2.5.

That's our blank canvas. Now there are some standard interface elements we'll need to account for, as shown in Figure 2.6.

Figure 2.5. An empty wireframe containing only the device shell

[5] http://graffletopia.com

Figure 2.6. Adding the operating system and browser chrome

On iOS, the status bar weighs in at 20px, and in Mobile Safari, the toolbar at the bottom of the screen takes up 44px of vertical space. On Android, the browser chrome disappears from the screen once the page has loaded, but the status bar takes up 25px; the same is true of the browser on webOS.

Let's ignore these elements for a minute and look at the layout of our application in an empty screen. To start things off, it's often useful to establish the distinct objects that make up the application at large. For StarTrackr, these are easy to identify: we have celebrities (stars) and locations (spots) that are linked together by sightings. However we end up combining them in our interface, those three objects form the basis of everything we do. If we've identified the three main features we're going to focus on, what information or actions might each one contain?

Finding Sightings By Location

This one really is about the context. Our users are out and about, so they might be able to act on the information our app provides and go to the spot where a star has been sighted. While it might seem handy for a user to see *all* the most recent sightings, finding sightings that have happened *nearby* is probably much more useful. With that in mind, we'll want a list of locations—ordered by distance—that our users can drill down into.

A list, eh? Well, that sounds familiar. In fact, the list pattern is perfect for presenting this information. We want to let our users quickly flick through a series of locations, and then move into a detailed view of that spot if it piques their interest.

Figure 2.7 shows a wireframe of our list of spots, ordered by distance from the user. We're showing the important information on the left—the name and distance—and on the right, we've added the number of sightings at that given location. This will probably mean very little to our users initially, but there's no need to force content on them. It's okay to let them discover that information on their own.

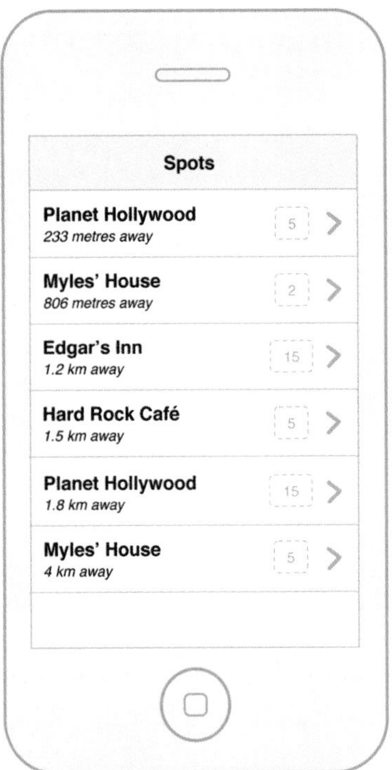

Figure 2.7. A wireframe of StarTrackr's "Spots" listing

Makes sense, right? The only problem is that to make this real, we need to know the location of our users. There are a couple of ways to go about this. The JavaScript Geolocation API exposes the functionality we need to access the device's location sensors, as many smartphones include a GPS. So, we can merely place a button in our interface that starts that process. Unfortunately, the Geolocation API isn't available on all mobile devices, so we'll need a fallback of some sort.

The addition of a fallback text field to our geolocation button has the advantage of giving our users the flexibility to modify their location if they so wish. Why would they want to do that? We'll go into the nitty-gritty of the implementation of the Geolocation API a little later on, but it's worth knowing that it's sometimes a bit like magic. Each device, and indeed each browser, has a different way of figuring out a location; information can sometimes be unreliable or inaccurate, so allowing a user to refine their position can be a useful feature. Furthermore, if we limited ourselves to using just the Geolocation API, it would mean that users would be limited to only exploring their actual physical location; so if they wanted to explore the hot spots in a different city, they'd have to actually go there!

Figure 2.8 shows the standard approach to asking a user for their location.

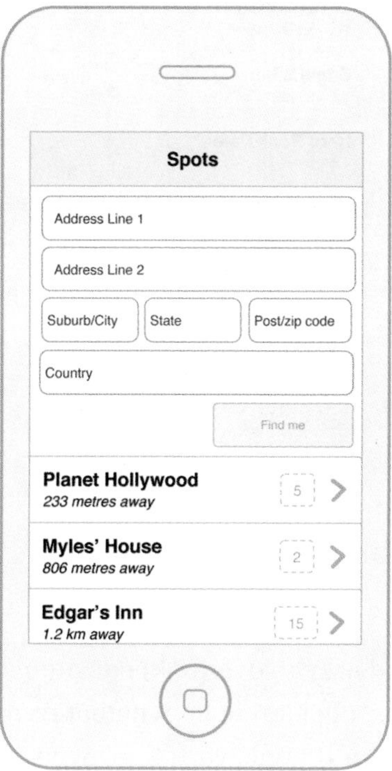

Figure 2.8. An excessive address form

That's not very friendly, is it? Entering data on a mobile device (especially one without a physical keyboard) is much harder than through a keyboard and mouse combination, so if we can reduce the effort our users have to make, we should.

A much better option—even outside of mobile context—would be to let our users enter information in a free text field, and then infer their location using a third-party service or API (we'll look at how to hook this up in Chapter 5). The canonical example of this kind of field is the Google Maps search interface.

Figure 2.9 shows an example of a simpler location entry interface.

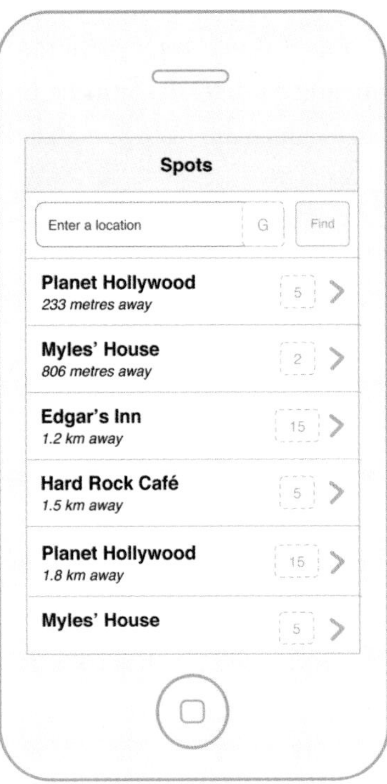

Figure 2.9. A simpler approach

That's much better!

This brings us to an important (and easy to overlook) consideration for touchscreen devices. The available area for our form changes, depending on whether or not the keyboard is displayed. Figure 2.10 shows a minimal form on an iPhone, with the keyboard active.

Figure 2.10. The on-screen keyboard can obscure a significant portion of a page

Our once blank canvas is now half-filled with a keyboard. In fact, in portrait mode, the iOS keyboard takes up 260px of the 480px space we have to play with, reducing our usable space to less than half of what we started with. When building forms for mobile devices, always keep this in mind, and make sure you're not hiding essential information or controls behind the keyboard.

Overview and Detail

So, if we're happy with our list structure, we can move on to creating what a detailed view for a given location will look like. This is an example of the master/detail pattern we touched on earlier. From the index of locations, our users have selected an area of interest. Once they click on that location, we can narrow the focus and show them information from that one spot. Let's take a stab at that—Figure 2.11 shows what we've come up with.

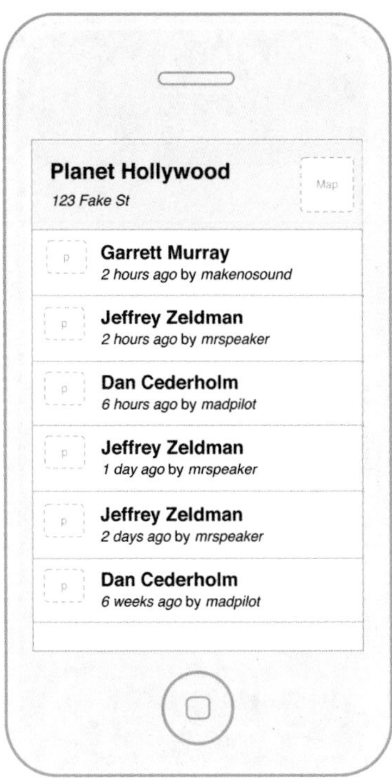

Figure 2.11. A wireframe for the detailed view of a spot

All the vital bits of information about a spot are present: the name, address, and a breakdown of the recent celebrity sightings that have occurred there. If there's a photograph associated with a sighting, we can include it as a thumbnail (and perhaps link to a larger version). There's plenty more we could include here—for example, a breakdown of the most-sighted celebs at this particular spot, or a perhaps a photo gallery of each sighting—but we're trying to keep it simple, right? The set of information we're showing here will let our users know who's been spotted recently—the most important piece of information we can provide them with.

Finding Sightings by Celebrity

We've now worked out the location-centric path through our application, but what if our users are only interested in a particular celebrity? Charlie Sheen showing up at their local bar every evening is irrelevant if they're only interested in what Brad Pitt is up to. Again, a master/detail view is the pattern we are going to use here, as it makes sense in this situation. An index of names ordered alphabetically is a familiar and easy-to-grasp interface for most users (mobile or otherwise). Figure 2.12 shows our wireframe for this screen.

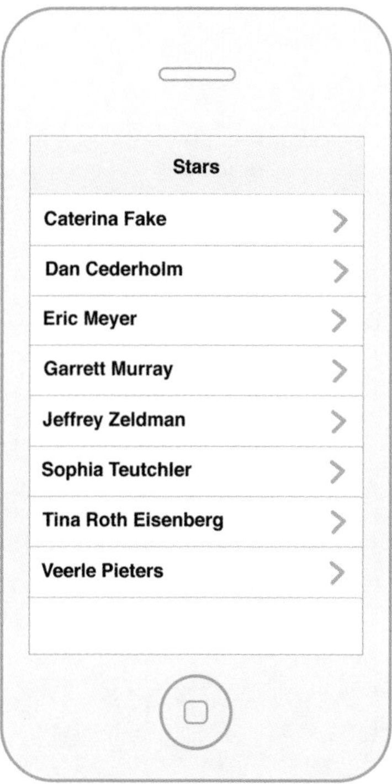

Figure 2.12. Wireframing the Stars listing

There we are: a dead-easy way for our users to find their celebrity of choice. It's worth noting that such a basic interface is potentially problematic; if our app becomes very popular and there are suddenly 1,000 stars in our database, a list like this becomes unwieldy.

It'd be fine if we were only interested in the Brad Pitts of the world, but if our taste changes to, say, Zach Braff, that's a whole lot of scrolling to do. The Android contacts application addresses this issue by including an additional scroll tab, allowing users to jump around the whole list (with lesser accuracy). iOS has an extra alphabetical scroll area that can be used to skip to the start of a single letter grouping. Both those platforms also let you narrow the list by searching within it. For our application, we're going to start simple, and deal with that problem if and when it becomes an issue for our users.

That's our master view. Now on to the detail for a single star, which you can see in Figure 2.13.

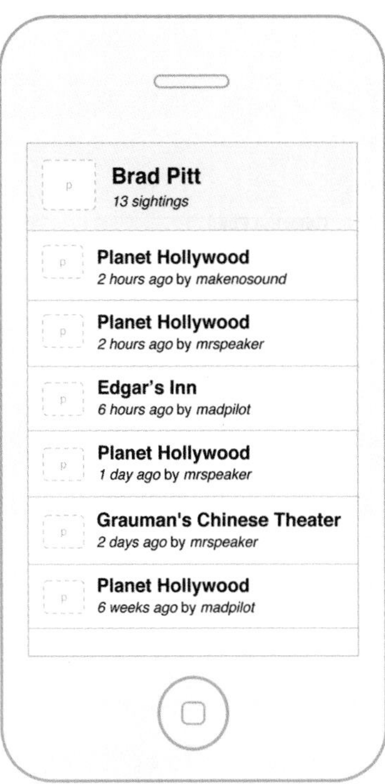

Figure 2.13. Viewing a single Star

The detail view for a star is basically the same as for a location, except the roles are reversed. Again, we have all the bits we need: the name of the star we selected, and a list of recent sightings with their locations. You can think of these pages as an index for sightings filtered by the context through which we arrived: one way is through spots, the other through celebrities.

Adding a Sighting

Now that we've catered for user movement through our application, we need a way for users to contribute to our content. The success of our application is going to depend on the amount of information we can provide people with. Imagine a café review application that has no cafés—what's the point of a celebrity-sighting service if no one can track their sightings?

Encouraging users to fill out forms online is difficult at the best of times, but it's exacerbated on mobile. The longer it takes for users to fill in a form on their mobile device, the higher the possibility that failures or errors will happen—say, losing network connectivity. Designing for efficiency is paramount.

We have to make sure we're including everything necessary to flesh out a sighting. A sighting is the combination of a star at a spot on a given date. Those three facts are all we really need.

Figure 2.14 shows a basic mockup for this form. It strikes a good balance by collecting all the information we need, while still being simple enough to not scare users away from using it.

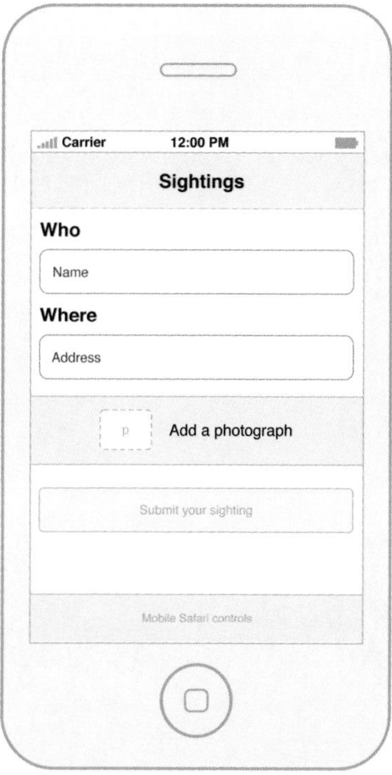

Figure 2.14. Adding a Sighting

Tying It All Together

So, we have all the components of our application in place. The problem is they're separate contexts, so we need a way for our users to flick between them easily. Luckily for us, there's a tried and tested solution out there that we can use—the tab bar. Let's review some of the features of the tab bar:

- establishes the structure of an application
- lets users easily move between an application's sections
- indicates the current state/location of the app

Sounds right up our alley! The flat hierarchy of the tab bar actually suits us here; we have three main sections that are of equal importance.

However, the implementation of a tab bar needs careful consideration, especially when thinking about a mobile web application. In a native app, the tab bar is usually a fixed element at the top or bottom of the screen. Inside the browser, though, this is trickier to accomplish. So what are our options? Placing the tab bar at the base of the viewport would mean placing it directly above the browser controls.

For a mobile web application, it makes more sense to place the tab bar at the top of the viewport, for the result shown in Figure 2.15.

Figure 2.15. Placing the tab bar at the top makes more sense

This improved placement has the added advantage of fitting the expectations of Android users, since tabs on that platform are generally at the top anyway. If we roll the tab bar out to each of the screens we've looked at already, we can see our application is starting to take shape. There's a consistent, flexible structure, and our users can easily identify which context they're in.

The Fix Is Out

Whether it appears at the top or bottom of the screen, the tab bar is often fixed in position, with the main content of the application flowing underneath it. This presents a couple of problems, the most obvious being that none of the current crop of mobile browsers support `position: fixed` in CSS. There are some JavaScript solutions that we'll look at Chapter 6, but they can be complicated (particularly across browsers and platforms), and can also cause performance problems. We need to determine whether the user experience benefits are worth this trade-off in performance. Do our users need access to each section of the app at all times? Will it be confusing if they don't have it?

As a general rule, erring on the side of simplicity is the best way to go. For the in-browser version of our application, we're going to let the tab bar scroll offscreen; users can simply scroll back to the top to change contexts.

Home Screen

On iOS, we have an extra mode that sits somewhere between a web application and a native application. iOS lets us set an option to run Mobile Safari in full-screen mode when our users bookmark our application on their home screen. We'll go into the details of implementing this behavior in Chapter 3, but for now, all we need to know is that full-screen mode removes all the browser chrome. Let's spend a bit of time designing a modified look and feel for this standalone mode. This gives us the opportunity to make our site conform more closely to the iOS user-interface paradigm.

None of the other platforms we're looking at offer this function, so when we're in standalone mode we can conform to the "iOS way" and move the tab bar down to the bottom. It's nice and close to our users' thumbs, as you can see in Figure 2.16.

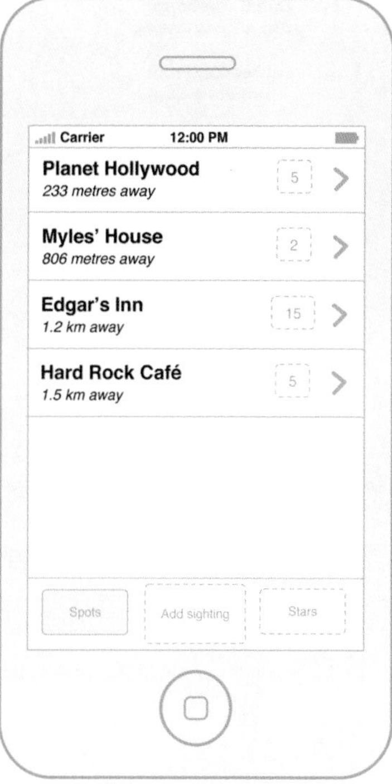

Figure 2.16. Wireframing the "standalone" mode of our app for iOS

That all sounds wonderful, right? And it is, but it's not without problems. The main design gotcha we need to think about at this stage is the lack of the standard browser controls. Our navigational model is drill-down, with the user's options being to move deeper, shift back up a level, or start at the top of the tree again. Without a back button, however, one of those options is impossible; there's no way for our users to go back, so we'd be forcing them to retrace their steps whenever they wanted to move up a level in our navigation. That means we have to include our own back button somewhere in our standalone mode interface. iOS users expect the back button in the top-left corner, so that's where we'll put it.

Figure 2.17 shows our full-screen wireframe with the addition of an iOS-style navigation bar and back button.

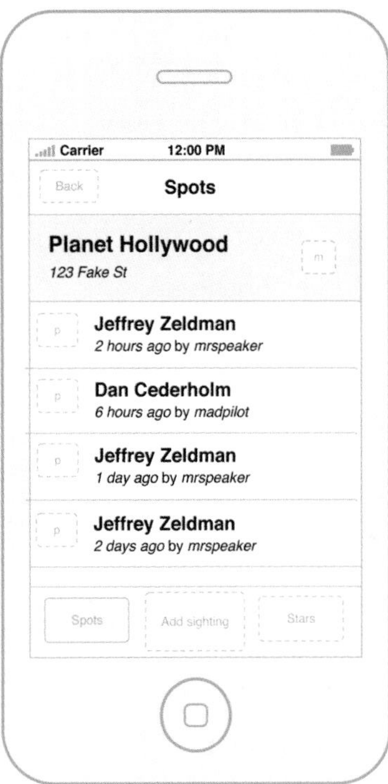

Figure 2.17. Adding a back button completes our standalone mode

Phew! Now that we're happy with the structure and flow of our application, let's attack the fun part: the style and aesthetics of our application.

Establish a Style

Finding a theme to riff on can give us a clarity of vision about the look of our app. In the case of StarTrackr, we can start by thinking about the sort of imagery we associate with celebrity. Here are a few ideas: money, the red carpet, sunglasses, flash photography, film, movies, music, awards shows, the Oscars, stars, gold, diamonds, paparazzi, glamor.

Which items on that list stand out as the strongest images? The colors. The red carpet is synonymous with celebrity, while the color gold brings to mind wealth and glamor. Luckily for us, those colors should work well together, so we can create a palette with which to build our design. What we've come up with is shown in Figure 2.18.

Figure 2.18. A color palette for our app, based on ideas of celebrity glamor

Of those colors the reds are much richer, so they're a more appropriate base for our application. A nice way of testing out multiple color choices is by putting together a basic *in situ* comparison. Let's look at one example, in Figure 2.19.

Figure 2.19. Playing around with colors in the context of our app

It gives us a sense of which colors work best together, and which ones clash. With the colors we've chosen, notice that even though they're completely flat, the darker red gives the impression of sitting *behind* the bright red. We can use this natural depth to our advantage, giving an implied structure to our interface without resorting to over-the-top effects.

Touchable Interfaces

Touchscreen devices let users interact directly and physically with an interface, so we want to build a design that *feels* touchable. One of the secrets to creating beautiful interfaces is to steal some tricks from the real world. Real objects have presence and volume, and their surfaces have variations in light and texture.

They also have a consistent light source. Nothing stands out more in a carefully crafted interface than a shine or shadow that's coming from the wrong direction. Always keep in mind where the light is coming from. We have some leeway—the angle of light doesn't need to be identical for all elements, and in some cases you'll need to change the direction subtly—but in general, we'll try to make sure our light source appears to be coming from above our interface elements. That means shine on the top, shadows on the bottom.

It's useful to imagine the objects in our interface sitting in the same room; that way we can understand how the light might affect them based on where they're located. We're going to follow convention a little here and build up an iOS-like tab bar, so let's have a look at the finished product and the various lighting effects used to build it up in Figure 2.20.

Figure 2.20. The style we'll be aiming for with our tab bar

Here are the key features of our design:

- light source from above
- gradient overlay to give the bar a round, physical presence
- highlight from above
- disappearing into shadow at the bottom
- hard line in the middle indicating the apex of the curve (when compared to the light)
- simple icons

That's our tab bar in its default state—but in fact it'll never look like that in use. Our users will always be somewhere in our application, which means that one of the items will always be selected. How might that look? Figure 2.21 gives an idea.

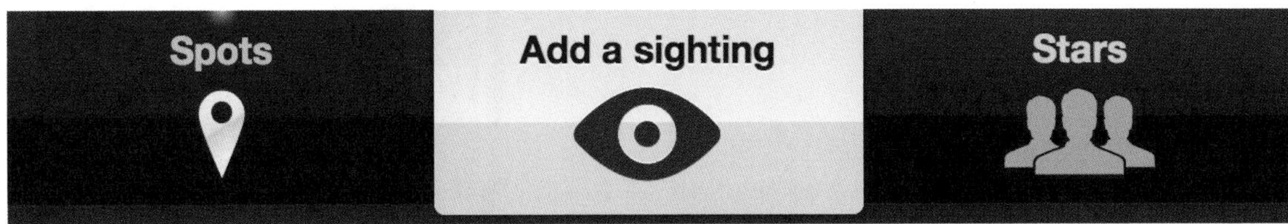

Figure 2.21. Our tab bar again, this time with an item selected

Here's a breakdown of the key features of the selected state:

- dark overlay to increase contrast on the selected button
- use of a contrasting color, in this case the gold color from our palette

- a subtle spot to draw attention
- added depth—highlights and shadow—to our interface icon

The task of styling the tab bar requires a delicate balance. We want to separate it from our content without having it disappear into the background completely. By using muted colours—or rather a lack of color—we're making the distinction between menu and content clear.

We're also doing something a little out of the ordinary with our tab bar. Usually, each item in the bar has the same style and weighting. This assumes that each of those items is conceptually similar, but in our case one of them isn't. "Spots" and "Stars" let our users view content, while the "Add a sighting" item lets them *add* content. We've played on that distinction and given the "Add a sighting" button a contrasting style in an attempt to encourage our users to contribute. There are a number of examples of native applications that use this pattern to draw attention to the function items in their tab bar, as shown in Figure 2.22.

Figure 2.22. Examples of tab bars with differentiated buttons, from Path, Instagram, and DailyBooth

Interface Icons

In our tab bar, we're using icons alongside text to reinforce the function behind each menu item, as well as adding graphical flair to the design. Both Android and iOS have similar design philosophies for their interface icons—namely that they're simple monochrome icons. This makes it easier to create a consistent iconography, and lets us use color in the icons to indicate selected (and other) states for each tab.

It's most important to find icons with the right metaphor to represent your content. As one of the tab bar items in our app is "Stars," using an actual star as that tab's icon would at first seem to make perfect sense. Yet, when you ponder over it more, problems begin to surface. The star has traditionally had a specific use in many applications: favorites (or "starred" items). If we used a star here, we'd essentially be asking our users to ignore their previous expectations. It makes more sense to use a closer representation of the actual content. In the case of "Stars," that content is a list of celebrities, so using human silhouettes is a better fit.

The other icons for our tab bar are a little easier to decide on. Spots are locations, so some sort of map-related symbol makes sense. We're going to use a Google Maps-style marker, as it's simple and recognizable. For sightings, we're trying to suggest the act of seeing a celebrity. We could use cameras, glasses, binoculars, or autographs—but they're all either hard to make out in the form of a tiny icon, or, as with stars, have associations with other common functions. An eye icon is the simplest and easiest to understand for that function, so that's what we'll use.

"But," you protest, "I'm terrible at drawing—my magnifying glasses always end up looking like spoons! Is there somewhere I can access icons?" Yes, there is! Recently, there's been a proliferation of great royalty-free interface icon sets released, making it incredible easy to find a consistent iconography for an application. Some of the most useful are:

Glyphish, http://glyphish.com/
: A set of 200 or so icons that are available as a free set with attribution requirements, or US$25 for the Pro version.

Helveticons, http://helveticons.ch/
: A lovely set of up to 477 icons based on the letterforms of the typeface Helvetica Bold. Costs are between US$279 and US$439, depending on the set.

Pictos, http://pictos.drewwilson.com/
: Pictos is actually three separate sets consisting of 648 icons! The vector packs for each set are between US$19 and US$29, and are an absolute steal at that price.

A Pixel is no Longer a Pixel

We can no longer assume that we're designing for a single resolution. The iPhone 3GS is 163ppi (pixels per inch), while the iPhone 4 is double that at 326ppi; the iPad is lower at 132ppi, and the Palm Pre sits around the middle at 186ppi. Android's developer guidelines split its devices into three categories: low density, medium density, and high density screens.

What that means for us is that we need to design in high resolution. More and more you'll have to create resolution-independent interfaces, so you can save yourself an enormous amount of time by building designs that way from the start. This doesn't necessarily require you to throw out your favorite bitmap tools and start jumping into a vector world, but it does mean thinking about the end product throughout the design process. For example, instead of creating gradients in Photoshop using, say, bitmaps layered on top of each other, you're better off making those effects using layer styles. That way you can resize those elements without losing definition.

Typography

Typography is central to good web design, yet it's a skill that's often glossed over in favor of shinier features. We're trying to communicate with people, and most of the time that means presenting information or options for them to read and then act upon. Text is user interface. Not only that, but a judicious choice and use of type can give your application meaning.

Unfortunately, the typographic landscape in the mobile space leaves much to be desired. For us web designers, this is nothing new: we're used to finding creative ways to work the limited palette of web-safe fonts. That palette is unfortunately significantly smaller in the world of mobile devices, but it's no excuse to eschew typographic discipline. There are exceptions to this rule, but many mobile devices will have an extremely limited choice of fonts, perhaps only one or two—and those fonts are often not the same from one platform to the next.

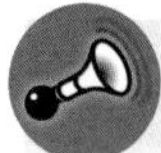

Your `@font-face` is Showing

Or rather, it's not. The world of web typography is an exciting place at the moment, mostly due to support for embedding additional fonts via the `@font-face` CSS rule. Whilst we'll avoid going into the specifics of `@font-face` here, we'd be remiss if we failed to mention the support for it in the mobile space. `@font-face` embedding is possible in most WebKit-based mobile browsers, and Opera mobile—though older versions of iOS require SVG fonts in order to work.

The biggest downside to using `@font-face` in a mobile application is performance. Font files are frequently very large; even using a subset of a single weight of a typeface can add an overhead of 100KB of data. For a project that's targeting mobile users, that's often too much to ask. Speed is a feature, so creating a bottleneck in the pursuit of a little extra flair often makes little sense.

Performance Considerations

It's easy to get carried away when designing a mobile app. There are so many examples of stunning interface design on all the native platforms, that it's hard to not want to compete. Alas, we need to be careful about how we use effects in our design. If we create an interface that requires lots of images to implement in HTML and CSS, we may run into performance problems, particularly in scroll-heavy applications. This is one of the unfortunate trade-offs between a native application and a web app. In a native application, we can create beautiful hardware-optimized and accelerated graphical effects using the drawing APIs available in the various native SDKs. The drawing tools available to web apps are a bit more limited. As much as possible, we should be thinking about designing interface elements that we can implement using mostly CSS.

"But we just made a beautiful tab bar! Do we have to throw that all away?" Well, no. Having some heavier graphical effects for the tab bar is no big deal. It will either remain on-screen in a static position all the time, or drop off the page promptly once a user scrolls down. The rows of our main lists, on the other hand, are elements that we should try to keep simple. We can still make them look beautiful, we just have to be a little more inventive. For our list rows, we're going to start with a solid color for each row, but using a slightly different shade for alternating odd and even rows, as Figure 2.23 shows.

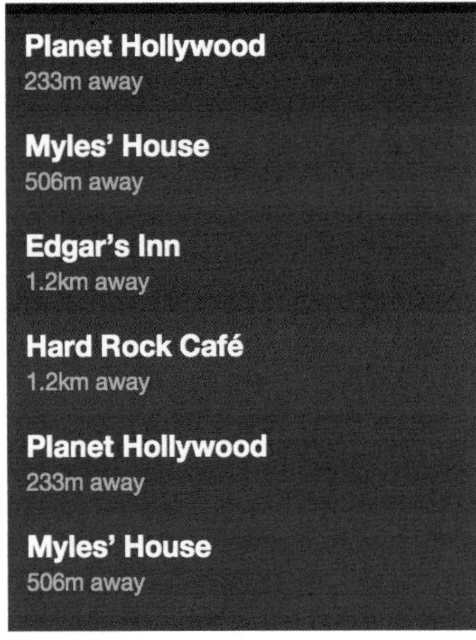

Figure 2.23. A basic list made up of solid alternating colors

Looks a bit flat, right? Let's give those rows a little "pop" with some lighting effects. The easiest way with an interface element like this—a multi-item list with content that could potentially vary in size—is to add a highlight to the top edge and an inset shadow to the bottom edge, as in Figure 2.24.

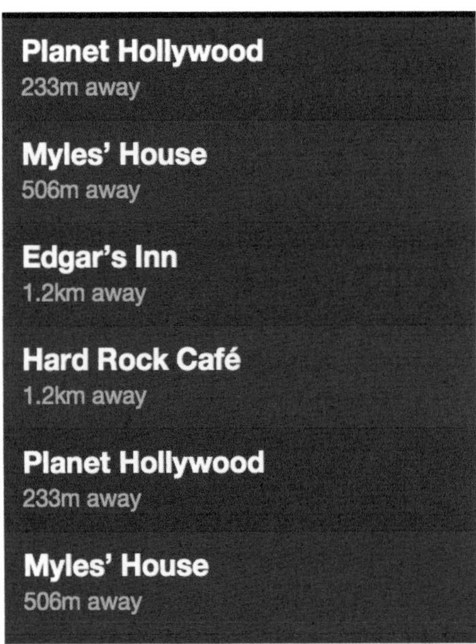

Figure 2.24. Adding a bit of depth to our list with highlights and shadows

That's much better! It's a subtle effect, but it really helps lift the interface and lets our users focus on the content. Plus, it can be implemented using only CSS border properties, so it passes our performance requirements. The problem now is that our text feels a little flat—because it appears to be unaffected by the same light that's adding the highlights and shadows to the rows of our list. Thankfully, we can use the same visual trick to give the text a little more physicality, as Figure 2.25 demonstrates.

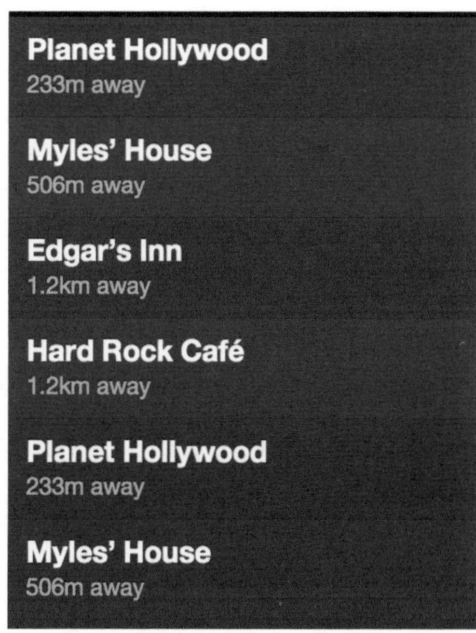

Figure 2.25. Adding shadows to our text gives it a stronger presence

Here we're just adding a one-pixel black shadow to the top edge of our letterforms. This gives the impression that the type has been physically stamped into the interface, the way a letterpress imprints onto paper. It's a simple effect, but it needs to be used carefully: if the text to which we're adding a shadow is too small, it can lose readability.

Remember, subtlety is one of the pivotal points to keep in mind for interface design, as Cameron Adams once said:[6] "Your maturity as a designer can be measured by the subtlety of your drop shadows."

Truer words were never spoken. A subtle interface lets the content of our application speak for itself. Using cheap and over-the-top effects will only distract our users from what we're trying to tell them. Our interface should define a structure for our content and help our users understand the function of our application. Great design is functional, not flashy.

---

[6] http://www.themaninblue.com/

Testing Design

It's impossible to design a great mobile application without seeing and "feeling" your interface on an actual device. There are some great tools for previewing your artwork on a mobile device. One of the most useful for the iPhone is LiveView (not least because it's free).[7]

LiveView is a remote screen-viewing application intended to help designers create graphics for mobile applications. The app is split into two parts: a screencaster application that you can run on your desktop machine, and an iPhone/iPad application that you can run on your phone. The screencaster lets you position a "window" over your desktop interface, and then broadcasts whatever graphics are under that window to your phone via Wi-Fi. It will even pass clicks from the device back to the screencasting computer. Unfortunately, LiveView is an OS X-only application, but there are similar remote desktop applications for Android and other platforms as well, which should be easy enough to find with a search through your marketplace of choice.

However you decide to do it—saving images to your device, or perhaps creating some image-only web pages—testing your designs and prototypes on your target device is an absolute must.

Reviewing Our Design

Alrighty, let's take a moment and assess where we're up to. We have a structure for our pages and a flow for our application; we have a theme we want to go with, and we've looked at some techniques we can use to give our design some flair. Let's roll out the design to the screens we've created.

Most of the pages use the techniques and structures we've outlined already, but lets break down a couple of these designs and look at them in further detail. First up is the Spots index, shown in Figure 2.26.

---

[7] http://www.zambetti.com/projects/liveview/

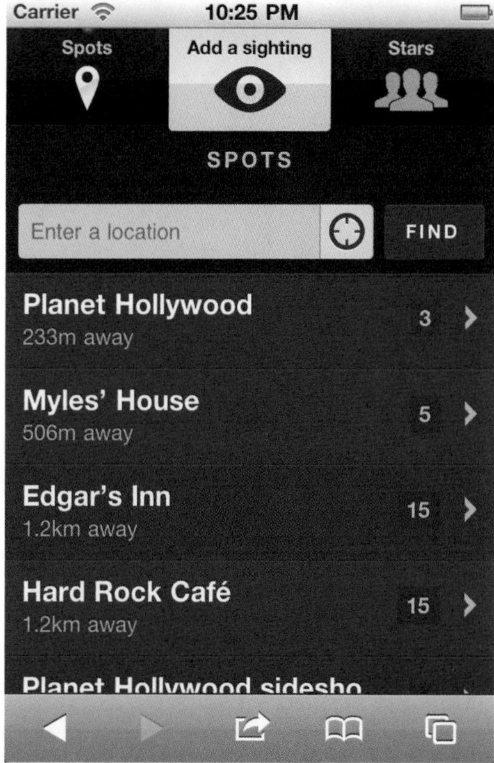

Figure 2.26. The complete Spots index page

Here's a quick review of the elements contained in this page:

- actionable list items have an arrow that suggests more content
- actionable list items have neutral text color, with the yellow reserved for hyperlinks
- a dark background with a lighter foreground
- a "find" button with the same highlights we're using for list rows
- a button for geolocation tied into the text field (this suggests those functions are linked—which they are—and reduces the number of separate elements in the form)

Figure 2.27 shows what the Spots listing will look like when scrolled down to the bottom.

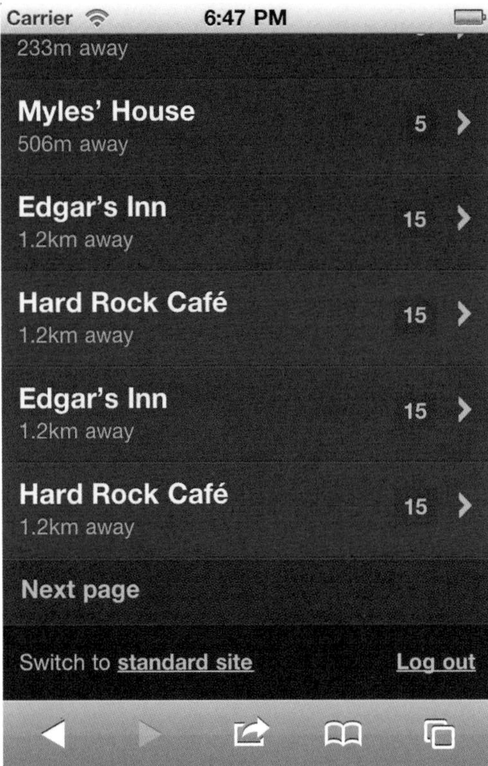

Figure 2.27. Spots index page, scrolled to the bottom

Some points to note here are:

- The footer at the bottom includes links to the full (non-mobile) site, and the ability to log out.
- The "Next page" link (because we don't want to load endless amounts of data over the mobile network, especially when those results might be irrelevant for our users, as the information is potentially old and out of date).

Next up is the detail view of a Spot, shown in Figure 2.28.

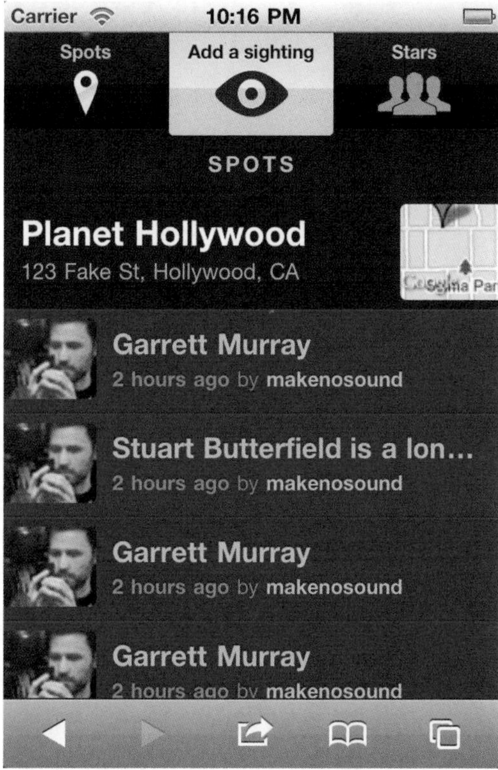

Figure 2.28. Viewing a Spot

In this design, notice:

- the main details are over the background, enabling the main content to sit in the foreground area
- that rows don't have to be limited to a single action (we're using a contrasting yellow for standard hyperlinks)
- a small thumbnail of a map (while practically useless at this size, a map is still instantly recognizable, so we can use it as an icon linking to a real map)

The final design to review is the full-screen or standalone mode. Let's look at our Spots index in standalone, as shown in Figure 2.29.

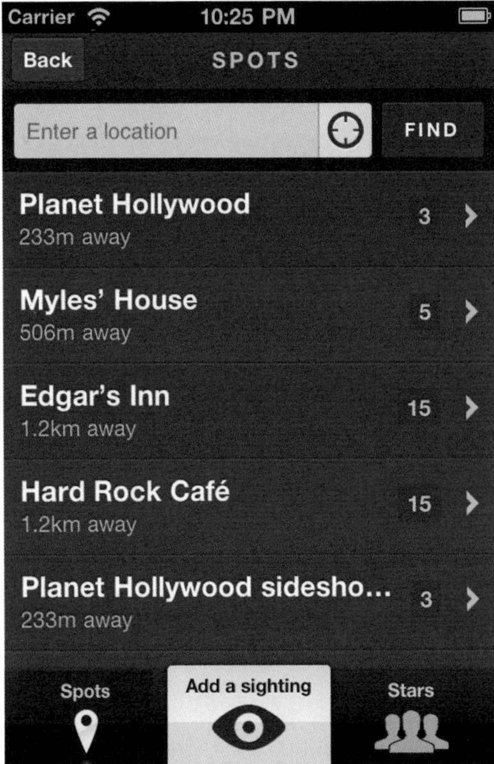

Figure 2.29. The full-screen mode of our Spots listing

All the changes we made in the wireframing stage are reflected here, notably that:

- our navigation is at the bottom
- we're bringing in a header element, which establishes the context and gives us room for more controls (such as our back button)

Application Icons

Now that we've built up our lovely design for StarTrackr, we'll need an icon to match. Our icon will eventually be used in a number of places, but primarily it'll end up on our users' home screens. In all likelihood, it'll be the part of our application that people will see most often, so we need to create a memorable icon that reinforces the function we're offering. In general, good application icons do one or more of the following:

- build from an existing brand iconography
- encapsulate the functionality of the application in a single image
- play off the name to reinforce the identity

Good examples of the first approach can be seen in the Facebook iPhone application, as well as the various mobile applications offered up by 37signals—seen in Figure 2.30. Facebook uses a white "f" on a blue background; it's incredibly simple, but the association with their standard logotype and the color scheme of their website is immediate and strong.

Figure 2.30. The application icons for Facebook, Campfire, and Basecamp

37signals have done a great job creating a set of consistent yet unique icons to match their suite of applications, and this applies to the icons for the two mobile applications they currently offer: Campfire and Basecamp. Campfire is a native application, and Basecamp a web app, but they share a consistency of shape (and thus brand) while staying different enough to be recognizable. The strong base color helps differentiate each icon from the other.

There are some excellent examples of this approach all over the place, particularly in some of the default applications on iOS, as you can see in Figure 2.31.

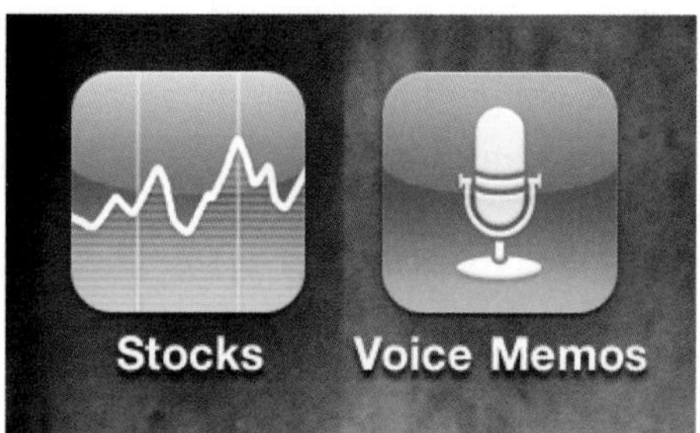

Figure 2.31. The icons for the Voice Memos and Stocks apps on iOS

Voice Memos, for example, uses an old-school microphone to make the connection between the application and its purposes. The iPhone Stocks app uses a graph to indicate the function—keeping track of ever-changing stock prices—and hint at the application's interface.

Unfortunately for us, StarTrackr is yet to have the same brand recognition as, say, Facebook, and the functionality of our app—finding and adding celebrity sightings—is difficult to distill in a single, comprehensible image. Instead, we're going to keep it uncomplicated and just use a star as the main graphic element for our icon. This gives us a strong image that helps reinforce the name of our application, and it has a nice association with the notion of celebrity. This concept also lets us build on the visual style that we've established with the application interface.

In our design to this point, we've been looking at the idea of the red carpet and trophy gold, awards, and glamor we associate with celebrity, and we can keep that flowing through the application icon. Figure 2.32 shows what we've come up with.

Figure 2.32. The application icon for the StarTrackr app

Icons should be, well, *iconic*, and our star fits the bill perfectly. Sure it's simple, but that's exactly what we're after. Some general rules when designing applications icons are:

- They should be forward-facing. We want volume and presence, so some perspective is nice, but don't go overboard.
- The light source should be top-down.
- Fill the entire background. While some platforms support transparent images, your app will look out of place on iOS without a complete background color.
- Consider the icon's appearance at small sizes, and create one that is recognizable at every resolution.
- Create artwork in a vector format. We'll see later on that there are a myriad of sizes for our icons.
- Subtle texture will make surfaces feel more real and less clinical.
- Above all, keep it simple.

Ready to Shine

That's it for the design of our application. We have a strong theme with a consistent feel, and a layout that's familiar to our users that establishes a navigational structure for the rest of the experience. Now let's learn how to make it real.

Chapter 3

Markup for Mobile

We have covered the process of sketching and designing our app. Now we're going to look at how to actually build it. Luckily, we have all the basic coding knowledge to begin developing mobile websites and applications: HTML, CSS, and JavaScript. This means, as always, that we're going to be designing and building with web standards. Using standards-based web development techniques will ensure the most consistent presentation and experience for our users, both now and as new devices arrive. A well-structured HTML page with clean, semantic markup will display correctly, and be both usable and accessible on any device—desktop or mobile.

In this chapter, we will focus on the most interesting parts of our application's CSS. There are a number of basic rules we'll be skipping over or only touching on briefly, either because they're self-explanatory, or because they have no particular bearing on mobile development. We'll be spending more time on the HTML5 and CSS3 features we'll be using, since some of those will likely be new to you, as well as those tricks that are specifically suitable or necessary for mobile.

What about WML?

For the uninitiated, in the early days of the mobile web, WML (or Wireless Markup Language) was the *de facto* standard for publishing web content on mobile devices, but it has long since gone the way of the dodo. Many of the new breed of phones and tablets, including iOS and Android, have no support for WML. Instead, they have full-featured web browsers that can understand and render HTML on par with their desktop equivalents. Consequently, there's really no need to look to new languages or different standards for the mobile web. For now and into the foreseeable future, HTML is going to be the markup language of choice for mobile web development.

Let's build up the HTML for our app. We'll start by establishing a basic skeleton for our pages:

spots.html *(excerpt)*

```
<!doctype html>
<!--[if IEMobile 7 ]><html class="no-js iem7"><![endif]-->
<!--[if (gt IEMobile 7)|!(IEMobile)]><!--><html class="no-js">
➥<!--<![endif]-->
  <head>
    <title>StarTrackr</title>
  </head>
  <body>
  </body>
</html>
```

We're beginning with the fundamentals, but this simple HTML is the basis for every page of our application. The first item to take note of is the doctype declaration. Doctypes are important: they tell the browser what sort of markup to expect and therefore how to parse the HTML we're giving it. We're using the HTML5 doctype, as we're going to be writing HTML and including some features from the HTML5 spec. If you're unfamiliar with HTML5, don't worry; for the most part it's identical to previous versions of HTML, although, as you'll have noticed, the doctype is much easier to remember!

If the above markup looks a little confusing, it's probably because we're using conditional comments to create classes, in order to give us the option of targeting Internet Explorer 7 mobile if we need to. While currently just a small player in the mobile field, Internet Explorer 7 mobile is the default browser in the current iteration of Windows Phone Series 7, so it's likely to gain some traction in the coming months and years.

The idea behind this technique is that Internet Explorer 7 mobile will understand the conditional comment and thus include an HTML element with an extra `class` of `iem7`. We can then use this `class` in our CSS to fix specific issues in the rather outdated IE7 rendering engine. For more information on this technique, and the various pros and cons of its usage, have a read of Paul Irish's post on the subject.[1] We're also including an extra `class`—`no-js`—that will be important later on in this chapter.

Style over Substance

Just as our markup is much the same as we would be writing for a regular website, our CSS will be relatively similar to what we're used to. Unfortunately, CSS support on mobile devices is less than terrific, and while the information is a couple of years old now, it's worth taking some time to read through Peter-Paul Koch's CSS compatibility tests for mobile devices for a good idea of what features

[1] http://paulirish.com/2008/conditional-stylesheets-vs-css-hacks-answer-neither/

of the CSS 2.1 specification are supported (or not).[2] Another good resource for information about support and compatibility for CSS properties, as well as HTML5 features and JavaScript APIs, is http://caniuse.com/. This site only includes information about a couple of mobile browsers—Mobile Safari, Opera Mini and Mobile, and Android's browser—but as this represents most of our target platforms, it's definitely worth a look.

Here are the basic principles for creating the stylesheets for our app:

- Keep our CSS completely separate from the HTML.
- Code for the most standards-compliant browsers first; then fix issues in IE and other devices where problems arise.

Let's set up our base CSS file and start layering some style on our app. First up, we'll need to update our HTML to include the reference to our CSS file:

spots.html *(excerpt)*

```
<!doctype html>
<!--[if IEMobile 7 ]><html class="no-js iem7"><![endif]-->
<!--[if (gt IEMobile 7)|!(IEMobile)]><!--> <html class="no-js"><!--<![endif]-->
  <head>
    <title>StarTrackr</title>
    <link rel="stylesheet" href="stylesheets/screen.css" media="screen">
  </head>
```

Nothing unusual there. Mobile browsers are no different from their desktop equivalents in that they all apply default CSS styles differently, so to get our CSS started, we'll begin with a very basic reset to clear out some of those various defaults:

stylesheets/screen.css *(excerpt)*

```
html, body, div, span, object, iframe, h1, h2, h3, h4, h5, h6, p,
blockquote, pre, abbr, address, cite, code, del, dfn, em, img, ins,
kbd, q, samp, small, strong, sub, sup, var, b, i, dl, dt, dd, ol,
ul, li, fieldset, form, label, legend, table, caption, tbody, tfoot,
thead, tr, th, td, article, aside, canvas, details, figcaption,
figure, footer, header, hgroup, menu, nav, section, summary, time,
mark, audio, video {
  margin: 0;
  padding: 0;
  border: 0;
  outline: 0;
  font-size: 100%;
  vertical-align: baseline;
```

[2] http://www.quirksmode.org/m/css.html

```
  background: transparent;
}

body {
  font-family: "HelveticaNeue", Arial, Helvetica, sans-serif;
}
```

Now that we have the shell of an HTML page and a stylesheet to work with, let's take a look at the construction of the various components of the StarTrackr application.

The Tab Bar

The HTML for the tab bar is quite simple. We're going to use the tried and true practice of marking up our navigation as an unordered list. This is old territory for most of us, but it's worth reminding ourselves why the `ul` element makes sense for navigation: it's the closest semantic representation of what our navigation really is, a list of pages:

spots.html *(excerpt)*

```
<ul id="tab-bar" class="page-spots">
  <li id="tab-spots">
    <a href="#">Spots</a>
  </li>
  <li id="tab-sighting">
    <a href="#">Add a sighting</a>
  </li>
  <li id="tab-stars">
    <a href="#">Stars</a>
  </li>
</ul><!-- #tab-bar -->
```

Points to note:

- We're giving the main tab bar element (`ul`) an `id` of `tab-bar`.
- Each of the list items (`li`) in the tab bar has an `id` as well, (we'll use this a little later on once we start to apply our styles).
- The main tab bar element has a `class` of `page-spots`, giving us a hook for adding a selected state to the navigation using CSS.
- We're keeping the HTML as clean and simple as possible. This structure gives us everything we'll need to implement our sexy tab bar design in CSS.
- There are comments to indicate the end of blocks; while they're unnecessary, they're nice for development purposes.

Why not nav?

At this point, you might well ask, "If we're using HTML5, why aren't we using the `nav` element here?" A perfectly valid question, to which the answer is that HTML5 support is still varied across the entire spectrum of mobile devices. If our target platforms were limited only to the current breed of smartphones, we could use the more semantic HTML5 elements with abandon. For the time being, it's best to keep it simple and use the tools we know will work across all browsers. Plus, there's nothing wrong with using only HTML 4 elements; they're still perfectly valid in HTML5.

CSS for mobile devices presents a relatively new concern for most digital designers: pixel density, or rather, resolution. Where desktop computers have been fairly stagnant in terms of screen resolution, the spectrum of mobile devices sees a whole range of resolutions. The solution is to use relative values for layout, and that means percentages and our old friend, the em.

Relative Units

A quick primer: an **em** is a unit of measurement in typography. In CSS, it's used as a measurement of the vertical space needed for any given letter in a font; hence, if the font size is 16 pixels, the value of 1 em will equal 16 pixels. The advantages to using relative units like ems and percentages is twofold. The use of percentages for layout means that our application is more likely to look correct across the broad spectrum of mobile devices. While we're expecting our target platforms to be generally similar in terms of their screen size, there's no way to we can used a pixel-based layout to target every platform. Secondly, with our interface and layout specified entirely in ems and percentages, we can adjust the overall scale of our interface by adjusting the `font-size` on our base element, which in our case will be the `body`. This becomes important as we look to adjust our interface on devices with different screen densities and physical sizes.

The CSS for the tab bar is a little more involved. To start with, we're going to build up the structure of the tab bar without the fancy visual fluff that we have in our design (don't worry, we'll reach the fancy parts a bit later on):

stylesheets/screen.css *(excerpt)*

```
#tab-bar {
  background: #050405;
  border-bottom: 1px #441d22 solid;
  position: relative;
  zoom: 1;
}

/* Clearfix to stop our floats escaping */
#tab-bar:before, #tab-bar:after {
  content: "\0020";
  display: block;
  height: 0;
```

```
  overflow: hidden;
}

#tab-bar:after {
  clear: both;
}

/* Float our three list items so they're evenly spaced */
#tab-bar li {
  display: inline;
  float: left;
  width: 33.333%;
}

/* Set a elements as blocks */
#tab-bar a {
  color: #cdcdcd;
  display: block;
  font-size: 0.875em; /* 12px / 14px */
  font-weight: bold;
  height: 4.583em; /* 55px / 12px */
  margin: 0 0.833em; /* 10px / 12px */
  overflow: hidden;
  padding-top: 0.428em; /* 6px / 14px */
  position: relative;
  text-align: center;
  text-decoration: none;
}
```

It's quite simple. We're floating the three list items so that each `li` takes up a third of the page, making sure to add a "clearfix" to the containing `#tab-bar` element so that it doesn't collapse.[3] We're not adding any margins or padding to the `li` elements, so we can be exact about their width—mixing margins with percentages for width can get a little tricky. Instead, we're applying the margins for our tab bar buttons to the `a` elements. This ensures they'll be bumped in from the boundaries of their containing `li`, and the delicate float balance is undisturbed.

We can add a temporary background color to the `a` elements for a look at how it's shaping up so far across a couple of different browsers and device resolutions—the results are shown in Figure 3.1.

[3] For more on this technique, see http://www.positioniseverything.net/easyclearing.html

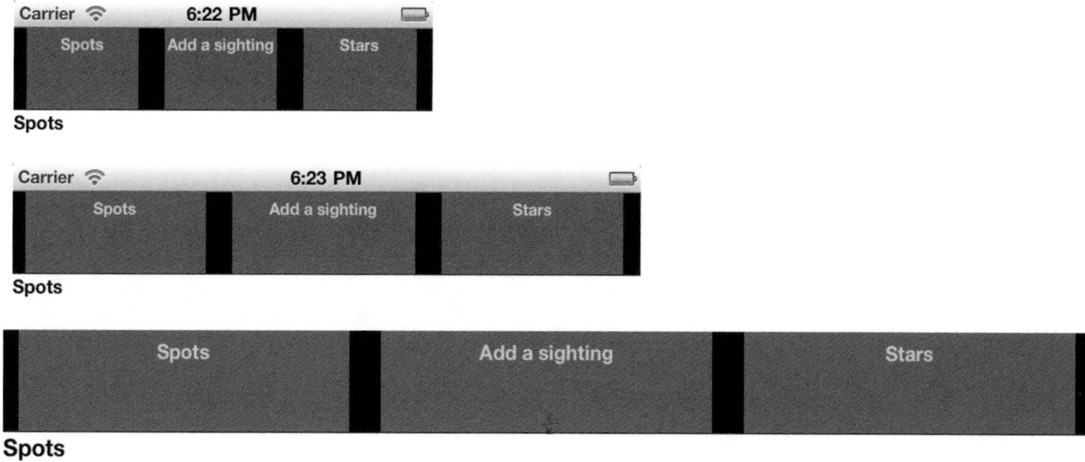

Figure 3.1. Top to bottom: iPhone in portrait orientation, iPhone in landscape orientation, Safari 5 on the desktop.

Some nice solid spacing so far. By using percentages, we have an evenly balanced tab bar across all these different browser widths; establishing this solid base means we can start to build more complex structures on top without worrying about breaking anything too badly. So let's go ahead and do this! Our design specifies that the "Add a sighting" tab needs to differ from the other two tabs—it extends beyond the tab bar and is reversed out. As we've given each of the tabs a unique ID, we can override the inherited styles thusly:

stylesheets/screen.css *(excerpt)*

```
#tab-sighting a {
  background: #d5d2d2;
  color: #111111;
  height: 4.95em;
  margin: 0 0 -0.367em;
}
```

By setting a height that's larger than the other tabs, the "Add a sighting" element will be taller. The problem is that the containing `ul` will grow to match this height, so instead of "Add a sighting" overlapping, the other tabs simply fall short. The trick to extending it is the negative bottom margin. By setting this to the difference between the height of the "Add a sighting" tab and the height of the standard tabs, we achieve the lovely little overlap we were after, as Figure 3.2 shows.

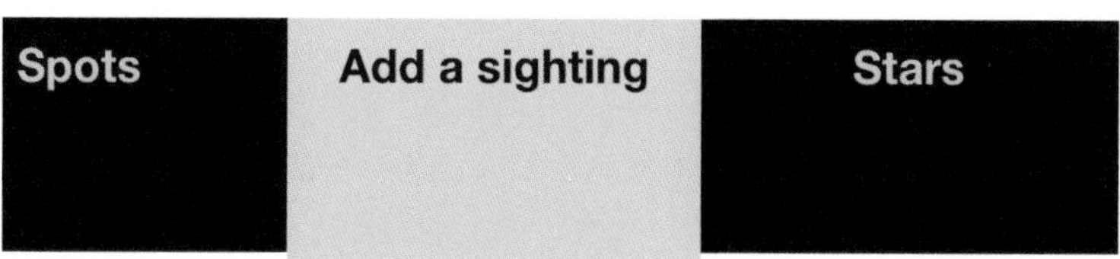

Figure 3.2. Negative margins allow our central tab to spill out of the tab bar

We noted before that we added an additional class to the tab bar as a hook for showing the state of the navigation. The technique is often used by applying an `id` or `class` to the `body` element, and then using that selector in CSS to make page-specific changes. We'll essentially be doing this, except we'll be limiting the scope so we have a bit more control. This will be useful down the track when we look at fancier methods of transitioning between pages. If we're on the "Spots" page, we want to make the "Spots" tab look selected, so our parent `class` will be `page-spots`. We can use the following code to change the color of the text on the selected tab:

stylesheets/screen.css *(excerpt)*

```
.page-spots #tab-spots a {
  color: #ebc466;
}
```

We're going to leave the tab bar there for now, but later on you'll see that we'll hook into this selector again to dress up our tab bar a little more. If you'd like to have a look at the full CSS used to create the final tab bar for StarTrackr, jump into the code archive and have a poke around the **screen.css** file.

Rows, Rows, Rows

The next part of our app we're going to look at are the main rows that make up the indexes of Spots and Stars. Once again, the HTML we're going to use is fairly basic. Here's the structure for the list of Spots:

spots.html *(excerpt)*

```
<ul id="spots-list" class="table-view table-action">
  <li>
    <a href="spot.html">
      <h2>Planet Hollywood</h2>
      <span class="relative-distance">233m away</span>
      <span class="sightings">3</span>
    </a>
  </li>
  <li class="even">
    <a href="spot.html">
      <h2>Myles&rsquo; House</h2>
      <span class="relative-distance">506m away</span>
      <span class="sightings">5</span>
    </a>
  </li>
</ul>
```

Some points worthy of note:

- We're using another unordered list as the base element for our list of Spots.

- This list has two classes that we'll use to target all the lists that have the same structure: `table-view` and `table-action`. We're using `table-view` to refer to all such lists, and `table-action` to identify indexes that have a single direct action.
- The block element (`h2`) inside our link (`a`) is valid HTML5. In previous versions of HTML and XHTML, block elements weren't allowed in this context, but HTML5 has no issue with it.
- We're identifying odd and even rows by an additional `even class` on the even rows (the absence of the class implies that the row is odd).
- The additional metadata for each "Spot"—the distance from the user and the number of sightings—are wrapped in `span` elements with semantic classes to identify them.

To start on the style for this index, we'll create some generic styles for all the `table-view` elements. These will be used for the indexes of "Spots," "Stars," and "Sightings":

stylesheets/screen.css *(excerpt)*

```
.table-view {
  background: #7c0c18;
}
.table-view li {
  border-top: 1px #8c2a34 solid;
  border-bottom: 1px #640913 solid;
}
.table-view .even {
  background: #830f1b;
}
```

At the design phase for this element, we mentioned that we need to keep performance in mind for these elements in particular. We're staying true to that here and keeping the styles as simple as possible—relying on basic CSS like borders to create the illusion of depth without heavy images. This brings us to the point shown in Figure 3.3; see how the simple dark-to-light borders gives the impression that each row has a slight bezel.

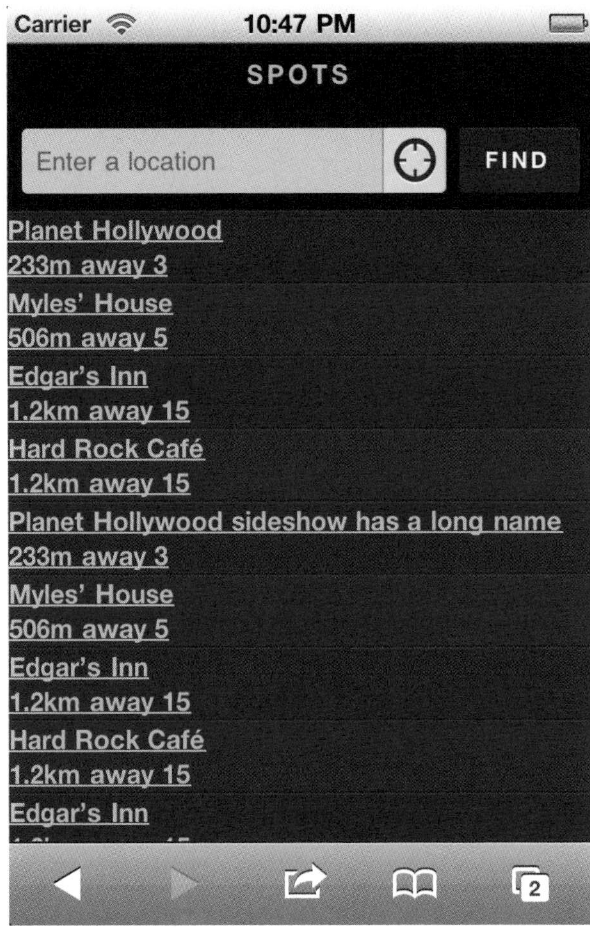

Figure 3.3. Simple techniques like using dark-to-light borders are effective in creating depth

Now we can flesh out the elements inside each row:

stylesheets/screen.css *(excerpt)*

```
.table-action li {
  position: relative;
}

.table-action a {
  color: #d6b69e;
  display: block; ➊
  padding: 0.5em 0.785em 0.714em;
  position: relative; ➋
  text-decoration: none;
  text-shadow: rgba(0, 0, 0, 0.4) 0 -1px 1px; ➌
}

.table-action h2 {
  color: white;
```

```
  font-size: 1.285em; /* 18px / 14px */
  width: 82%; ❹
}

.table-action .relative-distance {
  font-weight: normal;
}

.table-action .sightings {
  background: #6f0914;
  border: 1px #841420 solid;
  -webkit-border-radius: 0.143em; ❺
  -moz-border-radius: 0.143em;
  border-radius: 0.143em;
  color: #ebc466;
  font-weight: bold;
  position: absolute;
  padding: 0.214em 0.429em;
  right: 2.5em;
  top: 50%; ❻
  margin-top: -1.1em;
}
```

This code is all stock-standard CSS, but there are some points worth noting:

❶ We set the `a` to `display: block` so the whole row is clickable.

❷ Using `position: relative` here allows us to position child elements using absolute values.

❸ Using a `text-shadow` here makes the text look as though it's been imprinted into the interface.

❹ By limiting the width here, we have room for the metadata and icon.

❺ Everyone's favorite: rounded corners, repeated with vendor-prefixed properties for full support.

❻ We can center the element vertically by positioning it at 50% and applying a negative margin equal to half its height.

Our list is really starting to take shape now, as Figure 3.4 shows.

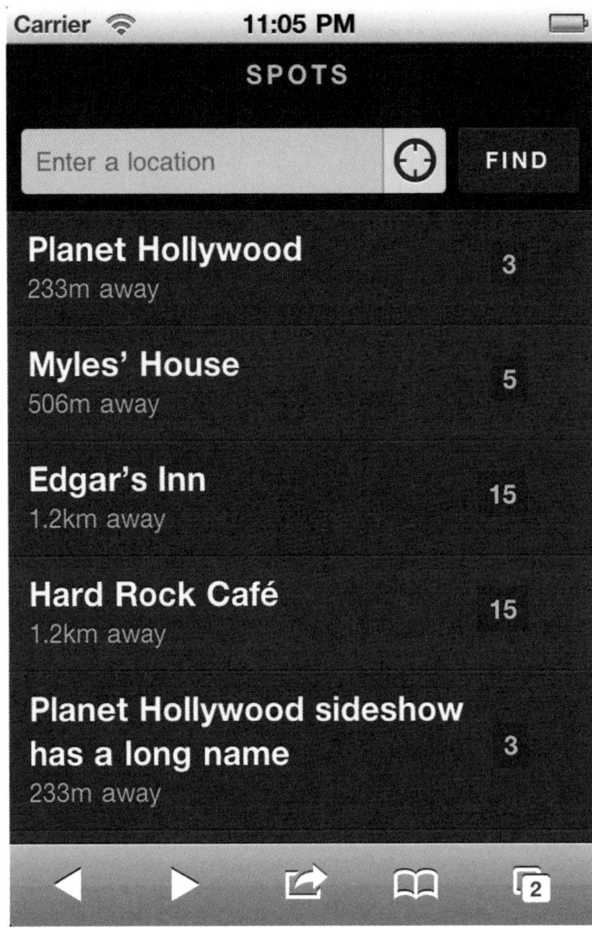

Figure 3.4. The elements in our list are now fully styled

This exact same code can be applied to our "Stars" list, as the underlying HTML is almost identical:

stars.html *(excerpt)*

```
<ul id="sightings-list" class="table-view table-action">
  <li>
    <a href="star.html">
      <h2>Caterina Fake</h2>
      <span class="sightings">5</span>
    </a>
  </li>
  <li>
    <a href="star.html">
      <h2>Dan Cederholm</h2>
      <span class="sightings">5</span>
    </a>
  </li>
</ul>
```

Without making any changes to our CSS files, the "Stars" index will now look like Figure 3.5.

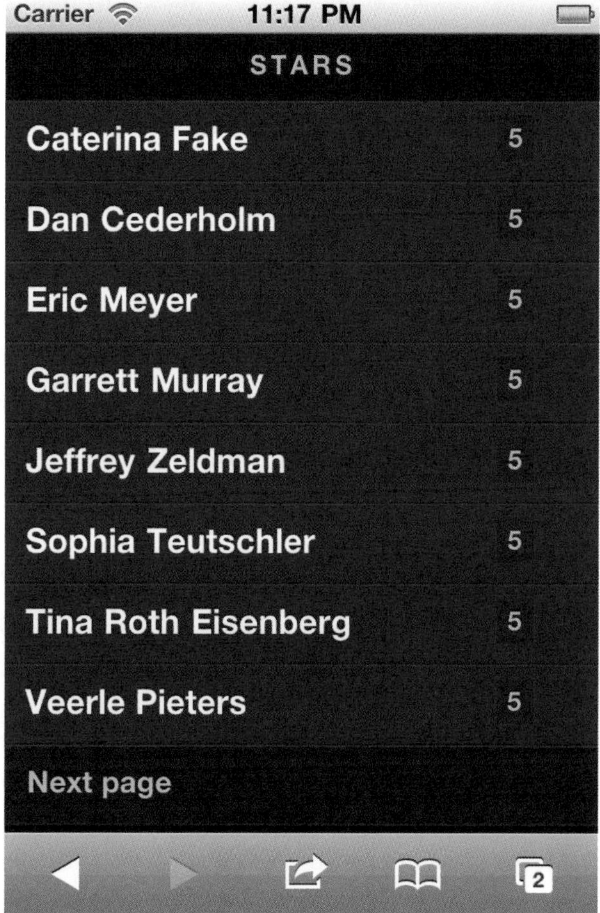

Figure 3.5. The same CSS applies to the listing of Stars

Writing modular and reusable CSS is as important as ever on mobile devices. The more generic we can make our CSS, the smaller the stylesheet our users have to download.

Validation

Remember to validate! While even the browsers on mobile devices will do their best to deal with malformed HTML, we can make their job (and ours) a whole lot easier by ensuring that our HTML meets the W3C specifications. By ensuring our HTML is well-formed, we increase our cross-platform compatibility and minimize rendering errors. This is especially important going forward—testing against the current crop of browsers is great, but what about the browser that's released six months from now? A year from now? Code that validates is the most reliable guarantee that future web platforms will handle it as designed.

Images and Pseudo-elements

We're going to make use of an **image sprite** for the icons in our application—that is, multiple images combined into a single graphic and then selectively cropped in different contexts. It's a technique that's often used in desktop web development, as it means there are fewer images for the browser to download. It may seem counterintuitive, but it's actually faster for a browser to download a single large image rather than several small images. That's because browsers can only download a limited number of resources in parallel from any server—so the more images, the longer the queue to download each one.

The usual process of implementing sprites is to create a single image that can then be used as a background image for multiple elements. This background image is then repositioned to show the correct sprite in the correct place. The problem with this approach is that it requires either:

- large, complex images that have enough padding around each sprite for the space they appear in (to ensure other parts of the sprite don't bleed in accidentally)
- unnecessary markup that gives us a hook to crop the sprite tightly in place

We're going to use a technique that avoids both these pitfalls, instead creating the additional elements we need using content generated in CSS pseudo-elements. This approach also lets us alter the source of the sprite using only CSS, which will come in handy down the track.

Before we tackle the code though, we need an image! The one we're going to use for our app contains all the icons we need, with extra copies for each additional state we require (in our case we're only using a selected state for the icons that appear in the tab bar). The image we've created is shown in Figure 3.6, and can be found in the code archive as **images/sprite.png**.

Figure 3.6. Our tightly packed sprite image.

We're going to use the "Stars" tab in our tab bar as the demo for this technique. The first step is to create the pseudo-element that's going to contain our sprite. Pseudo-elements can be used to insert "fake" elements into our page via CSS, allowing us to apply additional background images without affecting the markup of our page.

There are two pseudo-elements that we can use for the purpose of adding extra images, and the syntax for creating them is similar to what's used for pseudo-classes like `:hover` and `:visited` with which you're probably already familiar:

- `:before`, which can be used to insert content before the selected element

- :after, which can be used to insert content after the selected element

In the example below, these two selectors would place their respective content before and after each paragraph tag:

```
p:before {
  content: "I'm in front!"
}
p:after {
  content: "Bringin' up the rear!"
}
```

This may look a little odd if you're unfamiliar with the content property in CSS. It lets us generate additional content—like the text in the example above—using only CSS. Both the above pseudo-elements behave in much the same way, but we're going to use :after, because the icon will appear after the text in our tab bar element. Let's create our new element with our sprite image:

stylesheets/screen.css *(excerpt)*

```
#tab-spots a:after {
  content: url(../images/sprite.png);
}
```

A lesser-known feature of the content property is that it can be used to generate more than just text. If we give it the URL of an image, as we've done above, it'll create an img element using that URL as its src.

Figure 3.7 shows what this will look like.

Figure 3.7. Our sprite image, injected using the content property

"Wonderful," you say, "but how are we supposed to crop the image?" And again, the answer is with a little CSS magic. We're going to use the clip property to trim the sprite down to just the bit we want. clip lets us define a rectangle inside the bounds of an element and then crop the content of that element to the rectangle.

Let's look at a simple example so that you can understand the concept:

```
.example {
  background: #000;
  height: 100px;
  width: 100px;
}
```

This code will make a 100×100px box with a black background. By adding a `clip` property, we can crop its contents without altering the overall size of the element:

```
.example {
  background: #000;
  clip: rect(0 50px 50px 0);
  height: 100px;
  width: 100px;
}
```

Figure 3.8 shows a before/after comparison (note the original shape of the div has been included in gray to illustrate the difference).

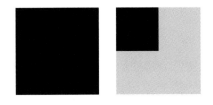

Figure 3.8. An example of the `clip` property in action

The element still thinks it's 100 pixels wide, but only 50 pixels of its content is visible. You can see how this property can be used to selectively show sections of our sprite image. The four values in the parentheses after `clip: rect`, in order, are the distance to crop from:

1. the top edge, measured from the top edge
2. the right edge, measured from the left edge
3. the bottom edge, measured from the top edge
4. the left edge, measured from the left edge

The values are in the same order as you're probably used to specifying for the `margin` or `padding` shorthand properties: top, right, bottom, left. The most important point to remember is that the origin for all crop values is the top-left corner of the element. It's done this way because the top-left corner is the only anchor point that won't change relative to the content in the clipped element. At first this will seem counterintuitive, but once you get the hang of the syntax, it does make sense.

For the Spots tab in our tab bar, we want to clip a rectangle that includes only the unselected state for the map pin icon, which works out to be:

- top: 0 pixels from the top edge
- right: 18 pixels from the left edge
- bottom: 33 pixels from the top edge
- left: 0 pixels from the left edge

So our `clip` value will be:

stylesheets/screen.css *(excerpt)*

```
#tab-spots a:after {
  content: url(../images/sprite.png);
  clip: rect(0 18px 33px 0px);
  position: absolute;
}
```

This gives us the nicely cropped icon we're after, as Figure 3.9 shows, though, note that `clip` only works on elements that are absolutely positioned.

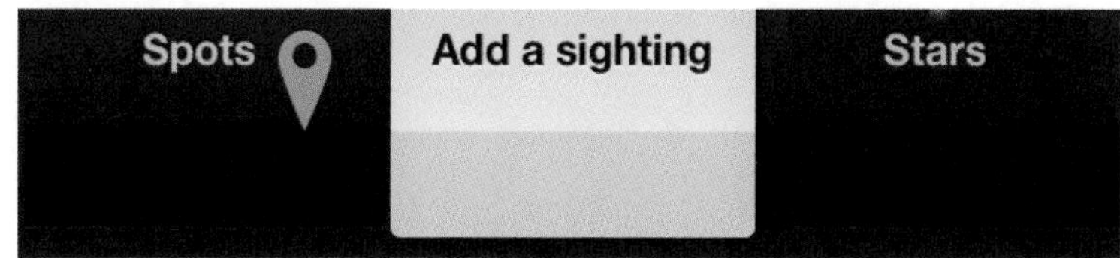

Figure 3.9. Our sprite image clipped to show only the relevant icon

All that's left to do now is to wrangle it into the position we want. Pseudo-elements can be manipulated in the exact same way as standard elements in the DOM, so we can position our sprite using regular techniques. In this case, we're going to use the 50% position and negative margin trick to center the icon in the middle tab:

stylesheets/screen.css *(excerpt)*

```
#tab-spots a:after {
  content: url(../images/sprite.png);
  clip: rect(0 18px 33px 0px);
  left: 50%;
  margin-left: -10px;
  top: 1.833em;
  position: absolute;
}
```

Perfect! Figure 3.10 shows the final appearance of our icon.

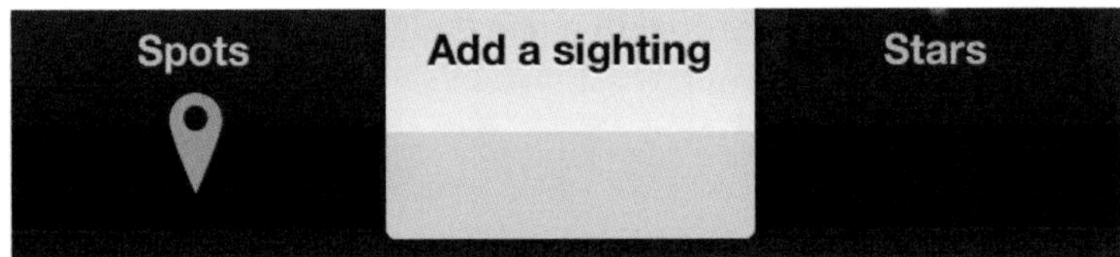

Figure 3.10. Our clipped sprite, now where it should be

One trick with this technique that's not immediately obvious is that we need to offset our pseudo-element by an additional amount equal to the distance we're cropping in from the left. This is because `clip` doesn't reduce the actual size of the element it's applied to—so if you're clipping a rectangle 40px from the left edge of an image, the resulting image will still show up 40px from where you've placed the image. To offset this, you'll need to apply a negative margin to pull the element back and line up the clipped section of the background image.

For the first icon we've placed above (the "Spots" icon), this turns out to be unnecessary, since that icon is the first one from the left in our sprite. But if you take a look at the code for the selected state of our "Spots" tab, you can see the additional value. Remember, we're using the class applied to the containing `ul` to note the selected state:

stylesheets/screen.css *(excerpt)*

```
.page-spots #tab-spots a:after {
  clip: rect(0 37px 33px 18px);
  margin-left: -29px;
}
```

Here we're cropping an area that's 19px wide, so we're using a negative left margin of 18px to wrangle it into the correct position—the last value in the `rect` function. Because we're already using a negative margin to center the image (half the total width, 10px), the total negative margin winds up being 28px. Whew!

So that's it! Now we can roll the same implementation out to all the places we need icons.

Understanding the Viewport

When building for mobile, it's essential to have an understanding of the **viewport**. On the desktop, the viewport is a clear concept: it's the visible space in the browser window. On mobile devices, it's a little more complicated, because the screen is usually smaller than the browser window.

In "A tale of two viewports—part two,"[4] Peter-Paul Koch breaks it up into two separate concepts: the **visual viewport** and the **layout viewport**. The visual viewport is the section of our page that's

[4] http://www.quirksmode.org/mobile/viewports2.html

currently visible; its size can be altered when a user scrolls or zooms to a different part of the page. The layout viewport refers to the size of the actual page.

On the desktop, the visual viewport and the layout viewport are one and the same, but on mobile devices the browser needs to set a default for the layout viewport that's larger than the visual viewport. These defaults differ between devices: Mobile Safari uses 980px; Opera Mini, 850px; Android WebKit, 800px; and IE, 974px. Why these larger values? Because otherwise, when you viewed a website designed for a desktop browser on your mobile device, the layout might break, since the content would be squeezed into a 320px window. By defining a large layout viewport, mobile browsers allow the CSS for these sites to be interpreted as if the screen were significantly wider than it is. Like it or not, we're living in a time of fixed-width layouts and 960px grids, so mobile browsers need to adapt to live in a desktop world.

This poses a problem for our mobile site, since we're specifically designing it to fill the viewport of a mobile device: it's a single column that looks stretched out of proportion if you view it in a desktop browser at 960px or more.

Thankfully, we're not limited by this behavior of mobile browsers. Using a `meta` tag, we can override the default width. If we wanted to create a site that's 500px wide, we could use the following to set the layout viewport to match our design:

```
<meta name="viewport" content="width=500">
```

That's great, but of course it's a contrived example. What if we wanted to make the visual viewport and layout viewport match? We're unable to specify a width, because we have no way of knowing exactly how wide the visual viewport of a user's device might be. If we set the viewport value to `width=320`, for example, it would achieve the result we want on an iPhone, but not all devices have this exact width. Lucky for us the browser manufacturers have already considered this problem, and have provided us with the `device-width` variable that we can use to set a dynamic width for each device:

```
<meta name="viewport" content="width=device-width">
```

This will set the width of the visual viewport and the layout viewport to the same value, making it appear as though the site is optimized perfectly for their device. The `viewport` meta key also lets us control other aspects of the viewport, such as:

`height`
: Unsurprisingly, this sets the height of the viewport in pixels. As with the `width` attribute, we can set it to the height of the screen using `device-height`.

`initial-scale`
: This is the initial scale of the viewport—in other words, the zoom level of the screen. This usually defaults to whatever value will fit the entire width of the page on the screen.

`minimum-scale`
: This sets the smallest scale the user can resize the viewport to. On iOS, the default for this is 0.25, but the value can be set anywhere between 0 and 10.

`maximum-scale`
: Funnily enough, this lets us specify the *maximum* zoom level the user can resize the viewport to. On iOS, the default for this is 1.6, but the value can be set anywhere between 0 and 10.

`user-scalable`
: This specifies whether we want to let our users resize the viewport—that is, zoom in or out. The default is `yes`, and to disable scaling we can change the value to `no`.

`target-densitydpi`
: An Android-only property for now, which gives us control over the rendered resolution of the target device. You can set it to `device-dpi` to match the screen density of the device, but this can have the effect of scaling your CSS pixel values up or down. If you're developing your CSS to be resolution-independent, as we've been doing so far, it's sensible to use the default value of 160dpi—so you don't need to specify this value.

To change some or all of these properties, use a single `meta` tag with comma-separated values. For example, if you wanted to set `width` to `device-width`, `minimum-scale` to `0.5`, and `maximum-scale` to `2`, you could use the following:

```
<meta name="viewport" content="width=device-width, minimum-scale=0.5,
➥maximum-scale=2">
```

Not all these are supported by every mobile browser, but you can use still them without too much worry. Other properties will be ignored by browsers that don't understand them. This is the final viewport `meta` tag for our app:

```
<meta name="viewport" content="width=device-width, minimum-scale=1,
➥maximum-scale=1, user-scalable=no">
```

We're setting the `width` to the width of the device, and ensuring users can't scale the interface by disabling it explicitly with `user-scalable=no`. Instead of using `initial-scale`, we're using a combination of `minimum-scale` and `maximum-scale`, which has the benefit of being better supported. The decision to disable features like zooming shouldn't be taken lightly—zooming is an important accessibility feature and is used by many —indeed, probably most—people. We're doing it because our application is designed specifically for small screens, and it will be perfectly usable at a scale of 1. If you're unable to guarantee that, don't break the standard behavior for your users.

Here's some further reading on configuring your viewport:

- Safari Web Content Guide: Configuring the Viewport [5]
- An introduction to meta viewport and @viewport[6]

Know Your (Resource) Limits

When building desktop applications, we hardly ever push our machines to the limit of their capabilities, but mobile devices are a different beast. To keep the devices small and their power usage down, mobile devices usually have extremely limited computing resources; this means we can hit the limits of those resources quickly.

Bandwidth is the limit we run into most often, and though the problem is accentuated in the mobile space, most web developers are accustomed to minimizing bandwidth usage. Limited memory is a more difficult issue and, though there are limits on all resources in mobile browsers, images are most likely to cause a problem here. You might have come across this when browsing a page with a large number of images; Mobile Safari will display a blue question mark [?] icon when the memory limit is reached. Pages with infinite scrolling are especially susceptible to this issue, as they continue to add resources to the page without freeing up any memory.

iOS imposes the following maximum sizes for resources loaded by web pages:

- 3 megapixels for GIF, PNG, and TIFF images
- 32 megapixels for JPEG (but any larger than 2 megapixels will be decoded to a smaller size, which may lead to unintended behavior)
- 3 megapixels for a `canvas` element
- under 10MB for individual resource files (applies to HTML, CSS, JavaScript, and any other non-streaming resources, including images)

In addition, JavaScript execution time is restricted to 10 seconds for each top-level entry point.

iOS imposes the following limits on resources loaded by web pages:

- The maximum size for GIF, PNG, and TIFF images is 3 megapixels.

---

[5] http://developer.apple.com/library/safari/#documentation/appleapplications/reference/safariwebcontent/UsingtheViewport/UsingtheViewport.html%23//apple_ref/doc/uid/TP40006509-SW24
[6] http://dev.opera.com/articles/view/an-introduction-to-meta-viewport-and-viewport/

- The maximum image size for JPEGs is 32 megapixels—but any JPEG images larger than 2 megapixels will be decoded to a smaller size, which may lead to undesired behavior.
- The maximum size for a `canvas` element is 3 megapixels.
- Individual resource files must be less than 10 MB. This applies to HTML, CSS, JavaScript, and any other non-streaming resources (including images).
- JavaScript execution time is limited to 10 seconds for each top-level entry point.

It's really important to be aware of these limitations, as breaking them can result in mysterious and mind-boggling errors. For example, if you hit the JavaScript execution limit on iOS, Mobile Safari will simply stop the script wherever it's up to—which may cause some odd results. It's hard to find concrete information for Android devices—especially as they vary greatly compared to Apple's offerings—but given that hardware specifications are quite similar across the spectrum of mobile devices, it's relatively safe to assume that the limits for other platforms are in the same range as for iOS devices.

Overarching resource limits are only part of the picture—there are also limits on what mobile browsers will be able to cache. The documentation from the various mobile browser vendors on these limits is slim or nonexistent; thankfully, Ryan Grove from Yahoo has made various attempts to divine those limits, and shared his learning on the Yahoo! User Interface (YUI) blog.[7] You can check out the post for the full breakdown of his findings, but the important points for us to take note of are:

- iOS will only cache external resources if they're smaller than 4MB, Android has a slightly lower limit at 2MB, and webOS is around 1MB.
- iOS cache limits for the content of an HTML page (the HTML itself) range from 25KB to 103KB, Android and webOS have the same limit as for external resources (though webOS's cache behavior is unreliable).

Thus, he recommends the following limits on resource size to ensure optimal cache performance across the current spectrum of available devices:

- Keep external resources like CSS, JavaScript, and images under 1MB.
- Limit the size of HTML pages to 25.6KB or less.

As with almost every feature in the mobile device space, these limits change on a daily basis. New devices and newer versions of operating systems can affect these restrictions, so it's imperative that you test, test, and test again if you want to be absolutely sure that your app is working as expected. That said, if we stay under these recommended limits we're likely to be safe for most use cases.

---

[7] http://www.yuiblog.com/blog/2010/07/12/mobile-browser-cache-limits-revisited/

Let's Get Progressive

When, as web developers, we first made the transition from table-based layouts to building websites with CSS, we were forced to employ a range of methods—complex CSS hacks and unreliable browser sniffing scripts—to ensure that our designs would function across the range of browsers and their varying implementations of both CSS and JavaScript. As time went on, it became clear that this approach was fragile and prone to failure: new browsers would be released and our careful hacks would be misapplied. In an attempt to create more durable sites, the practice of **graceful degradation** was established: building websites so that they provide the optimal user experience in more modern browsers, then degrading gracefully to a more limited level of user experience in older browsers. Basically, it was about just making sure that sites didn't break.

This idea has morphed into a newer philosophy: **progressive enhancement**. While conceptually similar to graceful degradation, progressive enhancement simply flips the methodology. We start by establishing a baseline of functionality that works across all browsers, then layer on additional style and functionality for browsers that include the features we want to target. How do we do that? By asking nicely. Central to the idea of progressive enhancement is the practice of **feature detection**: testing the users' browser to see if it can do what we want. This approach means we're only asking browsers that pass the test to use a given feature. If a browser fails the test, they receive the baseline template, and everyone is happy.

The only downside to using progressive enhancement is that setting up all those tests for the various features you might want to use is a complex and somewhat tedious affair. Or rather, it used to be.

Modernizr to the Rescue

If you're yet to come across Modernizr, you've been missing out. It's an open source JavaScript library that makes supporting different levels of experience based on the capabilities of our users' browsers a piece of cake. This allows us to take advantage of the shiny new features in HTML5 and CSS3 without having to worry about destroying the experience for users with older browsers.

Usage is dead simple. Start by downloading the latest release at http://modernizr.com—that's version 1.7 at the time of writing. Once that's done, we can embed it in the `head` of our page:

```
<script type="text/javascript" src="javascripts/vendor/modernizr-1.7.min.js">
➥</script>
```

First Things First

Because it adds behavior that other scripts and stylesheets may depend on, Modernizr *should* be included in the `head`, and not at the bottom of the document as is usually recommended.

You should ensure that you've added the `no-js` `class` to the `html` element of your page—remember that we did this when we first started building our page. This gives you the ability to target devices without JavaScript, as Modernizr recognizes this `class` and will change it to `js` if the browser supports JavaScript. When it loads, Modernizr will automatically run through a barrage of feature tests—all of which are outlined in the documentation—and then give you access to information on which features are supported, and which are not.

The first way this information is exposed is through a series of classes that are added to the `html` element. In the same way that JavaScript support can be discerned by the presence of either a `no-js` or a `js` class, Modernizr will add a class for each of the tests it completes.

Let's look at this in practice. Say we want to use custom fonts embedded via `@font-face` in our application. Running Modernizr in a browser with support for `@font-face` would result in the following `html` element:

```
<html class="js fontface">
```

And in a browser *without* `@font-face`, we'd have:

```
<html class="js no-fontface">
```

Because the `html` element is a container for all the other elements in our page, we can use that `class` as a hook in CSS to add the `@font-face` embedded typeface to our font stack only when we know it's supported:

```
@font-face {
  font-family: 'MyFontFamily';
  src: url('myfont-webfont.eot?') format('eot'),
       url('myfont-webfont.woff') format('woff'),
       url('myfont-webfont.ttf')  format('truetype'),
       url('myfont-webfont.svg#svgFontName') format('svg');
}

.fontface h1 {
  /* Yay, browser has @font-face support! */
  font-family: 'MyFontFamily', serif;
}

h1 {
  /* No @font-face, fall back to image replacement code */
}
```

Just to be clear: Modernizr will add these classes for *every test it supports*. So it's more than likely our `html` element will end up crowded like this:

```
<html class="js flexbox canvas canvastext no-webgl no-touch geolocation
postmessage websqldatabase no-indexeddb hashchange history draganddrop websockets
rgba hsla multiplebgs backgroundsize borderimage borderradius boxshadow
textshadow opacity cssanimations csscolumns cssgradients cssreflections
csstransforms csstransforms3d csstransitions fontface video audio localstorage
sessionstorage webworkers applicationcache svg no-inlinesvg smil svgclippaths">
```

This code is from Modernizr in Safari 5 on OS X. We can see there's support for properties and APIs like geolocation, border-radius, and box shadows. On the other hand, there's no support for WebGL or inline SVGs.

In addition to the classes we can use in our stylesheets, Modernizr creates a JavaScript object that can be used to easily test for the same set of features in your JavaScript code. The object is simply called `Modernizr`, and has `true` or `false` properties for every available test.

Let's continue with the `@font-face` example. Let's say that instead of using images as your fallback, you wanted to use Cufón—a canvas and VML text replacement library. You could do this:

```
if(Modernizr.fontface == false) {
  Cufon.now();
}
```

Modernizr sets the `fontface` property with a Boolean value, so we can easily test for it in JavaScript. The full list of supported properties and the details of how they work can be found in the Modernizr documentation.[8]

Weighing In

Modernizr is a handy tool, but it's always a good idea to think carefully before adding cruft to our application. At the time of writing, the current (minified) version of Modernizr weighs in at 8.8KB (though only 3.7KB when Gzipped). This is quite small as far as JavaScript libraries go, but remember: when building a mobile site or app, every kilobyte really counts.

We want to ensure that, as much as possible, we're only sending information that's absolutely necessary. Out of the box, Modernizr detects support for 41 different features—most of the time, you're only going to use a fraction of them. There's good news: Modernizr has begun providing a way to create a custom build of the library that includes only the tests you're interested in. It's still in beta, but it works fine. Head over to http://modernizr.github.com/Modernizr/2.0-beta/, tick the boxes corresponding to the features you want to test for, and generate your own personal Modernizr. Figure 3.11 shows what this looks like.

---

[8] http://www.modernizr.com/docs/

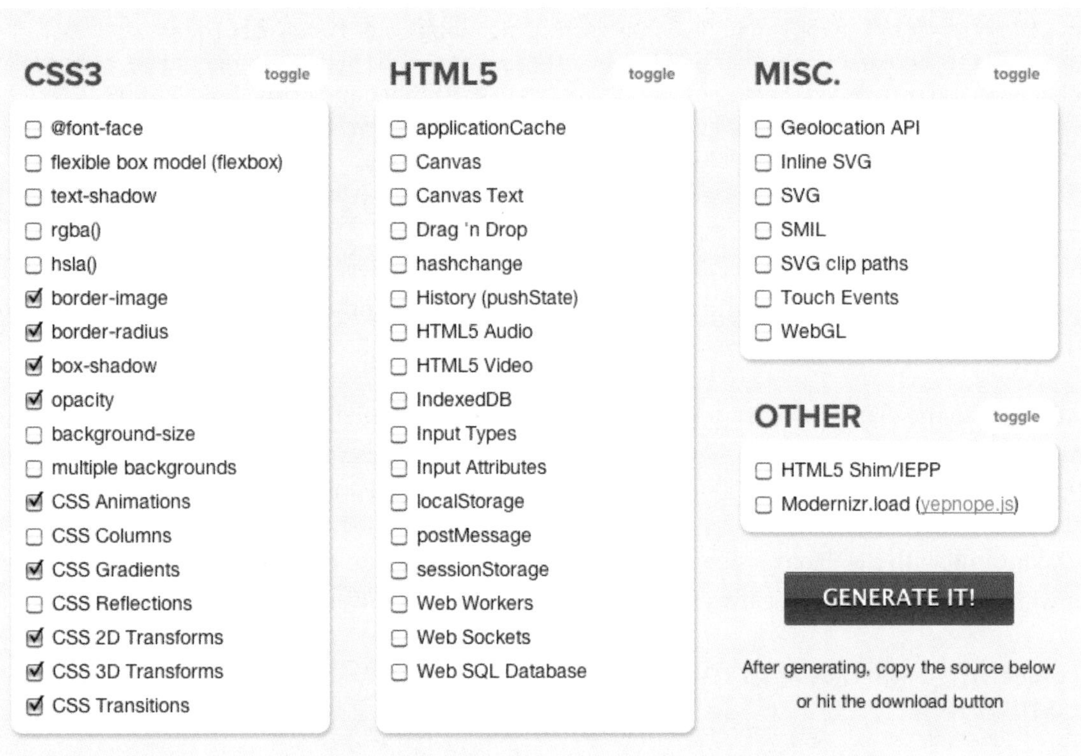

Figure 3.11. Modernizr lets us create a custom build with a subset of tests

Detecting Touch

Unfortunately, there's no robust way to detect whether or not a user's device is touch-capable. Modernizr includes a test for touch support, but all it tests for is the presence of the `touchstart` event. While this will give a consistent and positive result for devices with support for touch events, there are a number of browsers that *don't* use the `touchstart` event, even on touchscreen devices. This means it's impossible to be really sure whether our users are on a touchscreen device or not.

Building on Our Base

We have a good base of styles for our app. In the spirit of progressive enhancement, let's add some extra flavor with CSS3. First up: CSS gradients. Support for gradients generated using CSS is varied across mobile devices, but as we're using progressive enhancement techniques, there's no need to worry. First up, let's look at the syntax for CSS gradients. These were introduced by the WebKit project a few years ago, and the syntax has been in a state of flux since then. Luckily, it seems to have settled down now, and a consensus has been reached, evident in the new W3C specification. Still, there are enough older browsers out there (including the current versions of iOS and Android) to warrant specifying the older syntaxes as well.

Here's some example code that will create a linear gradient that transitions evenly between light gray (#CCC) and black (#000):

```
.gradient {
  /* Default for browsers that don't support gradients */
  background-color: #000;
  /* Original syntax for WebKit browsers */
  background-image: -webkit-gradient(linear, ❶ left top ❷, left bottom ❸,
➥from(#ccc), to(#000) ❹);
  /* New syntax for WebKit browsers: Chrome 10+, Safari 5.1+ */
  background-image: -webkit-linear-gradient(#ccc, #000);
  /* Syntax for Mozilla/Gecko browsers: Firefox 3.6+,  */
  background-image: -moz-linear-gradient(top, #ccc, #000);
  /* Syntax for Opera 11.10+ */
  background-image: -o-linear-gradient(top, #ccc, #000);
  /* Future proofing without vendor prefixes using W3C syntax */
  background-image: linear-gradient(top, #ccc, #000);
}
```

Since we're going to want to have our gradients appear in Mobile Safari and other WebKit browsers, we'll need to break down the now-outdated syntax. While it looks a little confusing, it's actually quite simple:

❶ The first value is the type of gradient, which can be `radial` or `linear`.

❷ We then specify the starting point of the gradient. This is an X/Y position from the top left of the element where the gradient will start. You can either use pixel values or keywords.

❸ The end point now needs to be designated, in the same way as the starting point.

❹ Finally, we specify any number of colors and their positions to make up the gradient. Colors can be specified either with the `from()` and `to()` functions for the starting and end colors, as we've done above, or using the `color-stop()` function. In a color stop, include the position (a number between 0 and 1) and the color. For example, `from(#CCC), to (#000)` is the same as `color-stop(0, #CCC), color-stop(1, #000)`.

The newer W3C-backed syntax is much the same, though it separates the two gradient types into separate functions—`linear-gradient` and `radial-gradient`—and a number of the values are optional. It's worth including the extra rules for the newer syntax, as it's likely that the mobile browsers based on WebKit will eventually be brought into line with the desktop versions.

It's important to realize that by creating gradients in CSS, we're actually getting the browser to generate an image and then insert that image into our page. As we mentioned in Chapter 2, image-heavy pages can cause performance problems on mobile devices; scrolling performance in particular can experience lag and feel unresponsive. This is why the tab bar is the only place in our design where we've used gradients heavily. We already have basic styling for our tab bar in place, so let's break down the CSS we'll need to implement the more design-rich parts of this element.

First up, we'll build the glossy, dark gradient that makes up the body of the tab bar. The Modernizr library gives us a hook via the `cssgradients class`, so we can do the following (for brevity, only the old WebKit style and W3C syntaxes are shown—but you can copy the `linear-gradient` value and add vendor prefixes as required to support other browser engines):

stylesheets/screen.css *(excerpt)*

```
#tab-bar {
  background: #050405;
}

.cssgradients #tab-bar {
  background-image:
    -webkit-gradient(linear, 0% 0%, 0% 100%,
      from(#353535),
      color-stop(0.55, #212021),
      color-stop(0.551, #090809),
      to(#050405));
  background-image:
    linear-gradient(top,
      #353535,
      #212021 55%,
      #090809 55.1%,
      #050405);
}
```

Where did those color values come from? In our case, since we built our gradient in Photoshop using a gradient overlay, we can just match the values of each color stop in the layer style to the color stop in our CSS code, as Figure 3.12 shows.

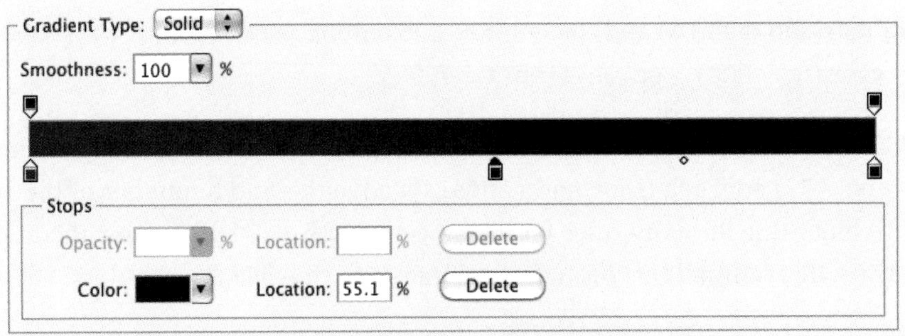

Figure 3.12. Each of the squares in the gradient editor represents a color stop between 0 and 100% location

If we note down the values from the gradient overlay, we have four stops:

- 0% with a hex value of #353535
- 55% with a hex value of #212021
- 55.1% with a hex value of #090809
- 100% with a hex value of #050405

These are the values we've used in the above CSS code to create our gradient. The results are shown in Figure 3.13.

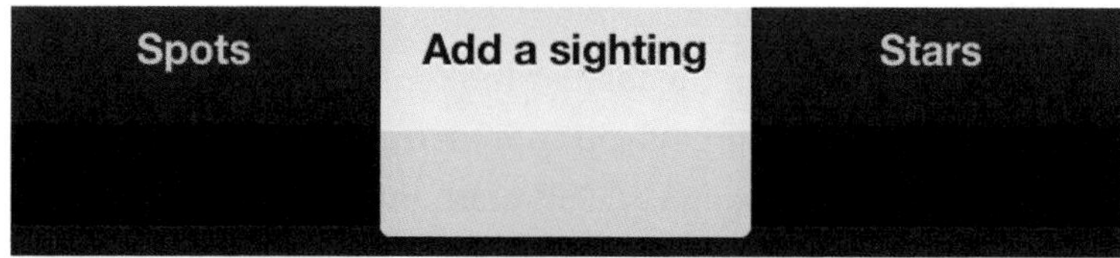

Figure 3.13. Re-creating our Photoshop gradient using CSS3 in the browser

Pixel perfect! Exactly what we're after. Now we can add a little extra love to the other bits in our tab bar to match our mockups. Let's gussy up the selected states for the individual list items:

stylesheets/screen.css *(excerpt)*

```
.page-spots #tab-spots a {
  ⋮
}

.cssgradients .page-spots #tab-spots a {
  background:
    -webkit-gradient(linear, left top, left bottom,
      from(rgba(40, 40, 40, .9)),
      color-stop(0.55, rgba(35, 35, 35, .5)),
      to(rgba(46, 46, 46, .1)));
  background-image:
    linear-gradient(
      rgba(40, 40, 40, .9),
      rgba(35, 35, 35, .5) 55%,
      rgba(46, 46, 46, .1));
}
```

It's the same trick, with some minor changes. The resulting gradient is shown in Figure 3.14.

Figure 3.14. A semi-transparent gradient to give the selected navigation item a bit more shine

RGBA Notation

In this case, we're using **RGBA** notation to specify our colors. The `rgba()` function allows you to specify the red, green, and blue values of your color using numbers from 0 to 255. The fourth value refers to the **alpha channel** or transparency, and is a number from 0 to 1; with 0 representing full transparency and 1 being fully opaque. This means we can have our gradient fade out to an almost transparent value that lets the background come through. It's not necessary, but it adds a little depth and complexity to the interface, making it feel that little bit more real.

We have one final fancy feature to make the tab bar look just right. Our design includes a subtle glowing spot to help anchor the selected navigation item to the top (or bottom) of the screen. We're going to combine our newfound knowledge of CSS gradients and pseudo-elements to create that spot without adding any extra markup to our HTML. Looking at our original CSS for the "Spots" element in the tab bar, we can see that we're using the `:after` pseudo-element to generate an additional element via CSS for our sprite icon.

Thankfully, that leaves another pseudo-element we can use for our glowing dot: `:before`. The setup is simple, and similar to the code we used for creating our icons; instead of inserting the sprite image into the generated element, though, we're going to create it with a blank string. Once that's done, we'll position it in the center of the selected tab using the negative margin trick again, and then add our generated gradient as a background image:

stylesheets/screen.css *(excerpt)*

```
.page-spots #tab-spots a:before {
  content: "";
  display: block;
  height: 0.5em;
  margin-left: -0.5em;
  left: 50%;
  position: absolute;
  margin-top: -1px;
  top: 0;
  width: 1em;
}

.cssgradients .page-spots #tab-spots a:before {
  background-image:
    -webkit-gradient(radial, 50% 0, 0, 50% 0, 7,
      from(rgba(236, 223, 156, 0.9)),
      to(rgba(0, 0, 0, 0)));
  background-image:
    radial-gradient(
      rgba(236, 223, 156, 0.9),
      rgba(0, 0, 0, 0));
}
```

The interesting change here is that we're using a radial rather than linear gradient. The syntax for radial gradients is similar to their linear brethren, though with a few more options. Again, you need to be aware that the syntax for mobile WebKit devices is different from the W3C specification. After specifying `radial`, you need to provide two sets of values representing the positions and radii of an inner and outer circle respectively, followed by a set of color stops.

The W3C syntax for other browsers is much simpler, especially in this case because our gradient is centered. We only need to provide the start and end color for the gradient, and we're done.

Gradients are tricky to master, so it's worth having a read through the W3C specifications to learn about all the available options. That said, let's take a look at how our fancy little radial gradient looks, in Figure 3.15.

Figure 3.15. Tab bar with "Spots" selected

Looks great, right? Unfortunately, webOS has incomplete support for generated images. While it passes Modernizr's test for CSS gradient implementation, and does *try* to render the gradient, it fails to do so correctly. In webOS, our radial gradient is rendered as a flat color, so our additional selected indicator looks out of place.

This brings home an important point when doing any sort of web development—but particularly for mobile devices: test, test, and test again on as many devices and emulators as you can get your hands on. Using progressive enhancement will help minimize these sorts of problems, but inevitably you'll come across some idiosyncrasies in implementation.

Unfortunately, there's no easy fix for this problem. Unless we were willing to remove the additional gradient, the best we can do is find a compromise that won't look too out of place on webOS. WebOS is rendering our gradient as a solid color somewhere in between our color stops. We're going to give this solid square of color some rounded corners, so that it feels more like an intentional design feature, rather than a mistake in rendering:

stylesheets/screen.css *(excerpt)*

```
.cssgradients #page-spots #tab-spots a:before {
  /* Snip previous styles */
  -webkit-border-bottom-left-radius: 0.143em;
  -webkit-border-bottom-right-radius: 0.143em;
  -moz-border-radius-bottomleft: 0.143em;
  -moz-border-radius-bottomright: 0.143em;
```

```
  border-bottom-left-radius: 0.143em;
  border-bottom-right-radius: 0.143em;
}
```

This will have no effect on the display of our radial gradient, as the rounded corners will only be cutting off transparent pixels. Interestingly, in webOS, the above change actually causes the gradient to disappear entirely! Problem solved, at least for that browser. Any other browsers that fail to render the gradient correctly (even when they appear to support them) will still see a nice round nub as a selected indicator. Remember the answer to the question, "Do websites have to look the same in every browser?" No!

Scalable Images

We've taken great care to this point to ensure our interface is resolution-independent by using relative units (ems). The only elements still stuck in bitmap land are the images in our interface. If we look at our in-progress application on, say, an iPhone 4, we can see that our icons are pixelated and blurry.

Serving high-resolution content images—that is, images embedded in the HTML rather than CSS background images—is a little tricky, but it can be done. Graphics that are included via CSS are a different story. There are a whole host of options for serving different resources to different resolutions. The problem is that these resolutions are changing at a furious pace. At the moment, even if we only target a limited selection of devices, we'll need to accommodate at least the resolutions shown in Table 3.1.

Table 3.1. A few common mobile device screen resolutions

iPhone 4	326ppi (pixels per inch)
iPhone 3G/3GS	163ppi
iPad/iPad 2	132ppi
Android devices	72–350ppi (varies)
HTC Touch Pro	287ppi
Palm Pre	186ppi

That's a lot of different resolutions to try and support—it could become messy quickly. Instead, we're going to take a relatively straightforward approach and use SVGs wherever possible to create an interface that works well on any resolution device—as long as they have SVG support, that is.

SVGs have a number of advantages over bitmap graphics. Firstly, they're an open and W3C-backed standard. Secondly, for simple graphics, they're often significantly smaller than their bitmap equivalents—a nice bonus for our users. Finally, and most importantly for us, they can be scaled to any size without losing detail and becoming pixelated. In-browser SVG is supported by iOS from version 2.1, and is included in Android as of version 3.0.

Once again, the Modernizr library has done some of the heavy lifting for us; it includes detection for SVG support, both inline and embedded, though we're only interested in the embedded support for now. As with CSS gradients, Modernizr adds a `class` to the `html` element of our page to indicate support (or lack thereof) for SVG. For embedded SVGs, this `class` is simply `svg`.

For devices supporting SVGs, this means that creating resolution-independent graphics is as simple as overriding the references to our **sprite.png** image with ones to **sprite.svg**. For example, with the tab bar, we can add another block to our CSS file:

stylesheets/screen.css *(excerpt)*

```
#tab-bar a:after {
  content: url(../images/sprite.png);
  position: absolute;
  overflow: hidden;
  left: 50%;
  top: 1.833em;
}

.svg #tab-bar a:after {
  content: url(../images/sprite.svg);
}
```

Easy! As long as the dimensions of our two sprite images match exactly, there's no need to make any more changes to our code. Figure 3.16 and Figure 3.17 show what the difference looks like on an iPhone 4.

Figure 3.16. Note the pixelation of the standard resolution icons

Figure 3.17. Our icons are perfectly crisp with SVGs, regardless of the device resolution

Pixel Perfection

SVGs are never going to appear exactly as we'd like them to. They're scalable graphics, which means that we're letting the browser do the work of resizing our graphics, and this can mean less than desirable results. Sometimes graphics can lose definition around the edges, particularly when there are small lines or fine detail. If we did want to go down the path of creating graphics that are optimized for each and every resolution we wanted to support, we could do so by using media queries based on the device's pixel density:

```
/* Target iPhone 4 and other high pixel ratio devices */
@media
  only screen and (-webkit-min-device-pixel-ratio: 1.5),
  only screen and (-o-min-device-pixel-ratio: 3/2),
  only screen and (min-device-pixel-ratio: 1.5) {
    /* Styles go here */
}
```

Dealing with the Media

In an attempt to keep it simple, we've refrained from having audio or video in our application. Most mobile devices lack support for Flash (or other plugins) for embedding rich media like audio and video, but it is still technically possible to include it. There has been a lot of work done over the last few years to create native capability in HTML; as a result, these APIs are quite mature, and relatively well-supported. They're also incredibly easy to implement—especially when compared to the same process in Flash. Here's a breakdown of the HTML you could use to embed a video using the the HTML5 `video` element:

```
<video width="480" height="320" autoplay controls> ❶
  <source src="video.mp4" type="video/mp4" /> ❷
  <source src="video.webm" type="video/webm" /> ❸
  <source src="video.ogv" type="video/ogv" /> ❹
</Video>
```

❶ `autoplay` and `controls` are Boolean attributes, so they don't require values. `autoplay`, unsurprisingly, will cause the media to load and play as soon as the page loads—though this is rarely a good idea—and the `controls` attribute tells the browser to provide native controls for the media.

❷ Multiple source elements are required to provide support for all platforms. The H.264-encoded MP4 needs to come first—otherwise the iPad experiences a bug and fails to play. It provides support for iOS, Android, and Safari on the desktop.

❸ WebM is supported in the latest versions of Chrome, Firefox, and Opera.

 Ogg Theora could be omitted, but provides support to older versions of Firefox, Opera, and Chrome.

At the time of writing, H.264 is the most common and well-supported format for native video playback on mobile devices; this is, in part, due to the preponderance of WebKit-based browsers. It may change in the relatively near future, though, as Google has put its weight behind its own WebM format, and is planning to remove H.264 support from Chrome on desktop. It's yet to be seen whether that decision will filter down to the Android OS.

The HTML to embed audio is much the same:

```
<audio autoplay controls>
  <source src="audio.ogg" />
  <source src="audio.mp3" />
</audio>
```

Audio on Android

Note that the default browser on Android 2.2 and below has incomplete support for HTML5 audio.[9] The 2.3 release fixes the issue, but if support for 2.2 devices is required, you can use the `video` element to play MP3 files as a stopgap measure.

For a detailed look at the ins and outs of the HTML5 audio and video APIs, have a read through SitePoint's *HTML5 & CSS3 for the Real World*,[10] or Mark Pilgrim's excellent *Dive into HTML5*.[11] Using native implementations for rich media is particularly important on mobile devices, as they're likely to be optimized for the specific device, and can be hooked into hardware decoders for the video codecs they support. iOS devices, for example, all include H.264 hardware decoders so that H.264-encoded video playback will perform well and use a minimum amount of power.

Another advantage with these native APIs is that building up the interface doesn't need to be a priority. Each browser or device has a set of native controls for the video and audio elements that we can automatically include, and users will be accustomed to seeing them on their device. Of course, we could create our own playback controls if we so desired—the JavaScript interface gives us the hooks we'd need—but sometimes it's best to leave well enough alone. Also note that if we wanted to do feature detection for video or audio, we could again turn to Modernizr, as the library includes support for both HTML5 audio and video.

---

[9] http://www.brianhadaway.com/html5-audio-support-on-android-devices/
[10] http://sitepoint.com/books/htmlcss1/
[11] http://diveintohtml5.org/video.html

Standalone Mode

Now that we've enhanced our app's appearance a little, we can give it an even more native feel by implementing the standalone mode we discussed in the last chapter. Most of the following information is specific to Mobile Safari (iOS), though some of it applies to the default Android browser as well. Our first task is to enable full-screen browsing; we can do this by including a `meta` tag in the `head` of our document, just as we did with the viewport settings:

spots.html *(excerpt)*

```
<meta name="apple-mobile-web-app-capable" content="yes" />
```

By setting this `apple`-prefixed `meta` tag to `yes`, our application will be able to launch in Mobile Safari without the browser chrome once it's been saved to the home screen by a user. What's important to remember is that once launched in this mode, the app acts like a single, standalone application in its own right; any links to other pages will open in the actual Mobile Safari application.

There's another `meta` tag that works in conjunction with the above code:

spots.html *(excerpt)*

```
<meta name="apple-mobile-web-app-status-bar-style" content="black" />
```

This is also an Apple/iOS-only property, and it lets us specify what style of status bar we'd like to use. In the above snippet, we're setting the status bar to the black style, with the content appearing below the status bar. If `content` is set to `default`, the status bar appears as the default gray style we'd usually see in Mobile Safari. If set to `black-translucent`, the status bar is black and slightly see-through, with the web content displayed on the entire screen but partially obscured by the status bar.

Now that we've added the code that enables our application to behave as a standalone app, we can add some additional rules to our stylesheet that target this version of our app. First, though, we'll need a hook for our CSS. Unfortunately, Modernizr doesn't detect standalone capability. The global `navigator` JavaScript object, however, will have a `standalone` property that evaluates to `true` when the browser is in standalone mode.

That's the first piece of the puzzle. The second piece is that Modernizr gives us the ability to extend it by adding new tests. To do so, we simply call the `addTest()` method on the `Modernizr` object. `addTest()` takes two arguments: a string that defines the name of the test (this will be used as the `class` that's added to the `html` element when the test runs), and a function that returns a Boolean value (`true` or `false`) indicating that the test has been passed or failed. In this case, we're simply returning the value of `navigator.standalone`:

javascripts/basic.js *(excerpt)*

```
Modernizr.addTest('standalone',function(){
  return window.navigator.standalone;
});
```

Of course, even if you weren't using Modernizr, you could still use the value of `navigator.standalone` to accomplish the same result:

```
if(!!navigator.standalone) {
  document.documentElement.setAttribute('class',
➥document.documentElement.getAttribute('class') + " standalone");
}
```

The above simply sets the `class` attribute of the `html` element to be whatever it was before, plus a space and the word `standalone`. Either way, with our test complete, we now have a `.standalone` hook that will allow us to change the layout of our app. As per the design we came up with in the last chapter, let's move our tab bar from the top of the interface to the bottom. Unfortunately—as we mentioned earlier—we can't use `position: fixed` to pin the tab bar to a spot in our interface. We're going to have to implement a JavaScript solution to this problem. We'll come back to this later on, but for the moment, for mockup purposes we can use `position: absolute` and `bottom: 0` as a temporary solution to make the rest of the layout right:

stylesheets/screen.css *(excerpt)*

```
#tab-bar {
  ⋮
}

.standalone #tab-bar {
  margin-top: .3em;
  position: absolute;
  width: 100%;
  bottom: 0;
  z-index: 200;
}
```

While the tab bar won't stay fixed, it is pinned to the bottom of the screen on first load; if we don't scroll we can mock up the rest of the elements and it will look correct. With the tab bar fixed at the bottom, we need to ensure that there's always enough room for it at the end of our main content—otherwise the tab bar will potentially obscure part of the interface. To do this, we just need a little extra padding on the `body` element:

```
.standalone body {
  padding-bottom: 4.5em;
}
```

There's no need for us to change the main gradient in the tab bar. The light still comes from the top when the tab bar is at the bottom. However, for the two regular items in the navigation—Spots and Stars—we're going to flip the gradient in their selected state so that it moves through from semi-transparent to fully opaque:

stylesheets/screen.css *(excerpt)*

```
.standalone.cssgradients .page-spots #tab-spots a {
  /* New gradient */
  background-image:
    -webkit-gradient(linear, 0% 0%, 0% 100%,
      from(rgba(46, 46, 46, 0),
      color-stop(0.55, rgba(35, 35, 35, 0.5)),
      to(rgba(40, 40, 40, 0.9))));
  background-image:
    linear-gradient(top,
      rgba(46, 46, 46, 0),
      rgba(35, 35, 35, 0.5) 55%,
      rgba(40, 40, 40, 0.9));
  /* New box shadow */
  -o-box-shadow: rgba(0, 0, 0, 0.8) 0 1px 1px 0;
  -webkit-box-shadow: rgba(0, 0, 0, 0.8) 0 1px 1px 0;
  -moz-box-shadow: rgba(0, 0, 0, 0.8) 0 1px 1px 0;
  box-shadow: rgba(0, 0, 0, 0.8) 0 1px 1px 0;
}
```

We're just changing the alpha values of the gradient so that it fades in rather than out, and then tweaking the shadow that's applied to the selected items as well. Whilst we'll skip going through every change needed to make the transition to a standalone app, the principle is exactly as we've applied above: use the `.standalone` CSS selector to override the normal rules.

Tell Your Users

All this work creating a standalone app is wonderful, but it's only going to be useful if our users actually add our application to their home screens. So make sure you give them some encouragement! We can see this sort of behavior in action in the web applications for Gmail, and Currency.io, and EightBit, shown in Figure 3.18.

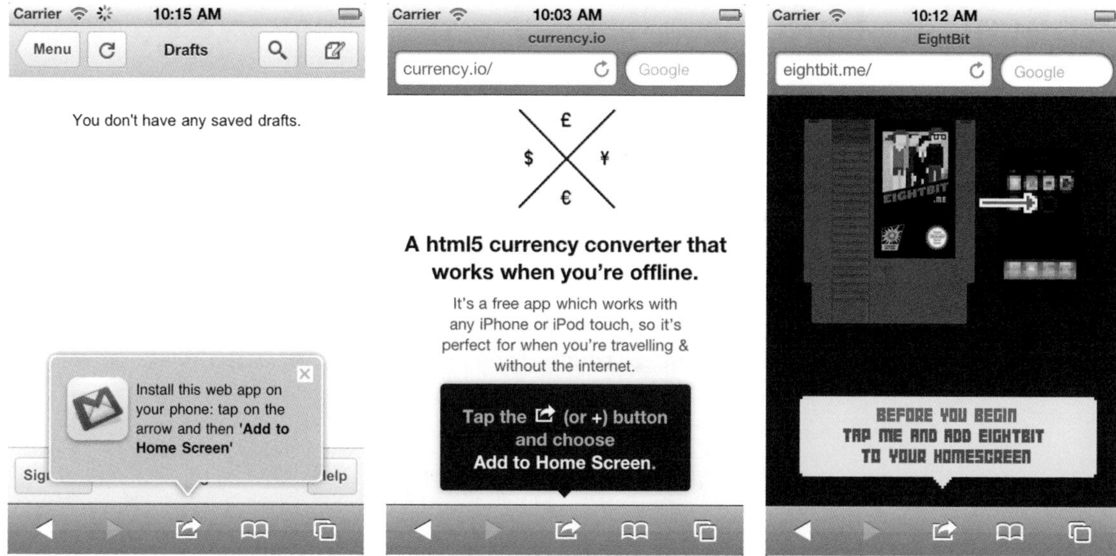

Figure 3.18. Encouraging users to add an app to their home screen

These three apps use the same design, a little pop-up bubble with a call to action asking the user to tap the bookmark button. This is potentially problematic, as it's tied to the interface layout of a single suite of devices—Apple's. That's less of an issue than you might think, though, because iOS is the only mobile platform that supports standalone web apps!

Before showing the message, we'll test for the presence of the `navigator.standalone` property; it will be `undefined` on devices without support standalone mode. If it's absent, there's no need to show the notification. Furthermore, it's best we avoid hassling our users each and every time they open our app—especially if they've already saved our app to their home screen! So we'll also check to make sure we're not currently in standalone mode:

```
if(navigator.standalone != undefined && !!!navigator.standalone) {
  // Show notification
}
```

We also don't want to hassle them if they've been shown the notification and then dismissed it. This means we'll need a way of remembering that they've decided not to add the app to their home screen before. We could do this by using a cookie, or by storing that preference in local storage (more on this in Chapter 6). If you're after an out-of-the-box solution for this problem, check out the Mobile Bookmark Bubble project from Google.[12] It's a little standalone— no pun intended—library for doing exactly this, and it's the code that's used by the Gmail application. It even includes support for the iPad and its top-positioned toolbar, and has configurable options for how many times we want to remind our users.

[12] http://code.google.com/p/mobile-bookmark-bubble/

Application Icons

If we're going to encourage our users to add our application to their home screen, we'll want to make sure our app looks right at home. This means we need an application icon. In the absence of such an icon, home screen bookmarks use a screenshot of the current page as their icon, but we can do better than that! In the previous chapter, we built up a whole range of icons for the various native applications.

iOS supports a couple of options for specifying home screen icons, done via the inclusion of a `link` element with a `rel` attribute of either `apple-touch-icon` or `apple-touch-icon-precomposed`, like this:

```
<link rel="apple-touch-icon" href="apple-touch-icon.png" />
<link rel="apple-touch-icon-precomposed" href="apple-touch-icon-precomposed.png"
➥/>
```

The only difference between these two tags is that the former will apply the default shine and drop shadow that you see on standard iOS application icons, and the latter will show the icon exactly as we've provided it—hence the `precomposed`. We can only use one of these tags at a time.

Interestingly, iOS ignores this setting in the multitasking bar, and always applies the default gloss when displaying home screen web apps there, so you'll want to check that your icon looks okay in this situation. Both iOS and Android support the `apple-touch-icon-precomposed` `link` element, so it's the preferred way of setting a cross-platform custom icon; be mindful, though, that BlackBerry 6 only supports the nonprecomposed tag, so you should always include it anyway. Be aware also that while Android supports home screen bookmarks, it will only display a custom icon if the path to the icon is absolute, meaning it includes the full http://domain.com/ before the location of the image. In addition, Android's implementation is at the mercy of the various device manufacturers; for example, on HTC devices that use the Sense UI, custom icons are included as a small overlay on top of a standard bookmark icon.

Each of Apple's devices requires a differently sized home screen icon:

- 114×114px for high-resolution displays like the iPhone 4
- 72×72px for iPad
- 57×57px for everything else

How do we specify different icons for each device? The simplest solution is to serve a single high-resolution icon for anyone and everyone. The obvious downside here is that all users will have to download the larger icon, even those with no need for the extra resolution. Never mind; as of iOS 4.2, we can specify multiple icons for different device resolutions by using the `sizes` attribute:

```
<!-- For iPad -->
<link rel="apple-touch-icon-precomposed" sizes="72x72"
➥href="apple-touch-icon-72x72-precomposed">
```

And we can cater to other devices, including pre-iOS 4.2 devices, by including a fallback without the `sizes` attribute. The key is that the fallback value has to come *after* all the others:

```
<!-- For iPad -->
<link rel="apple-touch-icon-precomposed" sizes="72x72"
➥href="apple-touch-icon-72x72-precomposed.png">
<!-- For pre-retina iPhone, iPod Touch, and Android 2.1+ devices -->
<link rel="apple-touch-icon-precomposed" href="apple-touch-icon-precomposed.png">
```

In the same way that most browsers will look for a **favicon.ico** file at the root of a domain to use as a favicon—regardless of whether or not it's specified in the `head`—iOS devices will scan the root of our domain for home screen icons and magically apply the correct one. An iPad, for example, would check for the presence of the following files in order:

1. **apple-touch-icon-72x72-precomposed.png**
2. **apple-touch-icon-72x72.png**
3. **apple-touch-icon-precomposed.png**
4. **apple-touch-icon.png**

This makes it incredibly easy to serve the correct icons to specific iOS devices. Alas, no other browsers support this as yet, so we'll need to use our HTML-based method. Taking into account all the devices we care about, as well as Android's fussy implementation, our final code for including a home screen icon is this:

```
<!-- For iPad -->
<link rel="apple-touch-icon-precomposed" sizes="72x72"
➥href="http://domain.com/apple-touch-icon-72x72-precomposed.png">
<!-- For iPhone 4 with high-resolution Retina display -->
<link rel="apple-touch-icon-precomposed" sizes="114x114"
➥href="http://domain.com/apple-touch-icon-114x114-precomposed.png">
<!-- For iOS 1- and Blackberry 6 -->
<link rel="apple-touch-icon" href="http://domain.com/apple-touch-icon.png">
<!-- For pre-retina iPhone, iPod Touch, and Android 2.1+ devices -->
<link rel="apple-touch-icon-precomposed"
➥href="http://domain.com/apple-touch-icon-precomposed.png">
```

Figure 3.19 reveals what it looks like when we've added it our home screen.

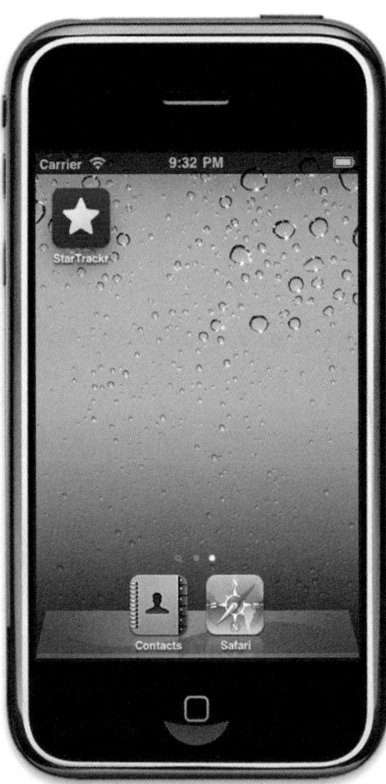

Figure 3.19. The StarTrackr icon sitting comfortably on our home screen

Mobile Safari supports one more feature for making web applications feel a little more native: startup images. By adding a `link` element with a `rel` value of `apple-touch-startup-image` in exactly the same manner as the home screen icons above, we can specify an image that will be shown while the application loads:

```
<link rel="apple-touch-startup-image"
➥href="http://domain.com/apple-touch-startup-image.png">
```

Adding this code means a startup image will be shown every time our application is launched or switched to from the multitasking bar (unless it's been closed for a very short period of time). While you might be tempted to use the startup image as an opportunity to reinforce the brand of your application—resist the temptation! It can be jarring or annoying for users, making them feel like they're sitting through a splash screen for no reason.

A better approach is to use an image of the interface that's emptied of content. This creates the illusion that the shell of our app has loaded the instant it's opened, and creates a smooth visual transition for our users once the application really does load. This method is the one Apple uses for the default native applications on iOS—you can see it an action when opening Mail—just make sure you kill the process in the multitasking bar first.

When going with this approach, we need to make sure that our empty startup image matches our fully loaded interface with pixel precision, otherwise the illusion will be broken. The easiest way to make the image match exactly is to use the interface itself as the canvas and take a screenshot. This is simply a matter of hiding the elements we want to be invisible using `visibility: hidden` in our CSS file, and then taking the screenshot. Figure 3.20 shows one we prepared earlier.

Figure 3.20. Our perfectly matching empty interface chrome

Note that we're hiding everything except the backgrounds for the main elements. We can't include the items in the tab bar, as it's impossible to be sure of the state they're meant to be in. Removing all the interactive elements also means that our users can't be confused about the state of the app: if there are no buttons to click, they won't try and click them. The image must be 320×460 pixels—the full screen resolution of a pre-Retina iPhone minus the 20 pixels taken up by the status bar. The `apple-touch-startup-image` flag is rather dumb, as it has no way of differentiating between different resolutions or device orientations—all devices receive the same image. If our application was landscape orientation only, we'd have to rotate our startup image 90° clockwise to have it appear correctly.

Neither iOS or Android require that any of these properties be set for the application to be added as a shortcut on a user's home screen. So if we didn't want to go the whole way with a standalone app, we could just include a home screen icon and omit the `apple-mobile-web-app-capable` `meta` tag. Considering that the extra steps are fairly easy, though, it's worth the additional effort to give our users the most polished experience we can.

Extra Credit

There are a few other techniques and mobile-specific properties that we can use to make our app feel a little more native.

Text Overflow with Ellipsis

On a small screen, it's possible for a layout to quickly become unusable as a result of content that's too long for its intended container. Each row in our list of Stars, for example, is only designed to cope with relatively short names. If we were to add an item with a lengthier name, the text would wrap over to another line and take up a lot of the screen space, as Figure 3.21 illustrates.

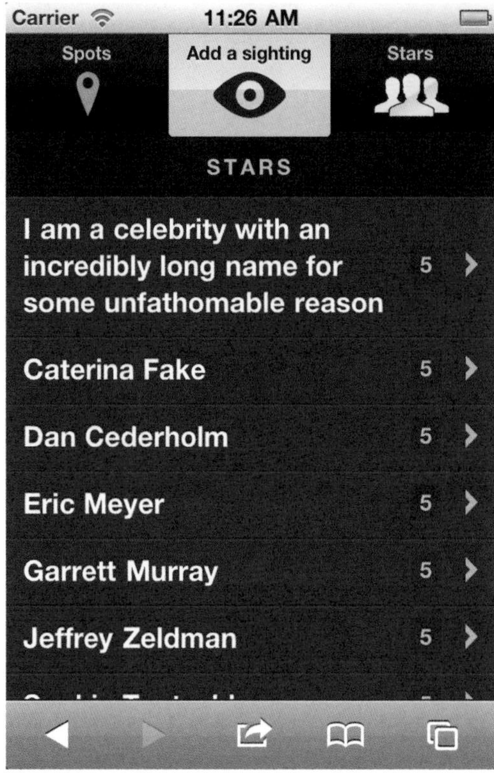

Figure 3.21. A long name will break the vertical rhythm of our list of Stars

What we want to do is truncate that text once it reaches the end of the line. The easiest way to do this is to use `overflow: hidden` and limit the width of the element that might wrap:

stylesheets/screen.css *(excerpt)*

```
.table-action h2 {
  overflow: hidden;
  white-space: nowrap;
  width: 82%;
}
```

Note that we need to ensure that the text won't wrap onto a new line. We achieve this by setting the `white-space` value to `nowrap`. Unfortunately, as it stands, this is hardly a graceful solution. We're unable to guarantee that the text will be truncated at the limit of a letter, so we may end up with similar situation to Figure 3.22.

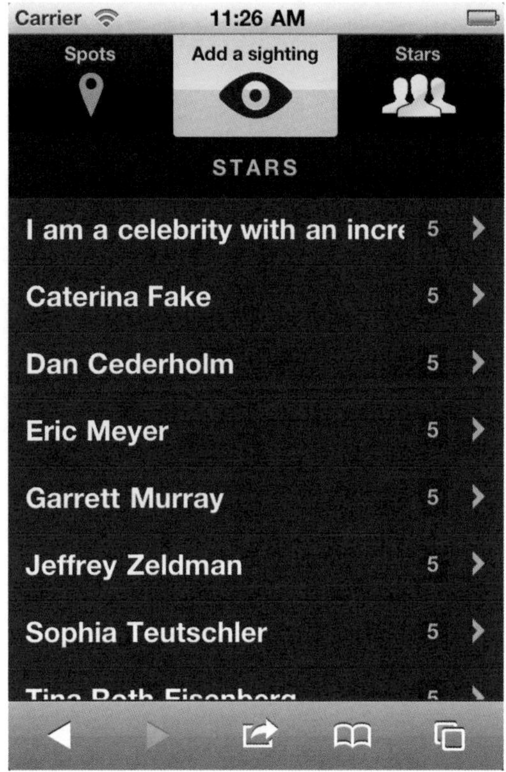

Figure 3.22. `overflow: hidden` can create hard crops at the boundary of the containing element

We have one more trick up our sleeves to make this truncation a little more graceful: `text-overflow: ellipsis`. By setting the value of this property to `ellipsis`, the browser will append an ellipsis at the boundary of the truncated text. Our new rule looks like this:

stylesheets/screen.css *(excerpt)*

```
.table-action h2 {
  text-overflow: ellipsis;
  overflow: hidden;
```

```
  white-space: nowrap;
  width: 82%;
}
```

And now, instead of the hard slice through the middle of a letter, we have a nicely shortened name, letting our users know there's more text available, as you can see in Figure 3.23.

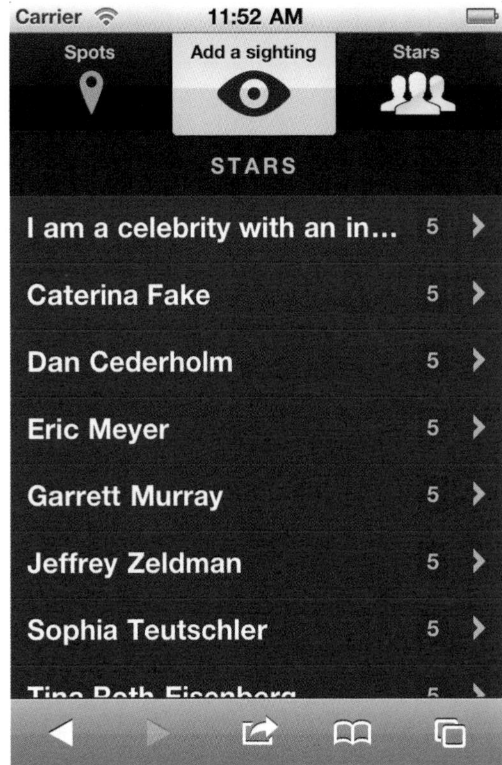

Figure 3.23. `text-overflow: ellipsis` gives us a much nicer approach to truncating text

Text Size Adjust

Mobile Safari does a little magic behind the scenes to adjust the text size as the orientation of the device changes. If we leave this value as its default and view our app in landscape, you'll see that the text increases in size. This increase is unnecessary for our app, so we're going to disable it by setting the value to 100%:

stylesheets/screen.css *(excerpt)*

```
html {
  -webkit-text-size-adjust: 100%;
  -ms-text-size-adjust: 100%;
}
```

Tap Highlight Color

By default, Mobile Safari applies a highlight color when the user taps a link or another clickable element. This is quite dark by default, so we're going to lighten it up a little using an RGBA color value:

stylesheets/screen.css *(excerpt)*

```
a:link {
  -webkit-tap-highlight-color: rgba(0,0,0,.2);
}
```

To disable the highlight entirely, just set the value to `transparent`, or an RGBA value with 0 alpha.

Touch Callout

In Mobile Safari, touching and holding onto a link brings up a dialog that offers various actions for that link: **Open**, **Open in New Page**, **Copy**, and **Cancel**. This is unnecessary for the standalone version of our app (these options make no sense in the context of a self-contained app) so we're going to use the `-webkit-touch-callout` property to disable them via CSS:

stylesheets/screen.css *(excerpt)*

```
.standalone * {
  -webkit-touch-callout: none;
}
```

Standalone Only

Note that we're only applying this rule to elements in our standalone app. Best not to mess with our users' normal browser controls without good reason!

User Select

iOS lets users copy and paste content from web pages by touching and holding on elements for a second or so. While we don't want to break this behavior entirely, there are some situations where we might want to disable text selection. In StarTrackr, there's no reason why our users would want to copy the text from the tab bar, so let's disable text selection there:

stylesheets/screen.css *(excerpt)*

```
#tab-bar {
  -webkit-user-select: none;
}
```

Performance Matters

Throughout this chapter, we've noted a number of techniques that help to create interfaces in a manner that is clean and semantic, while still performing well. Many—if not all—of these techniques are the same as what we'd use in a desktop web development, but let's summarize them briefly so they're a little easier to check off:

- Minimize HTTP requests by combining JavaScript files and stylesheets, and using image sprites wherever possible.
- Put stylesheets in the `head` to allow the page to render our layout as the HTML loads.
- Include JavaScript files at the bottom of the page (just inside the `body`) to ensure that parallel downloads aren't blocked.
- Keep JavaScript and stylesheets in external files so that the browser can cache our files between requests.
- Be aware of the resource and cache limits on mobile browsers; there's no point reducing HTTP requests in order to create a file that's too big to be cached on a mobile device.
- Optimize images, and minify JavaScript and CSS.
- Gzip all resources on the server side.

Moving On

While we haven't actually covered every single bit of markup or styling that went into the StarTrackr mobile website, we trust that we've covered all the essentials and given you the tools you need to create your own mobile websites and apps. In the next few chapters, we'll move on to discussing JavaScript, including its role both in giving our app even more native-like polish, and in tapping into new HTML5 APIs that are particularly handy for mobile apps.

Chapter 4

Mobile Web Apps

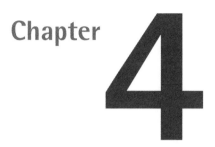

Now that we have a beautiful mobile website up and running, it's time to give it that extra touch of interactivity. Our client wants more than a simple mobile version of their website; they want an application on par with anything the app marketplaces have to offer.

It's a tall order, but device providers have given us a tantalizing set of capabilities that not only allow us, but encourage us to reproduce native behaviors in a web setting. If we play carefully with this double-edged sword—that is, knowing our limitations and exploiting our strengths—we can transform our websites into full-fledged apps that are a joy to use.

Setting up Shop

As a first pass for *app-ifying* our mobile website, we'll set up our environment, hook up a couple of common DOM events, and use the native-like features gifted to us for some gratifying "quick wins." These should help us get well on the way to creating a usable app that we can build on with more advanced features.

Frameworks and Libraries

First of all, we need to make some tough decisions. The mobile web app development landscape has no yellow brick road; it's more like strolling through a dense, twisted forest of super-cool devices and browsers—all with wildly varying capabilities. To help us out, new frameworks and libraries for mobile app development are sprouting up like mushrooms.

A framework can greatly simplify our task by taking care of cross-device and cross-browser inconsistencies, and offering prebuilt UI widgets and designs that we can patch together as an application. Sencha Touch[1] and jQuery Mobile[2] are two big players, but there are scores of others, and there is certainly no "winning" framework at the moment. All the big frameworks have benefits and drawbacks, so you'll need to carefully test and evaluate the options to see if they meet your needs for performance, compatibility, and customization. In the interests of teaching you the underlying concepts of developing for the mobile web, we'll be writing our own UI code in this book.

Okay, but how about a DOM library? Surely there's no need for us to write our own DOM manipulation code, right? Over the last few years, JavaScript libraries have changed the way we work with the DOM. We can modify and animate our documents with some terse, elegant APIs, and maintain some level of confidence that we won't be spending the majority of our workdays troubleshooting inconsistencies across desktop browsers.

So, does it make sense to bring this convenience to mobile? The answer is, of course, "it depends." Most of the major DOM libraries take great care to ensure they function across all the desktop browsers, including IE6. But when working on a mobile web app, IE6 is a non-issue. Again—you need to evaluate your options. For the remainder of the book, we'll stick with jQuery as it's very well known, but all of the concepts (and most of the code) convert easily between libraries—or to plain JavaScript.

A Slimmer jQuery

If you like jQuery, but are hesitant about its file size, you might like to check out the interesting Zepto project.[3] It has a jQuery-compatible (though not full-featured) API, but is only about 4k when minimized. This is possible because it only targets mobile WebKit browsers, rather than wasting hundreds of lines of code getting IE6 on board.

Debugging Mobile JavaScript

We've settled on jQuery, so let's add our library to the bottom of the HTML document, as low as you can before the final `</body>` tag. We'll also throw in a quick alert to verify that jQuery is up and running:

ch4/01-jquery.html *(excerpt)*

```
<script src="javascripts/vendor/jquery-1.6.1.min.js"></script>
<script type="text/javascript">
  $(document).ready(function(){
```

---

[1] http://www.sencha.com/products/touch/

[2] http://jquerymobile.com/

[3] http://www.zeptojs.com/

```
    alert("StarTrackr loaded!");
  };
</script>
```

What if you didn't receive an alert? What went wrong? Well, there are a few ways to troubleshoot and debug. The first is to test it on your desktop browser. Safari or Chrome (or another WebKit-based browser) will do a good job of emulating an iPhone or Android phone, and their built-in tools for debugging will save you a lot of headaches.

A rudimentary console is also available on the iPhone, though it's disabled by default. Switch it on in the Safari preference screen via the general phone preferences. Not only will the console show you any errors that occur on the page, you can also throw your own messages in there—which is far more convenient than spawning alert boxes throughout your code. There are a few different "types" of logs available to us:

```
console.log("General log item");
console.info("Just some information.");
console.warn("Oooh, be careful here…");
console.error("We've got a problem!");
```

Figure 4.1 shows what the output of these logs looks like on an iPhone.

Figure 4.1. Checking out the console on an iPhone

We've just output strings here, but you can also print the value of variables. On the iPhone, you'll only get the value of simple types (strings, numbers, and so on)—not objects. It's still very useful, though—just remember to remove these messages before you go live. If a user's device lacks a `console` object, it will throw an error and stop your scripts.

If you're testing on an Android device, you can enable USB debugging on your phone, and then use the Android Debug Bridge that comes with the Android SDK to log messages from your device to your computer's terminal. (We'll cover installing the SDK in Chapter 7.) To view these logs, run `adb logcat` from the **platform-tools** directory of your SDK.

Events

For many users, the most noticeable difference between a website and a native application is the way each one transitions between screens or pages. Native applications respond instantly, sometimes sliding or fading content on and off the screen, whereas websites show a few seconds of white screen before the next page's content starts loading in.

There are a number of ways we can make our web app feel more responsive. As you've probably guessed, using Ajax to pull in page components to avoid a refresh is an important component of our strategy. This approach will pay dividends in Chapter 7 when we use PhoneGap to bring our app into the native world.

Before we load in content with Ajax, and use transitions and animations to swoosh things around, we'll need to capture some events. For the most part, handling events on mobile is no different from the desktop, but there are a few key points worth learning about, so we'll start there.

Let's begin by capturing click events on the links in our tab bar. As a quick refresher, here's the markup for the navigation:

ch4/02-clicks.html *(excerpt)*

```
<ul id="tab-bar">
  <li id="tab-spots">
    <a href="#page-spots">
      Spots
    </a>
  </li>
  <li id="tab-sighting">
    <a href="#page2">
      Add a sighting
    </a>
  </li>
  <li id="tab-stars">
    <a href="#page3">
      Stars
    </a>
  </li>
</ul><!-- #tab-bar -->
```

To verify that we can capture click events on each list item, we'll fire off another alert message:

javascripts/ch4/02-clicks.html *(excerpt)*

```
$("#tab-bar li").click(function(e){
  e.preventDefault();
  alert("Coming soon!");
});
```

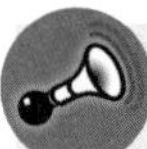

Running Scripts

All the code snippets that follow will assume the code is either inside, or is called from inside the `ready` function. That way, we're sure that our document is loaded before we run any code that relies on its presence.

We've attached our function to the click event on all the list items, and we've prevented the event's default behavior from occurring, so the browser won't navigate away to the link address. Fire that up on your mobile phone to make sure it's working. It might be a boring alert message, but seeing your code running in the palm of your hand is fairly cool. Figure 4.2 shows the output on the Android browser.

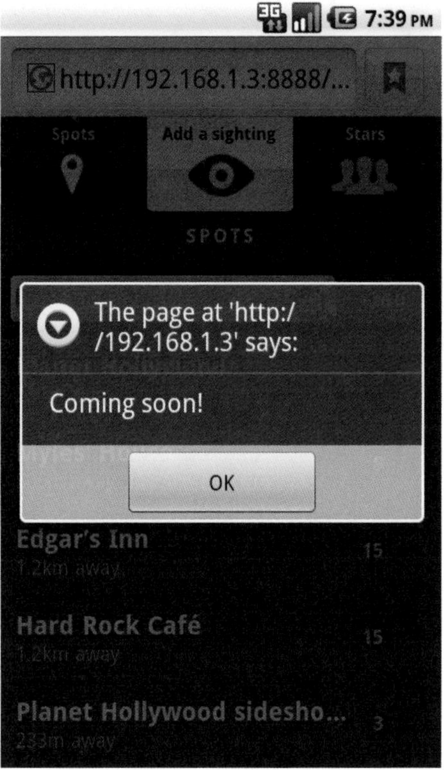

Figure 4.2. We've captured the click event and used it to display a message

The DOM `click` event comprises two separate steps: a `mousedown`, followed by a `mouseup`. Evidently, it's an event designed for a mouse, where clicking takes just a fraction of a second, and is done after the user has moved the mouse into the correct position. This interaction doesn't always replicate so well on the touch screen, and the click can end up feeling a bit sluggish on some devices.

For a slight improvement, only target the `mouseup` event; however, the `mouseup` event is independent of the `click` event, so we still need to stop the click from following the link to another page. Once we've curtailed the hyperlink, we can run our code in the `mouseup` event handler, which we attach using jQuery's `bind` method:

javascripts/ch4/03-mouseup.js *(excerpt)*

```
// Stop clicks from following links
$("#tab-bar li a").click(function(e){
  e.preventDefault();
});

// Do our magic on mouse-up!
$("#tab-bar li").bind("mouseup", function(){
  alert("Coming soon!");
});
```

Simple Touch Events

Although mobile devices can pretend that your finger is a mouse pointer, and fire regular click events, they also generate *touch* events, which are more accurate and useful. However, these come loaded with so many cross-browser booby traps, that you'll start wishing you could go back to developing for IE6!

Fortunately for us, detecting a touch is simple enough:

javascripts/ch4/04-touchend.js *(excerpt)*

```
$("#tab-bar li").bind("touchend", function(e){
  alert("Coming soon!");
});
```

Most recent mobile touch devices will fire the `touchend` event. This fires when the user lifts their finger from the screen after touching it. There are also a few other events that map quite nicely to the mouse equivalents, as Table 4.1 summarizes.

Table 4.1. Touch events and their corresponding mouse events

Touch event	Mouse event
`touchstart`	`mousedown`
`touchmove`	`mousemove`
`touchend`	`mouseup`
	`mouseover`

Notice that there's no `mouseover` event on a mobile device—after all, it's impossible to know where you're hovering your finger! It might be a small detail, but it has some interesting implications for user interaction design, as we discussed briefly in Chapter 2. No hover states or tooltips means the user can no longer move their mouse around the screen looking for help, so you have to make your interfaces nice and self-explanatory.

So far, we've wound up a subset of mouse events—nothing too fancy. In the next chapter, we'll explore some advanced touch features of mobile devices like swiping and gesturing. In the meantime, let's continue our investigation of simple touch events.

Clicking with Feature Detection

Touch events can be more responsive and accurate, but they're not supported on all devices. We may be focusing our attention on the latest generation of super-duper phones, but it's always a good idea to provide support for as many browsers as possible. In addition, relying solely on touch events makes it impossible to test your app on a desktop browser. It's great fun to see your hard work displayed on a phone, but not so fun having to switch between desktop and mobile phone copious times as you're testing features.

You can (and should) use the various device emulators that will interpret your mouse clicks as touch events, but if you're used to desktop web development, being able to test your apps in your desktop browser is very convenient.

To make our code run on both new and old mobile browsers—and desktop browsers too—we'll implement a piece of **feature detection**. Feature detection involves probing the user's browser to see which cool features we can use, as well as (we hope) providing adequate fallbacks for features that are missing.

We can do this by assigning a few variables:

javascripts/ch4/05-touchdetect.js *(excerpt)*

```
var hasTouch = "ontouchend" in document,
    touchEndEvent = "touchend";
```

```
// Default to mouse up, if there's no touching
if (!hasTouch) {
  touchEndEvent = "mouseup";
}
```

If a browser supports touch events, the window's `document` object will have the `ontouchend` event in it. We create a variable called `touchEndEvent`, which initially contains the string `"touchend"`; we replace this with `"mouseup"` if our touch detection turns up nothing.

Now that we have a variable containing the event we want to target, we can bind the variable instead of a static string, and the correct event will be handled based on the device's capabilities:

javascripts/ch4/05-touchdetect.js *(excerpt)*

```
$("#tab-bar li").bind(touchEndEvent, function(){
  alert("Coming soon!");
});
```

Ternary Operator

There's a shortcut in JavaScript (and in many other programming languages) that allows you to set a variable conditionally as we did above. It's called the **ternary operator**. It has the syntax `a ? b : c`, which translates to: if `a` is true, return `b`; otherwise, return `c`.

So we could have written the `touchend` assignment above as:

```
var touchEndEvent = "ontouchend" in document ? "touchend" : "mouseup";
```

This reads as "if `document` contains the property `ontouchend`, return `"touchend"`; otherwise, return `"mouseup"`." The result is then assigned to the `touchEndEvent` variable. Ternary operators are a terse (some would argue "cryptic") way to do a conditional assignment, and, as with the traditional programmer battle of tabs versus spaces, you either love the ternary operator or hate it!

Without trying to scare you, there is still more to say on the topic of clicking. Even the simple click has a raft of new problems when moving from the mouse to the finger, one being the implications of the double-click. Your mobile device needs to wait a relatively long time to see if your click is going to become a double-click, and that delay manifests itself as a small but noticeable lag. In Chapter 6, we'll have a look at removing this, with the "quick click." For the rest of this chapter, though, we'll err on the side of simplicity and rely on the good old `click` event.

Quick Wins

As we move though the book, we're going to meet some relatively complex code for recreating native effects and behaviors. Thanks to some (fairly) standard hooks and APIs, however, there are a few tricks we can employ to add a bit of pizzazz to our apps without having to do much work at all.

Nifty Links

For security reasons, mobile web applications are sandboxed away from many built-in features of the mobile device; for example, unlike native apps, they're not able to retrieve a list of a user's contacts, or take a photo with the device's camera (yet). However, they do have the ability to open a few core applications and fill them with data just by using some carefully constructed hyperlinks.

Email

The simplest of these is the well-known `mailto:` URI scheme. On the desktop, these will launch your default mail application—and a smartphone does the same:

ch4/06-links-forms.html *(excerpt)*

```
<a href="mailto:feedback@startrackr.com?subject=Complaint">
  Send complaint
</a>
```

This will bring up the device's email app, with the subject line filled out with the variable we passed in, as Figure 4.3 shows.

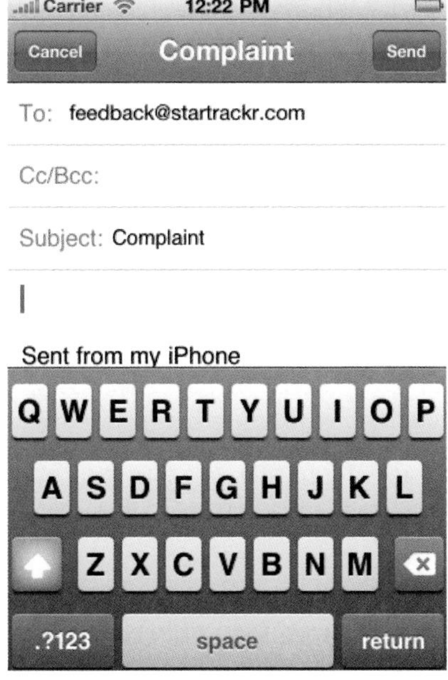

Figure 4.3. `mailto:` links will bring up the phone's email app

Phone Numbers

We can also assist in dialing a phone number using the `tel:` URI scheme. This will bring up (but not dial, of course) a phone number:

ch4/06-links-forms.html *(excerpt)*

```
<a href="tel:1-408-555-5555">
  Call in a sighting!
</a>
```

In fact, for the iPhone, there's no need to even wrap the number in a hyperlink. Mobile Safari includes a feature that automatically detects phone numbers in a page and turns them into links for you. "Excellent," you may think—until the first time it tries to turn your product IDs into "dialable" phone numbers! Similarly, there's a feature that turns address-like text into map links. But like any automagic feature, it's not always what you want. If that's the case, you can include `<meta>` tags in the head of your page to disable these features:

```
<meta name="format-detection" content="telephone=no"/>
<meta name="format-detection" content="address=no"/>
```

Again supported by the iPhone but not Android is the `sms:` URI scheme, which also takes a phone number, but opens up the text message application. At this point you might be worried about the limited support—fortunately, it's not a big problem if a device fails to recognize a URI scheme, as nothing will break; the link will simply do nothing.

Maps

Turning now to maps, the situation is a little less ideal. If you want to open a map and zoom to a given location, there's no widely implemented, standards-defined way to do it. A common method is to simply construct a URL that points to http://maps.google.com/ with a properly formatted latitude and longitude. Both iOS and Android will open this using the built-in mapping application rather than following the link in the browser:

ch4/06-links-forms.html *(excerpt)*

```
<a href="http://maps.google.com.au/maps?q=sitepoint">Visit us!</a>
```

A more standards-friendly version is the `geo:` URI, which accepts a variety of values that will be interpreted as map data by the device's mapping application. You can pass a latitude and longitude:

ch4/06-links-forms.html *(excerpt)*

```
<a href="geo:-33.87034,151.2037">Visit us!</a>
```

Or a street address or business name and location:

```
<a href="geo:0,0?q=123+Fake+St">Visit me!</a>
```

This is certainly nifty, but it's currently only supported on Android.

Form Field Attributes

With our links all polished up, let's turn to forms. HTML5 drags the basic form into the future with a quiver of shiny new input types and form attributes, which are well-supported on the current crop of mobile devices.

The HTML5 `placeholder` attribute of an input field will populate the field with a user prompt, which disappears when the user focuses on it. This is commonly used to avoid the need for a field label, or to offer additional help text to the user:

ch4/06-links-forms.html *(excerpt)*

```
<fieldset>
  <label for="name">
    <span>Who</span>
    <input type="text" name="name" placeholder="Star's name"/>
  </label>
  <label for="tags">
    <span>Tags</span>
    <input type="text" name="tags" placeholder="Tag your sighting"/>
  </label>
</fieldset>
```

The iPhone's keyboard tries to help out users by capitalizing the first letter in a form field. Most of the time, this is what you want—but not always; for example, in the tags field in our sample form. The iPhone will also attempt to correct words it fails to recognize, which can become a problem for our celebrity name field. These features can be disabled via the `autocorrect` and `autocapitalize` attributes:

ch4/06-links-forms.html *(excerpt)*

```
<fieldset>
  <label for="name">
    <span>Star</span>
    <input type="text" autocorrect="off" placeholder="Star's name"/>
  </label>
  <label>
    <span>Tags</span>
    <input type="text" autocapitalize="off" placeholder="Tag your sighting"/>
  </label>
</fieldset>
```

Note that these attributes are nonstandard, in that they're not in the HTML specification—at least for now.

Turn off the Automagic

If the majority of your form's fields require these attributes, you can also add them to the `<form>` tag itself, to apply them by default to all fields in that form. You can then override this setting on any given field as required.

Another HTML5 feature that's useful for mobile sites is the addition of a number of new input types. Beyond the traditional `type="text"`, HTML5 provides email, number, url, date, and even color inputs. These will all display as simple text fields on most browsers, but the iPhone cleverly provides appropriate keyboards for the data in question—for example, including shortcut keys for @ and . (period) when you use `type="email"`. For `type="number"`, it will provide a number pad instead of a traditional keyboard, as shown in Figure 4.4. The BlackBerry browser even provides date and color pickers for `date` and `color` input types.

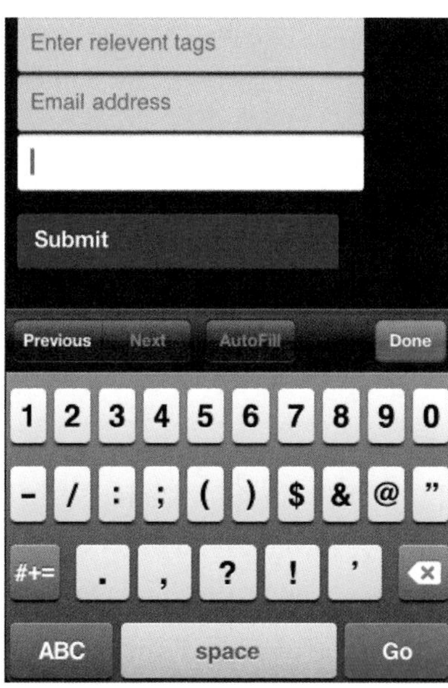

Figure 4.4. A numeric keypad appears when focusing a number input on the iPhone

Here's an example of these input types in action:

ch4/06-links-forms.html *(excerpt)*

```
<label>
  <span>Tags</span>
  <input type="text" autocapitalize="off" placeholder="Relevant tags">
</label>
<label>
```

```
  <span>Number of celebs</span>
  <input type="number" placeholder="Number of celebs">
</label>
<label>
  <span>Tags</span>
  <input type="email" placeholder="Your email address">
</label>
```

Support for all these features is inconsistent, so you'll need to test your target devices. The good news is that even when support is lacking, the app won't appear broken. Unsupported input types will simply behave as regular text fields, and users will be none the wiser.

Because the iPhone was the first to market, many of the iOS proprietary tricks have wide support on other devices; yet, not everyone wants to implement a competitor's features! Thankfully, support for the HTML5 standard is growing, and that should trickle down to all the big mobile players soon.

Loading Pages

Now that we've learned the basics of handling touch screens, and picked up a couple of quick wins by optimizing our links and forms, it's time to roll up our sleeves and get to work on the biggest component of just about any mobile web app. Unless your application is very basic, chances are you're going to need more than a single page, and therefore, you need to think about how to switch between pages. As we discussed earlier, our client is unlikely to be impressed with the web-like page reloads that currently exist in our app, so we need a way to hide the request/response cycle from the user. There are three main ways we can do this:

1. putting everything on one page, and then hiding and displaying sections as required

2. loading in new pages via Ajax

3. including only the complete skeleton of the app up front, and then bringing in data as required

The approach you take will depend heavily on the application. We'll start by looking at the first (and simplest) approach, and load all our content up front. This will let us look at how we can handle transitions between the various states. Of course, for a real app that depended on the user's location to fetch up-to-date information, you'd want to opt for one of the other two methods; we'll look at them at the end of this chapter.

Swapping Pages

If all our content is loaded in a single HTML page, a "page" from the point of view of our application is no longer a full HTML document; it's merely a DOM node that we're using as a container. We need to choose a suitable container and an appropriate way to group our pages, so that our scripts can manipulate them consistently.

We'll start by creating a container div (called pages), which contains a number of child div elements that are the actual pages. There can only be one page visible at a time, so we'll give that element a class of current. This class will be passed to whichever page is the active one:

```
<div id="pages">
  <div id="page-spots" class="current">
    <!-- Spots Index -->
  </div>
  <div id="page-spot">
    <!-- Spot Detail -->
  </div>
  <div id="page-sightings">
    <!-- Add Sighting Form -->
  </div>
  <div id="page-stars">
    <!-- Stars Index -->
  </div>
  <div id="page-star">
    <!-- Star Detail -->
  </div>
</div>
```

This list of pages will sit below the tab bar—so no need to change the markup of our navigation. We have, however, hooked up the links to point to the various sections by way of their id attributes; this will let us use a sneaky trick to show pages in the next step:

```
<ul id="tab-bar">
  <li>
    <a href="#spots">Spots</a>
  </li>
  <li>
    <a href="#sightings">Add a sighting</a>
  </li>
  <li>
    <a href="#stars">Stars</a>
  </li>
</ul>
```

After this, we need a couple of styles for hiding and showing pages. In our markup, every page is a first-level child of the main #pages container, so we can rely on that fact and use a child selector (>). First, we'll hide all the pages; then we'll unhide the page that has the current class:

stylesheets/transitions.css *(excerpt)*

```
#pages > div {
  display: none;
}
```

```
#pages > div.current {
  display: block;
}
```

To actually select some pages, we need to intercept the navigation menu clicks. We'll be using the code we wrote earlier to capture the event and prevent the browser from navigating to the link:

javascripts/ch4/07-swap.js *(excerpt)*

```
$("#tab-bar a").bind('click', function(e) {
  e.preventDefault();
  // Swap pages!
});
```

And here's the trick: the links point to our page elements by using the anchor syntax of a hash symbol (#), followed by a fragment identifier. It coincidently happens that jQuery uses that exact same syntax to select elements by `id`, so we can funnel the `hash` property of the `click` event directly into jQuery to select the destination page. Very sneaky:

javascripts/ch4/07-swap.js *(excerpt)*

```
$("#tab-bar a").bind('click', function(e) {
  e.preventDefault();
  var nextPage = $(e.target.hash);
  $("#pages .current").removeClass("current");
  nextPage.addClass("current");
});
```

With the target page acquired, we can hide the current page by removing the `current` `class` and passing it to the destination page. Swapping between pages now works as expected, but there's a slight problem: the selected icon in the tab bar fails to change when you navigate to another page. Looking back at our CSS, you'll remember that the tab bar's appearance is due to a `class` set on the containing `ul` element; it's a `class` that's the same as the current page `div` element's `id`. So all we need to do is slice out the hash symbol from our string (using `slice(1)` to remove the first character), and set that as the `ul`'s `class`:

javascripts/ch4/07-swap.js *(excerpt)*

```
$("#tab-bar a").bind('click', function(e) {
  e.preventDefault();
  var nextPage = $(e.target.hash);
  $("#pages .current").removeClass("current");
  nextPage.addClass("current");
  $("#tab-bar").attr("className", e.target.hash.slice(1));
});
```

Fading with WebKit Animations

The page swap we just implemented is as straightforward as it gets. This has its advantages—it stays out of our users' way, for one. That said, well-placed transitions between pages not only make your apps sexier, they can provide a clear visual cue to the user as to where they're being taken.

After the original iPhone was released, web developers leapt to re-implement the native transition effects in JavaScript, but the results were less than ideal, often containing lags and jumps that were very noticeable and distracting to users. The solution largely was to ditch JavaScript for moving large DOM elements, and instead turn to the new and hardware-accelerated CSS3 transitions and animations.

Before we worry about the transitions, though, we need to lay some groundwork. To fling DOM elements around, we need to be able to show, hide, and position them at will:

stylesheets/transitions.css *(excerpt)*

```
#pages {
  position: relative;
}
#pages > div {
  display:none;
  position: absolute;
  top: 0;
  left: 0;
  width: 100%;
}
```

By positioning the elements absolutely, we've moved every page up into the top-left corner, giving us a neat stack of invisible cards that we can now shuffle around and animate. They're not all invisible, though; remember that in our HTML, we gave our default page the `class` of `current`, which sets its `display` property to `block`.

The difference this time is that we're going to apply CSS animations to the pages. The incoming (new) page, and the outgoing (current) page will have equal but opposite forces applied to them to create a smooth-looking effect. There are three steps required to do this:

1. Set up the CSS animations.
2. Trigger the animation by setting the appropriate classes on the pages.
3. Remove the non-required classes when the animation is finished, and return to a non-animating state.

Let's start on the CSS. There are many approaches you can take with the problem of emulating native page transitions. We'll adopt a flexible method that's adapted from the jQTouch library. This is a modular approach, where we control transitions by applying and removing the relevant parts of an animation to each page.

Before we dive into that, though, a quick primer on CSS3 animations. These are currently supported only in WebKit browsers with `-webkit-` vendor prefixes. A CSS3 animation is made up of a series of keyframes grouped together as a named animation, created using the `@-webkit-keyframes` rule. Then we apply that animation to an element using the `-webkit-animation-name` property. We can also control the duration and easing of the animation with the `-webkit-animation-duration` and `-webkit-animation-timing-function` properties, respectively. If you're new to animations, this is probably sounding more than a little confusing to you right now; never mind, once you see it in practice, it'll be much clearer.

So let's apply some animations to our elements. First up, we'll set a timing function and a duration for our animations. These dictate how long a transition will take, and how the pages are eased from the start to the end point:

stylesheets/transitions.css *(excerpt)*

```
.in, .out {
  -webkit-animation-timing-function: ease-in-out;
  -webkit-animation-duration: 300ms;
}
```

We've placed these properties in generic classes, so that we can reuse them on any future animations we create.

Next, we need to create our keyframes. To start with, let's simply fade the new page in:

stylesheets/transitions.css *(excerpt)*

```
@-webkit-keyframes fade-in {
  from { opacity: 0; }
  to { opacity: 1; }
}
```

In the above rule, `fade-in` is the name of the animation, which we'll refer to whenever we want to animate an element using these keyframes. The `from` and `to` keywords allow us to declare the start and end points of the animation, and they can include any number of CSS properties you'd like to animate. If you want more keyframes in between the start and end, you can declare them with percentages, like this:

stylesheets/transitions.css *(excerpt)*

```
@-webkit-keyframes fade-in-out {
  from { opacity: 0; }
  50% { opacity: 1; }
  to { opacity: 0; }
}
```

With our keyframes declared, we can combine them with the previous direction classes to create the final effect. For our fade, we'll use the animation we defined above, and also flip the `z-index` on the pages to make sure the correct page is in front:

stylesheets/transitions.css *(excerpt)*

```
.fade.in {
  -webkit-animation-name: fade-in;
  z-index: 10;
}
.fade.out {
  z-index: 0;
}
```

By declaring `-webkit-animation-name`, we're telling the browser that as soon as an element matches this selector, it should begin the named animation.

With this CSS in place, we can move to step two. We'll start by applying our animation to a single navigation item, then broaden it out later so that it will work for our whole tab bar.

The page we're fading to (`#sightings`) will need to have three different classes added to it: `current` to make the page visible, `fade` to add our animation, and `in` to apply our timing function and duration. The page we're fading from (`#spots`) is visible, so it will already have the `current class`; we only need to add the `fade` and `out` classes:

```
var fromPage = $("#spots"),
    toPage = $("#sightings");

$("#tab-sighting a").click(function(){
  toPage.addClass("current fade in");
  fromPage.addClass("fade out");
});
```

This gives us a nice fading effect when we click on the "Add a sighting" tab, but now the pages are stuck—stacked atop one another. This is because those `class` names are still there, so the pages now have `current` and they're both visible. Time to remove them! We'll do this by binding to the `webkitAnimationEnd` event, which fires when the transition is complete. When this event fires, we can remove all three classes from the original page, and the `fade` and `in` classes from the new page.

Additionally, we must remember to unbind the `webkitAnimationEnd` event so that we don't go adding on extra handlers the next time we fade from the page:

```
var fromPage = $("#spots"),
  toPage = $("#sightings");

$("#tab-sighting a").click(function(){
  toPage
    .addClass("current fade in")
    .bind("webkitAnimationEnd", function(){
      // More to do, once the animation is done.
      fromPage.removeClass("current fade out");
      toPage
        .removeClass("fade in")
        .unbind("webkitAnimationEnd");
    });
  fromPage.addClass("fade out");
});
```

There we go. Our page is now fading nicely; however, there are a few problems with our code. The first is structural. It will become quite ugly if we have to replicate this same click handler for each set of pages we want to transition to! To remedy this, we'll make a function called `transition()` that will accept a page selector and fade from the current page to the new one provided.

While we're at it, we can replace our `bind()` and `unbind()` calls with jQuery's `one()` method. This method will accomplish the same task—it binds an event, and then unbinds it the first time it's fired—but it looks a lot cleaner:

javascripts/ch4/08-fade.js *(excerpt)*

```
function transition(toPage) {
  var toPage = $(toPage),
    fromPage = $("#pages .current");

  toPage
    .addClass("current fade in")
    .one("webkitAnimationEnd", function(){
      fromPage.removeClass("current fade out");
      toPage.removeClass("fade in")
    });
  fromPage.addClass("fade out");
}
```

Generalizing Functions

You might spy that we've hardcoded the current page selector inside our function. This makes our code smaller, but reduces the reusability of the function. If you are building a larger framework intended for more general use, you'd probably want to accept the *fromPage* as a parameter, too.

Great. Now we have a reusable function that we can employ to fade between any of the pages in our app. We can pull the link targets out of the tab bar the same way we did earlier, and suddenly every page swap is a beautiful fade:

javascripts/ch4/08-fade.js *(excerpt)*

```
$("#tab-bar a").click(function(e) {
  e.preventDefault();
  var nextPage = $(e.target.hash);
  transition(nextPage);
  $("#tab-bar").attr("className", e.target.hash.slice(1));
});
```

There's still a major problem, though, and it's one you'll notice if you try to test this code on a browser that lacks support for animations, such as Firefox. Because we're relying on the `webkitAnimationEnd` event to remove the `current` class from the old page, browsers that don't support animations—and therefore never fire that event—will never hide the original page.

Browser Testing

This bug—which would render the application completely unusable on non-WebKit browsers—highlights the importance of testing your code on as many browsers as possible. While it can be easy to assume that every mobile browser contains an up-to-date version of WebKit (especially if you own an iPhone or Android), the real mobile landscape is far more varied.

This problem is easy enough to solve. At the end of our `transition()` function, we'll drop in some feature detection code that will handle the simplified page swap in the absence of animations:

javascripts/ch4/08-fade.js *(excerpt)*

```
function transition(toPage) {
  ⋮
  // For non-animatey browsers
  if(!("WebKitTransitionEvent" in window)){
    toPage.addClass("current");
    fromPage.removeClass("current");
    return;
  }
}
```

With this code in place, our app now produces our beautiful fade transition on WebKit browsers, but still swaps pages out effectively on other browsers.

There's still one slightly buggy behavior, one you might notice if you become a little excited and start clicking like crazy. If you click on the link to the current page—or if you tap quickly to start an animation when the previous one has yet to complete—the `class` attributes we're using to manage the application's state will be left in an inconsistent state. Eventually, we'll end up with *no* pages with the `current class`—at which point we'll be staring at a blank screen.

It's relatively easy to protect against these cases. We just need to ensure our `toPage` is different from our `fromPage`, and that it doesn't already have the `current class` on it. This safeguard goes after the variable declaration, and before any class manipulations:

javascripts/ch4/08-fade.js *(excerpt)*

```
function transition(toPage) {
  var toPage = $(toPage),
    fromPage = $("#pages .current");

  if(toPage.hasClass("current") || toPage === fromPage) {
    return;
  };
  ⋮
```

Sliding

Awesome work—our first animated transition is up and running! Let's move on to the next one: an extremely common mobile interaction for master-detail pages, such as our Spots and Stars listings. On mobile devices, it's common for the detail page to slide in from the right side of the screen, as if it had been hiding there the whole time. When the user returns to the master page, the transition works in reverse, providing the user with a clear visual model of the app's information hierarchy.

Creating a slide or "push" transition is very easy now that we've learned to fade—we just need to update our CSS animations. To perform a push, we need to animate the current page off the screen to the left while simultaneously moving the new page in from the right. It's a bit trickier than just fading, but only just.

First, we'll create an animation for moving the current screen away. We'll use the `-webkit-transform` property to animate the `div` element's horizontal location via the `translateX` command.

CSS Transforms

If you're unfamiliar with CSS3 transforms, don't worry. They're simply an easy way to act on the position and shape of an element as its rendered. In addition to the translateX transform we're using here, you also have access to translateY (unsurprisingly), translate (for both X- and Y-axis translation), as well as `rotate`, `skew`, and `scale` functions. For the full list and examples of how they can be used, check out the W3C's CSS 2D Transforms Module.[4]

The screen starts at X=0 and then moves out of sight by translating to -100%. This is a nifty trick. If we translate by a negative amount, the screen moves to the left. By moving 100% to the left, the screen is gone. Once we've defined the keyframes, we can then assign the animation to the `.push.out` selector (remember that our existing `out class` provides a default duration and timing function for our animations):

stylesheets/transitions.css *(excerpt)*

```
/* Screen pushes out to left */
@-webkit-keyframes outToLeft {
  from { -webkit-transform: translateX(0); }
  to { -webkit-transform: translateX(-100%); }
}
.push.out {
  -webkit-animation-name: outToLeft;
}
```

Similarly, we'll define an animation for the new screen to fly in from the right, taking the place of the old one:

stylesheets/transitions.css *(excerpt)*

```
/* Screen pushes in from the right */
@-webkit-keyframes inFromRight {
  from { -webkit-transform: translateX(100%); }
  to { -webkit-transform: translateX(0); }
}
.push.in {
  -webkit-animation-name: inFromRight;
}
```

For the JavaScript, we could recycle the transition function we made for the fade, calling it `transition_push()`, for example. We'd then just need to change all the instances of `fade` to `push`. And then again for `flip` when we want to implement flip transitions, and so on. On second thoughts, it would be nicer to pass the transition type in as a parameter to our `transition()` function:

[4] http://www.w3.org/TR/css3-2d-transforms/#transform-functions

javascripts/ch4/09-slide.js *(excerpt)*

```
function transition(toPage, type) {
  ⋮
  toPage
    .addClass("current " + type + " in")
    .one("webkitAnimationEnd", function(){
      fromPage.removeClass("current " + type + " out");
      toPage.removeClass(type + " in");
    });
  fromPage.addClass(type + " out");
}
```

Now when we create CSS animations for a new transition, they'll automatically be available to use in our script. We just pass the new name in:

```
transition(nextPage, "push");
```

We'd like the push transition to be used for navigating down from a list to a detail page, so we need to add some new click handlers for the list items:

javascripts/ch4/09-slide.js *(excerpt)*

```
$("#spots-list li").click(function(e){
  e.preventDefault();
  transition("#page-spot", "push");
});
$("#stars-list li").click(function(e){
  e.preventDefault();
  transition("#page-star", "push");
});
```

With this, the detail pages will slide in from the right to replace the list pages. As we outlined earlier, though, what we'd also like is for the reverse to occur when the user is navigating back *up* the app's hierarchy. Next up, we'll look at building out that functionality, and, while we're at it, adding support for going "back."

Going Backwards

The user is now looking at a page of details about some crazy celebrity, and they're bored. They want a new crazy celebrity to read about, so they go looking for the Back button. But going back is more than just swapping the source and destination pages again, because the animations we applied need to be reversed: the old page needs to slide back from the left into view.

But that's getting ahead of ourselves; first, we need a Back button. We've provided one up in the header of each page in the form of an a element that's styled to look all button-like:

ch4/10-back.html *(excerpt)*

```
<div class="header">
  <h1>Spots</h1>
  <a href="#" class="back">Back</a>
</div>
```

And of course, we must have a handler to perform an action when the button is clicked:

javascripts/ch4/10-back.js *(excerpt)*

```
$("#spot-details .back").click(function(){
  // Do something when clicked …
});
```

Next, we need to recreate all our CSS animations—but in reverse. We've already created `inFromRight` and `outFromLeft` animations; we need to add two more to complement them: `inFromLeft` and `outToRight`. Once these are defined, they have to be attached to our elements with CSS selectors. We'll continue the modular approach, and use a combination of class selectors to leverage our existing properties:

stylesheets/transitions.css *(excerpt)*

```
@-webkit-keyframes inFromLeft {
  from { -webkit-transform: translateX(-100%); }
  to { -webkit-transform: translateX(0); }
}
.push.in.reverse {
  -webkit-animation-name: inFromLeft;
}
@-webkit-keyframes outToRight {
  from { -webkit-transform: translateX(0); }
  to { -webkit-transform: translateX(100%); }
}
.push.out.reverse {
  -webkit-animation-name: outToRight;
}
```

The next step is to work the new `class` into our `transition()` function. We'll add a third parameter, *`reverse`*, that accepts a Boolean value. If the value is `false`, or if it's not provided at all, we'll do the forward version of the transition. If the value is `true`, we'll append the `reverse` `class` to all the class manipulation operations:

javascripts/ch4/10-back.js *(excerpt)*

```
function transition(toPage, type, reverse){
  var toPage = $(toPage),
    fromPage = $("#pages .current"),
    reverse = reverse ? "reverse" : "";

  if(toPage.hasClass("current") || toPage === fromPage) {
    return;
  };
  toPage
    .addClass("current " + type + " in " + reverse)
    .one("webkitAnimationEnd", function(){
      fromPage.removeClass("current " + type + " out " + reverse);
      toPage.removeClass(type + " in " + reverse);
    });
  fromPage.addClass(type + " out " + reverse);
}
```

If we pass in `true` now, the new page will be assigned the `class` attribute `push in reverse`, and the old page will be assigned `push out reverse`—which will trigger our new backwards animations. To see it in action, we'll add a call to `transition()` in our Back button hander:

javascripts/ch4/10-back.js *(excerpt)*

```
$("#page-spot .back").click(function(e){
  e.preventDefault();
  transition("#page-spots", "push", true);
});
```

Managing History

The Back button works, but it's a bit "manual" at the moment. For every page in our app, we'd have to hook up a separate handler to go back. Worse still, some pages could be reached via a number of different routes, yet our current solution only goes back to a fixed page. To combat these problems, we'll create our very own history system that will keep track of each page users visit, so that when they hit the Back button, we know where we should send them.

To start with, we'll create a `visits` object, which will contain a `history` array and some methods to manage it:

javascripts/ch4/11-history.js *(excerpt)*

```
var visits = {
  history: [],
  add: function(page) {
```

```
    this.history.push(page);
  }
};
```

Our `visits` object will maintain a stack of visited pages in the `history` array. The `add()` method takes a page and prepends it to the stack (via the JavaScript `push()` function, which adds an element to the end of an array). We'll call this method from inside our `transition()` function, so that every page will be added before it's shown:

javascripts/ch4/11-history.js *(excerpt)*

```
function transition(toPage, type, reverse) {
  var toPage = $(toPage),
    fromPage = $("#pages .current"),
    reverse = reverse ? "reverse" : "";

  visits.add(toPage);
  ⋮
}
```

Centralizing Page Changes

The assumption that every transition corresponds to a page change is convenient for us, otherwise we'd have to call `visits.add()` everywhere we do a transition. However, there might be times when you want to do a transition to a new page, but not include it as a page change—for example, if you have some kind of slide-up dialog. In this case, you could create a `changePage()` function that handles both history management and transitioning. We'll be doing this in the next section.

The next item to think about is our Back button. We only want it to be shown if there's a history item to revert to. We'll add a helper method to the `visits` object to check for us. Because the first page in the history will be the current page, we need to check that there are at least two pages:

javascripts/ch4/11-history.js *(excerpt)*

```
var visits = {
  ⋮
  hasBack: function() {
    return this.history.length > 1;
  }
}
```

Now that we have this helper, we can use it in our transition code to show or hide the Back button accordingly. The `toggle()` jQuery function is very useful here; it accepts a Boolean value, and either shows or hides the element based on that value:

javascripts/ch4/11-history.js *(excerpt)*

```
function transition(toPage, type, reverse) {
  var toPage = $(toPage),
    fromPage = $("#pages .current");
    reverse = reverse ? "reverse" : "";

  visits.add(toPage);
  toPage.find(".back").toggle(visits.hasBack());
  ⋮
```

Good! Now we need some logic in our `visits` object to handle a back event. If there is history, we'll pop the first item (the current page) off the top of the stack. We don't actually need this page—but we have to remove it to reach the next item. This item is the previous page, and it's the one we return:

javascripts/ch4/11-history.js *(excerpt)*

```
var visits = {
  ⋮
  back: function() {
    if(!this.hasBack()){
      return;
    }
    var curPage = this.history.pop();
    return this.history.pop();
  }
}
```

Push and Pop

The `push()` and `pop()` methods add or remove an element from the end of an array, respectively. Both methods modify the original array in place. The `pop()` method returns the element that has been removed (in our example, we use this to get the previous page), whereas the `push()` method returns the new length of the array.

Finally, we can wire up all our application's Back buttons. When a request to go back is issued, we grab the previous page and, if it exists, we transition back to it. We just replace our hardcoded click handler with a general-purpose one:

javascripts/ch4/11-history.js *(excerpt)*

```
$(".back").live("click",function(){
  var lastPage = visits.back();
  if(lastPage) {
    transition(lastPage, "push", true);
  }
});
```

There's still a problem, though: we never add the *initial* page to the history stack, so there's no way to navigate back to it. That's easy enough to fix—we'll just remove the `current class` from the initial `div`, and call our transition function to show the first page when the document loads:

javascripts/ch4/11-history.js *(excerpt)*

```
$(document).ready(function() {
  ⋮
  transition($("#page-spots"), "show");
});
```

To hook up that "show" transition, we'll reuse our fade animation, but with an extremely short duration:

stylesheets/transitions.css *(excerpt)*

```
.show.in {
  -webkit-animation-name: fade-in;
  -webkit-animation-duration: 10ms;
}
```

Many native apps only track history between master and details pages; in our case, for example, a list of stars leads to the star's details, and the Back button allows you to jump back up to the list. If you change areas of the application (for example, by clicking on one of the main navigation links), the history is reset. We can mimic this behavior by adding a `clear()` method:

javascripts/ch4/11-history.js *(excerpt)*

```
var visits = {
  ⋮
  clear: function() {
    this.history = [];
  }
}
```

This simply erases our history stack. We'll call this method whenever the user moves to a new section:

javascripts/ch4/11-history.js *(excerpt)*

```
$("#tab-bar a").click(function(e){
  // Clear visit history
  visits.clear();
  ⋮
});
```

This has a very "app" feeling, and, as an added bonus, we don't have to wire up so many Back button events!

Back with Hardware Buttons

Our current Back button system is good, but it doesn't take into account the fact that a mobile device will often have its own Back button—either in the form of a physical button, or a soft button in the browser. As it stands, if a user hits their device's Back button after clicking a few internal links in our app, the browser will simply move to the last HTML page it loaded, or exit completely. This will definitely break our users' illusion of our site as a full-fledged app, so let's see if we can find a fix for this problem.

What we really need is to be able to listen to, and modify, the browser's built-in history, instead of our own custom stack of pages. To accomplish this, the HTML5 History API[5] is here to help us out.

The History API lets us add pages to the history stack, as well as move forward and backwards between pages in the stack. To add pages, we use the `window.history.pushState()` method. This method is analogous to our `visits.add()` method from earlier, but takes three parameters: any arbitrary data we want to remember about the page; a page title (if applicable); and the URL of the page.

We're going to create a method `changePage()` that combines both adding a page using the history API, and doing our regular transition. We'll keep track of the transition inside the history, so that when the user presses back, we can look at the transition and do the opposite. This is nicer than our previous version, where we'd only ever do a reverse slide for the back transition.

Here's a first stab at writing out this new method:

javascripts/ch4/12-hardware-back.js *(excerpt)*

```
function changePage(page, type, reverse) {

  window.history.pushState({
    page: page,
    transition: type,
    reverse: !!reverse
  }, "", page);

  // Do the real transition
  transition(page, type, reverse)
}
```

[5] http://www.w3.org/TR/html5/history.html

The first parameter to `pushState()` is referred to as the **state object**. You can use it to pass any amount of data between pages in your app in the form of a JavaScript object. In our case, we're passing the page, the transition type, and whether or not it's a reverse transition.

To use this new function in our code, we merely change all occurrences of `transition()` to `changePage()`, for example:

```
changePage("#page-spots", "show");
```

Now, as the user moves through our application, the history is being stored away. If they hit the physical Back button, you can see the page history in the URL bar, but nothing special happens. This is to be expected: we've just pushed a series of page strings onto the history stack, but we haven't told the app how to navigate back to them.

The `window.onPopState` event is fired whenever a real page load event happens, or when the user hits Back or Forward. The event is fed an object called *`state`* that contains the state object we put there with `pushStack()` (if the state is undefined, it means the event was fired from a page load, rather than a history change—so it's of no concern). Let's create a handler for this event:

javascripts/ch4/12-hardware-back.js *(excerpt)*

```
window.addEventListener("popstate", function(event) {
  if(!event.state){
    return;
  }

  // Transition back - but in reverse.
  transition(
    event.state.page,
    event.state.transition,
    !event.state.reverse
  );
}, false);
```

Where's jQuery?

For this example, we've just used a standard DOM event listener rather than the jQuery `bind()` method. This is just for clarity for the `popstate` event. If we bound it using `$(window).bind("popstate", …)`, the event object passed to the callback would be a jQuery event object, not the browser's native `popstate` event. Usually that's what we want, but jQuery's event wrapper doesn't include the properties from the History API, so we'd need to call `event.originalEvent` to retrieve the browser event. There's nothing wrong with that—you can feel free to use whichever approach you find simplest.

Fantastic! The animations all appear to be working in reverse when we hit the browser Back button … or are they? If you look closely, you might notice something strange. Sometimes we see "slide" transitions that should be simple "show" transitions, and vice versa. What's going on?

Actually, we have an off-by-one error happening here: when moving backwards, we don't want to use the transition of the page we are transitioning *to*, but the page we are transitioning *from*. Unfortunately, this means we need to call `pushState()` with the *next* transition that happens. But we're unable to see the future … how can we know what transition is going to happen next?

Thankfully, the History API provides us with another method, `replaceState()`. It's almost identical to `pushState()`, but instead of adding to the stack, it *replaces* the current (topmost) page on the stack. To solve our problem, we'll hang on to the details of the previous `pushState()`; then, before we add the next item, we'll use `replaceState()` to update the page with the "next" transition:

javascripts/ch4/12-hardware-back.js *(excerpt)*

```
var pageState = {};
function changePage(page, type, reverse) {
  // Store the transition with the state
  if(pageState.url){
    // Update the previous transition to be the NEXT transition
    pageState.state.transition = type;
    window.history.replaceState(
      pageState.state,
      pageState.title,
      pageState.url);
  }
  // Keep the state details for next time!
  pageState = {
    state: {
      page: page,
      transition: type,
      reverse: reverse
    },
    title: "",
    url: page
  }
  window.history.pushState(pageState.state, pageState.title, pageState.url);

  // Do the real transition
  transition(page, type, reverse)
}
```

We also need to update our `pageState` variable when the user goes back; otherwise, it would fall out of sync with the browser's history, and our `replaceState()` calls would end up inserting bogus entries into the history:

javascripts/ch4/12-hardware-back.js *(excerpt)*

```
window.addEventListener("popstate", function(event) {
  if(!event.state){
    return;
  }
  // Transition back - but in reverse.
  transition(
    event.state.page,
    event.state.transition,
    !event.state.reverse
  );
  pageState = {
    state: {
      page: event.state.page,
      transition: event.state.transition,
      reverse: event.state.reverse
    },
    title: "",
    url: event.state.page
  }
}, false);
```

There we go. The physical Back button now works beautifully. But what about our custom application Back button? We can wire that up to trigger a history event, and therefore tie into all that History API jazz we just wrote using a quick call to `history.back()`:

javascripts/ch4/12-hardware-back.js *(excerpt)*

```
$(".back").live("click",function(e){
  window.history.back();
});
```

Now our application Back button works exactly like the browser or physical Back button. You can also wire up a Forward button and trigger it with `history.forward()`, or skip to a particular page in the stack with `history.go(-3)`. You might have noticed that we've been a bit quiet on the Forward button handling. There are two reasons for this: first, most mobile browsers lack a Forward button, and second, it's impossible to know if the `popstate` event occurred because of the Back or the Forward button.

The only way you could get around this pickle would be to combine the `popstate` method with the manual history management system we built in the previous section, looking at the URLs or other data to determine the direction of the stack movement. This is a lot of work for very little return in terms of usability, so we'll settle for the history and back functionality we've built, and move on to the next challenge.

Ajax

We've now learned how to transition between pages smoothly and without reloading, but so far we've only done this with static content. We need to be able to load our pages dynamically, and *then* transition to them.

The good news is that there's comparatively excellent support for Ajax on high-end mobile devices—so Ajax work remains largely the same as you're used to on the desktop. Of course, you have to consider that the average data connection will be an order of magnitude slower (and more expensive), so it's best to keep your bandwidth use to an absolute minimum.

There are two approaches we could take to loading dynamic data into our application. We could load in the raw data (such as a list of JSON objects representing recently spotted celebrities) and merge it into the application's HTML—creating list elements and appending them to the page. Or, we could load the entire HTML contents straight from the server and dump it directly into our page. The latter approach sounds more straightforward—so let's try that first to become familiar with Ajax in the mobile environment. After that, we'll take a look at handling other data formats.

Fetching HTML

The first thing we'll need if we want to retrieve data from a server is … a server! If you try and grab data from a file:// protocol URL (which will be the case if you're testing pages by double-clicking an **index.html** file), you'll hit the dreaded "Access-Control-Allow-Origin" error.

Servers

As this is a book about building mobile web apps in HTML, CSS, and JavaScript, covering the details of setting up a server to deliver your data is unfortunately beyond our scope. We'll spend the rest of this chapter looking at examples of Ajax functionality we can add to Startrackr, but if you want to try these examples for yourself, you'll need to set up a server to deliver the appropriate data.

Assuming we have a server—be it running on our machine locally, on a VM, or on the Internet—we now need somewhere to dump the HTML chunks when they're returned from the server. For this we only require a skeleton of the page we've been working with, to act as a container that we fill. Because we'll be returning the same markup as before, our original CSS will apply to the contents without needing to be modified. Here's that skeleton:

ch4/13-ajax.html *(excerpt)*

```
<div id="pages">
  <div id="page-spots" class="page-spots"></div>
  <div id="page-spot" class="page-spots"></div>
  <div id="page-sightings" class="page-sightings"></div>
```

```
  <div id="page-stars" class="page-stars"></div>
  <div id="page-star" class="page-stars"></div>
</div>
```

All the content for each of those sections is back in the **spots.html**, **new.html**, and **stars.html** files—just like a regular website, except that now we'll be using Ajax to load that content into this empty skeleton.

With this basic HTML in place, the next step is to stop the link from being followed when clicked, as we did with our transition function earlier—with `preventDefault()`. Then we can execute our Ajax. The jQuery `load()` function is perfect for our needs: it loads HTML from a URL, and provides a mechanism for choosing which part of the document to return. This is great, because we have no need for the whole page, with the `head` and `meta` tags—we only want the contents of the `body`. Using `load()` means we don't need a special version of our HTML page for Ajax, and any updates will only have to be made in one place.

To accomplish this, we use the `load()` function with a string parameter consisting of the URL we want, followed by a space, followed by a jQuery selector string. The contents of the element matched by that selector will be inserted into the element from which `load()` was called. The content we want to insert is contained in the `.wrapper` `div` of the target page. So, when the Spots link is clicked, we want to call `load()` on our `#spots` container and pass in the string `"spots.html .wrapper"`:

javascripts/ch4/13-ajax.js *(excerpt)*

```
$("#tab-spots a").click(function(e){
  e.preventDefault();
  $("#page-spots").load("spots.html .wrapper");
});
```

Loading HTML Snippets

If you're unfamiliar with jQuery, you might be wondering how it loads in a small section of HTML via Ajax. There's no magic here; it actually loads the entire page and dumps it into a `div` element that exists outside the DOM. The filtering is done on this element, and the results are inserted in the correct position. Very handy, although of course it means transmitting more data over the network than you actually end up using. For most real-world applications, you'll probably want to pull data in XML or JSON format and insert it into your HTML on the client side. We'll be looking at how this can be done shortly. For now, though, we'll stick with using `load()` to keep it simple, and focus on demonstrating how the various Ajax methods work, as well as how they're best used in the context of a mobile app.

This will load the relevant HTML into the right container, but there are a few more tasks that need attention—most notably, making the new content visible! Fortunately, `load()` allows you to specify a callback function that will be executed once the Ajax call has completed. Inside this callback, we'll transition the page into view:

javascripts/ch4/13-ajax.js *(excerpt)*

```
$("#tab-spots a").click(function(e){
  e.preventDefault();
  $("#page-spots").load("spots.html .wrapper", function() {
    transition('#page-spots', "fade", false);
  });
});
```

Ajaxifying Links

Adding events to each navigation item is a tedious way to wire up our site. We made an Ajax loader for the Spots page just now, but we'd have to duplicate this code multiple times for it to work for all the links. Instead, we can take advantage of our site's consistent structure and concoct a system to do it programmatically, based on the contents of the navigation elements. Doing this gives us a level of progressive enhancement: our links are designed to work as normal, but our system intercepts them when clicked and loads the content via Ajax. This method is sometimes known as **Hijax**.

We'll then generalize the Ajax code we wrote so that it can be applied to any link we pass it. There are two pieces of data needed for that: the URL to load, and the name of the container to dump it in. This is where having conventions is important. As long as our pages and classes are named in a consistent manner, we can easily create code that targets all our links:

javascripts/ch4/14-hijax.js *(excerpt)*

```
function loadPage(url, pageName) {
  $("#" + pageName).load(url + " .wrapper", function(){
    console.log(this);
    transition("#" + pageName, "fade", false);
  });
};
```

This function is almost identical to the code from before, except we've replaced the page names and URLs with variables. Now we can load a page programmatically, for example:

```
loadPage("spots.html", "spots");
```

If fact, we need to load a page by default when the application loads, so we can place that line of code inside the `document.ready` handler. This will load up the Spots page via Ajax as our home page.

Data Caching

Because the `load()` method pulls in an entire HTML file, the results can be cached by the browser, which means that changes you make in the page being loaded may not be reflected right away. You can disable the cache globally (for all Ajax requests) with `$.ajaxSetup({ cache: false });`, or, if it's just for one particular call, you can append a timestamp to the URL so that each request will be seen by the browser as different. So, instead of loading `url + " #wrapper"`, you can load `url + "?" + new Date().getTime() + " #wrapper"`.

Finally, we want to call our function whenever any navigation items are clicked. Remember, we have to extract two pieces of data to pass to our function: the URL and the page name. The URL is simple—it's the `href` value of the link itself. For the page name, there are many approaches we could take: we could give our containers the same names as the files (minus the **.html**), or we could add some extra data into the link itself. The latter has become easier with the addition of custom data attributes in HTML5, which let us annotate elements with key/value pairs:

ch4/14-hijax.html *(excerpt)*

```
<ul id="tab-bar">
  <li>
    <a data-load="spots" href="spots.html">Spots</a>
  </li>
  <li>
    <a data-load="sightings" href="new.html">Add a sighting</a>
  </li>
  <li>
    <a data-load="stars" href="stars.html">Stars</a>
  </li>
</ul>
```

A data attribute starts with `data-` and is followed by your key name. You can then provide it with whatever value you like. According to the spec, these values should be retrieved using the element's `dataset` property; however, this is yet to be widely supported, so your best bet is to use the standard `getAttribute()` function (as in, `myElement.getAttribute("data-load")`), or, if you're using jQuery, the `attr()` method:

javascripts/ch4/14-hijax.js *(excerpt)*

```
$("#tab-bar a").click(function(e){
  e.preventDefault();
  var url = e.target.href;
  var pageName = $(this).attr("data-load");
  loadPage(url, pageName);
});
```

Et voilà! Any link inside the `#tab-bar` element will fire our `loadPage()` function, and we'll transition from the current page to the new page. You can easily extend this system to also specify the transition type, if you like.

One current problem is that if the page takes a long time to load, the user has no idea what's going on (and they'll probably become click-happy and try to load another page). The obvious solution is a "loading" indicator; jump over to Chapter 6 if you're keen to add one now.

Templating

Pulling in an entire dollop of ready-to-go HTML via Ajax makes it nice and easy to stick in your page, but typically this isn't the data format you'll receive from a web service or API. This means it's our responsibility to turn data into markup. Even if you're in control of the back end, it still makes sense to transmit your site data in XML or JSON rather than HTML, since those files will usually be much smaller, and require less of your mobile users' precious bandwidth.

So, how will this work? We start by receiving a list of data from the server. For each item in the list, we want to create an HTML fragment (such as a list item) and inject some values from the data. Finally, we want to add each fragment into the correct place in the page. There are a few common ways to approach this situation:

- build the HTML fragments ourselves, in JavaScript
- duplicate a "template" DOM element and change the contents of the relevant tags
- use a templating engine

We'll quickly visit each approach and see what works best in which contexts. We'll be assuming our data source is in the JSON format, and looks a little like this:

data/spots.json *(excerpt)*

```
[{
  "id": 4,
  "name": "Planet Bollywood",
  "distance": "400m",
  "sightings": 10
}, {
  "id": 7,
  "name": "Soft Rock Café",
  "distance": "1.1Km",
  "sightings": 3
}]
```

It's a simple array, with each element consisting of an object containing details about locations. This is a very common (albeit simplified) format for the data that we're likely to receive. To fetch it into our application, we can use jQuery's `getJSON()` method:

javascripts/ch4/15-templating.js *(excerpt)*

```
$.getJSON("../data/spots.json", function(data){
  // Got JSON, now template it!
});
```

With some data in our pocket, it's time to show it to the world. The first of our three approaches is to loop over the `data` array, building up HTML strings that can then be added into the DOM:

javascripts/ch4/15-templating.js *(excerpt)*

```
$.getJSON("../data/spots.js", function(data){
  // Got JSON, now template it!
  var html = "";
  for(var i = 0; i < data.length; i++) {
    html += "<li><a href='#'>";
    html += "<h2>" + data[i].name + "</h2>";
    html += "</a></li>";
  }
  $("#spots-list").append(html);
});
```

This is a very old-school approach, and while it can work for very simple examples, it tends to scale poorly: it's error-prone, difficult to maintain, and degenerates fairly quickly into a huge mess of mashed-together HTML and data.

The separation of data and presentation is important, and this is especially true for web applications. Using the previous method, if a designer wanted to make changes to the HTML, they'd either have to know some JavaScript (and potentially risk breaking something), or come and bother you about it. We would prefer to avoid being bothered, so a better solution is to include the HTML where it belongs—in the HTML page:

ch4/16-templating-2.html *(excerpt)*

```
<div id="tmpl-simple" style="display:none;">
  <li>
    <a href="spot.html" data-load="spot">
      <h2></h2>
      <span class="relative-distance"></span>
      <span class="sightings"></span>
    </a>
  </li>
</div>
```

We've constructed a generic fragment that's empty of any data. When we receive data from the server, we can clone this template and fill it with our data. It can be as complex as it needs to be, as long as there are some hooks for us to inject our data into. Of course, you don't want an empty row in the list shown to the user—so the template needs to be hidden. In the above example, this is done using `display: none;`.

To make use of the fragment, we'll clone it with jQuery's `clone()` method, and then inject all the pieces of data into their correct elements using the `text()` method:

javascripts/ch4/16-templating-2.js *(excerpt)*

```
$.getJSON("../data/spots.json", function(data){
  // Got JSON, now template it!
  $.each(data, function(){
    var newItem = $("#tmpl-simple").clone();

    // Now fill in the fields with the data
    newItem.find("h2").text(this.name);
    newItem.find(".relative-distance").text(this.distance);
    newItem.find(".sightings").text(this.sightings);

    // And add the new list item to the page
    newItem.children().appendTo("#spots-list")
  });
  transition("#spots", "show");
});
```

This solution works well, leaving all the HTML in one file and all the JavaScript in another. It's much nicer than our first approach, and is suitable for small static templates. But it's less ideal if the HTML is continually changing, and for large pages it requires us to write a lot of generic JavaScript to replace all the field values.

This is the kind of mind-numbing code that we want to automate away. Perhaps we could add some tokens in the HTML that could be automatically replaced from a given data object? That's quite a good idea, and it turns out plenty of developers have had it before: it's called a **templating engine**. Choosing a templating engine is like choosing a text editor: there are a lot out there, they have a many different features, most of them are fine, and ultimately it's up to you which one you (or your company) likes the best.

One "big one" that you'll see mentioned time and time again is Mustache.[6] It's available for many programming languages, and the template format is the same for all of them—which makes it worth becoming familiar with (though it also means that we're unable to use JavaScript's dot notation because it clashes with some other languages).

---

[6] http://mustache.github.com/

However, given that we're already using jQuery, we're in luck. In 2008, John Resig (the creator of jQuery) released a novel and extremely small templating engine made up of around 20 lines of JavaScript. It has since been expanded into a full jQuery library that is considered the officially sanctioned jQuery templating engine: the code is available from the jQuery repository on GitHub[7] and the documentation is located on the jQuery plugin site.[8]

To use the library, download the archive from GitHub and extract the minimized file. It will be called **jquery.tmpl.min.js**, and is only about 8KB in size. Copy this into your project to load it up:

```
<script src="jquery.tmpl.min.js" type="text/javascript"></script>
```

Twitter Integration with Templating

Having brought out the big guns—the jQuery templating engine—we need something a bit more juicy to use it on. The client has been toying with the idea of integrating some Twitter data into the app. Specifically, they noticed that Twitter does a good job of celebrity stalking too—and they want to harness that stalking power in their app.

The plan is to use a public search on the query term "celeb spotting," and display any tweets that match. Generally, you can't make cross-domain Ajax requests (it's a security issue—in fact, the same security issue that prevents you from placing Ajax requests to file:// URLs)—but Twitter provides data in **JSONP** format. JSONP is a common trick to grab data across domains by loading it inside a `<script>` tag. For this to work, we need to append the string `"callback=?"` to the URL request.

We've had a look at the Twitter API documentation,[9] and found the appropriate URL to conduct a search: http://search.twitter.com/search.*format*?q=*query*. All we need to do is call `getJSON()` with that URL and our search string:

javascripts/ch4/17-twitter-templating.js *(excerpt)*

```
var twitQuery = "celeb+spotting",
    twitUrl = "http://search.twitter.com/search.json?q=";

$.getJSON(twitUrl + twitQuery + "&callback=?", function(data){
  // Show some tweets
});
```

Now we have some data from Twitter! The tweets are stored in the `results` property of the `data` object as an array, so we can use them directly in our template system.

[7] https://github.com/jquery/jquery-tmpl
[8] http://api.jquery.com/category/plugins/templates/
[9] http://dev.twitter.com/doc/

Templates used in templating engines are defined in the same manner as the simple template we put together earlier: as elements inside our HTML file. The jQuery templating engine uses a clever trick to prevent the template from becoming a regular part of the DOM: it hides inside a `<script>` tag with `type="text/x-jquery-tmpl"`. Browsers don't know how to handle this type of "script," so they don't try to execute it, but we can still extract the content and use it as a template:

ch4/17-twitter-templating.html *(excerpt)*

```
<script id="tmpl-tweet" type="text/x-jquery-tmpl">
  <li>
    <a class="avatar" href="#"><img src="${profile_image_url}"
➥alt="${from_user}"></a>
    <a href="http://twitter.com/${from_user}"><h2>${from_user}</h2></a>
    <span class="details">
      ${text}
    </span>
  </li>
</script>
```

Template Types

Even if you're not using the jQuery templating engine, you can use the `<script>` trick with your own templates. You should use a different option to `x-jquery-tmpl` though; you can make up your own `type` if you want, but you'll often see the `text/html` used.

You'll notice that inside the HTML there are some odd-looking bits. These are are our tokens that will be replaced with data. The strings inside the curly braces aren't made up: they are the names of the values that are returned to us from Twitter. To find out exactly what data is returned by a given API call, you can either read the documentation, or simply log the data object to the console using `console.log(data);`.

All that's left to do now is to call the templating function. Just select the template item by `id` (we've called ours `tmpl-tweet`), and call the `tmpl()` method, passing the `data.results` array we retrieved via Ajax. The engine will see that our array has multiple items; for each item it will generate a clone of the template and replace all the tokens with the corresponding values from the data array. The result is a jQuery object containing the constructed DOM node, which we can inject into the page as we'd normally do:

javascripts/ch4/17-twitter-templating.js *(excerpt)*

```
$.getJSON(twitUrl + twitQuery + "&callback=?", function(data){
  $("#tmpl-tweet")
    .tmpl(data.results)
```

```
    .appendTo("#spots-list");
    transition("#spots", "show");
});
```

No need to do any looping or manual value insertion. The combination of data-rich APIs and simple templating engines gives you a lot of power as a developer, easily enabling you to enrich your applications with information from a variety of sources. A sample result from our Twitter search is shown in Figure 4.5.

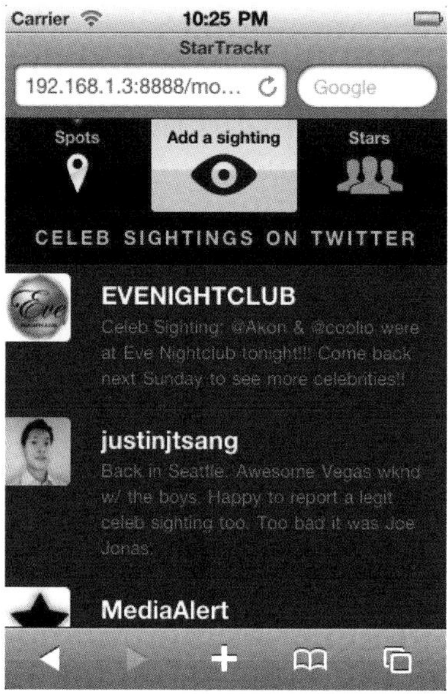

Figure 4.5. Pulling in celebrity spottings from Twitter

The jQuery template engine also includes tags for conditional evaluation like `{{if}}` and `{{else}}`, so you can show different parts of your template according to the situation. Check out the documentation for the full breakdown of available functionality.[10]

We Have an App!

We've taken our mobile website and transformed it into a decent mobile app that our users are going to love. Not too shabby, and we've only just picked at the surface. There's infinite room for creativity and experimentation, and a million ways we can tie everything together—we'll look at managing that soon. But be warned now: making mobile apps is addictive!

[10] http://api.jquery.com/jquery.tmpl/

Chapter 5

Using Device Features from Web Apps

We've morphed our simple mobile website into a basic app, but to meet the insatiable expectations of our users (and our client), we have to do better than that! Fortunately, that will be both easy and fun, because so far we've only been using a fraction of the functionality afforded to us. Today's mobile devices are filled to the brim with futuristic features: multi-touch screens, gyroscopes, cameras, accelerometers … You might think that access to this kind of device functionality would be the exclusive province of the native app—but that's not the case. Thanks to some emerging standards that are being implemented surprisingly quickly by mobile browsers, web apps have access to a sizable portion of a mobile device's functionality.

The way we interact with most of these features is the same: we listen for a specific set of events that provide information from the device's hardware. As web developers, we're accustomed to event-driven programming: we handle clicks, key presses, window loads, and page scrolls. It makes sense, then, that the APIs for interacting with new hardware utilize the same model.

As always, though, it's not quite that simple. Where there are gaps in compatibility between desktop browsers, there are giant craters between mobile devices. Even considering just the devices that run WebKit-based browsers, you'll find many potholes and traps.[1]

Thankfully, JavaScript is flexible enough to allow us to navigate this minefield, and many features do work reliably across a wide number of devices. In fact, taking advantage of most of the coolest phone features is so easy that the only real issue is thinking up a killer app to use them in!

---

[1] If you want to see *just how many* potholes, check out PPK's "Great WebKit Comparison Table." [http://www.quirksmode.org/webkit.html]

Geolocation

StarTrackr, like so many of today's fledgling social networking startups, relies heavily on users' physical location. The inclusion of geolocation functions in many new mobile devices—combined with the fact that mobile devices are, well, *mobile*—has paved the way for some fascinating and useful, (not to mention creepy) applications. The best examples of location-based services can seem like magic to the end user, and thankfully for us the most common API is very simple. Let's see how we can add some location-based functionality to our app.

Fetching Location

Geolocation is to position as information is to data. We can have a raw position (latitude and longitude), but unless we put it in some context, with some meaning, it's of little value. Once we know the user's location, we need to use it in a practical way. The StarTrackr database is growing larger every day, but we're still lagging behind the likes of foursquare,[2] who have huge numbers of people "checking in" to locations all around the world.

To help us catch up, we'll grab the user's location and mash-up nearby foursquare data into our Spots page, which will greatly increase the number of relevant locations our application displays. Before we dive into the foursquare API, though, we need to find out more about our user.

The Geolocation spec defines a method, `getCurrentPosition()`, that takes one to three parameters and asynchronously tries to fetch the current location of the device. Sounds fun! The `geolocation` object can be found as a property of the `navigator` object. Because `getCurrentPosition()` is an asynchronous function, the first two parameters are callbacks—the first when it's successful and the second when it fails:

```
navigator.geolocation.getCurrentPosition(
  function(pos) {
    // Successful!
    alert(
        pos.coords.latitude + ":" +
        pos.coords.longitude + ":" +
        pos.coords.accuracy
    );
  },
  function(error) {
    alert("Error!");
  }
);
```

[2] http://www.foursquare.com/

Naturally, there are some security and privacy protections around these features. The first attempt by your application to access these features will display a prompt to the user, asking for permission to access their location, as shown in Figure 5.1.

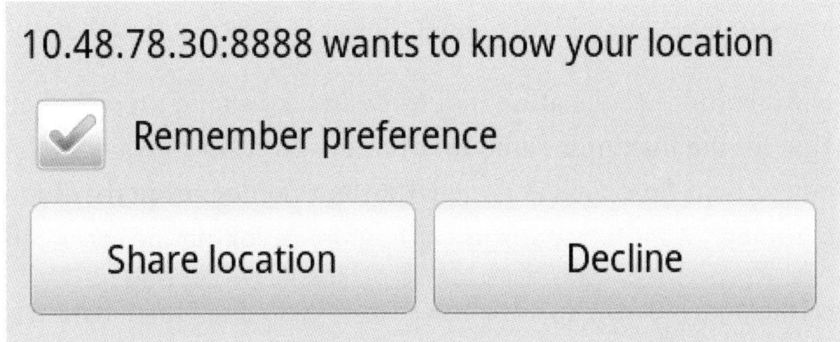

Figure 5.1. A prompt asking your permission to use your location

Resetting Permissions

If you accidentally hit **Don't Allow**, your page will be banned from accessing your location. To reset your permissions on iOS, go to **Settings** > **General** > **Reset** > **Reset Location Warnings**. On Android, open the browser settings (available from the context menu within the browser app), and find the **Clear location access** item.

Once you've got the all-clear, you're free to track away.

Your geo-enabled device will return for you its best guess of your current location. How good is its best guess? You need to examine the `accuracy` property to find out. The result is measured in meters, with a 95% confidence level. If the number that's returned to you is unacceptable, you may have to try again, but if the user has the GPS functionality of their device turned off, or is otherwise unable to be located, there's little you can do about it. However, there are a few extra parameters that the geolocation methods accept, which can give you better results:

javascripts/ch5/01-geolocation.js *(excerpt)*

```
navigator.geolocation.getCurrentPosition(
  function(pos){ },
  function(error){ },
  {
    // Options for geolocation
    maximumAge: 10000,
    timeout: 10000,
    enableHighAccuracy: true
  }
);
```

The third parameter to `getCurrentPosition()` is an object literal that contains various additional option flags. The first is `enableHighAccuracy`. This is a hint to the device that you'd like the best information possible. The drawbacks to this setting are that it may take longer to receive a response, and it may drain a device's battery faster. It defaults to `false`—but you probably want to set it to `true` for most purposes, unless you only care about the general area, rather than the specific location.

Like HTTP requests, sometimes geolocation requests can take a long time. To help counter this, it's possible to set a value for the maximum amount of time you want to wait, so that it abandons the request if it takes longer than this. This is done with the `timeout` property of the options object, and it specifies the number of milliseconds to wait before invoking the error callback.

The last option, `maximumAge`, lets you specify how "fresh" you need the location to be. For example, if the `maximumAge` is 10 seconds (as above), and you make multiple calls to the geolocator within that time, a cached value will be returned, so there's no need for the device to make another attempt to determine its location. If you call after 10 seconds, the cached value will have expired, and the device is forced to grab a new reading.

The important part is your success callback, though. It will be passed a `Position` object containing all kinds of juicy location data. Here's the structure of that object:

```
Position = {
  timestamp,
  coords: {
    latitude,
    longitude,
    accuracy,
    altitude,
    altitudeAccuracy,
    heading,
    speed
  }
}
```

The `timestamp` field contains a `DOMTimeStamp`[3] value that tells us the exact time the position was extracted. The `coords` object holds all the good stuff. Not all of it will be available on every device, but we should at least be able to get the latitude, longitude, and accuracy of the position—and that's enough to build some cool features.

Back to our app. Let's extract the latitude and longitude from the position object inside our success callback; we'll then pass them along to a `fetchLocations()` method that we'll write to interface with foursquare:

---

[3] http://www.w3.org/TR/DOM-Level-3-Core/core.html#Core-DOMTimeStamp

javascripts/ch5/01-geolocation.js *(excerpt)*

```
function fetchGeo() {
  navigator.geolocation.getCurrentPosition(
    function(pos) {
      // Succesfully got location
      var lat = pos.coords.latitude,
          lng = pos.coords.longitude;
      // Do something with the position!
      fetchLocations(lat, lng);
    },
    function(error) {
      alert("Error fetching geolocation.");
    }, {
      // Options for geolocation
      maximumAge: 10000,
      timeout: 10000,
      enableHighAccuracy: true
    }
  );
}
```

Foursquare has a JSONP-enabled search facility for venues. To use it, however, we have to pass it our special **client ID** and **client secret** details, so we'll need to sign up. Head to https://foursquare.com/oauth/register and fill out the form shown in Figure 5.2. The **Callback URL** field is intended for server-side applications that require users to authenticate with their foursquare accounts. In our case, since we're just querying the public search results, it doesn't matter and we can just fill it out with our site's URL.

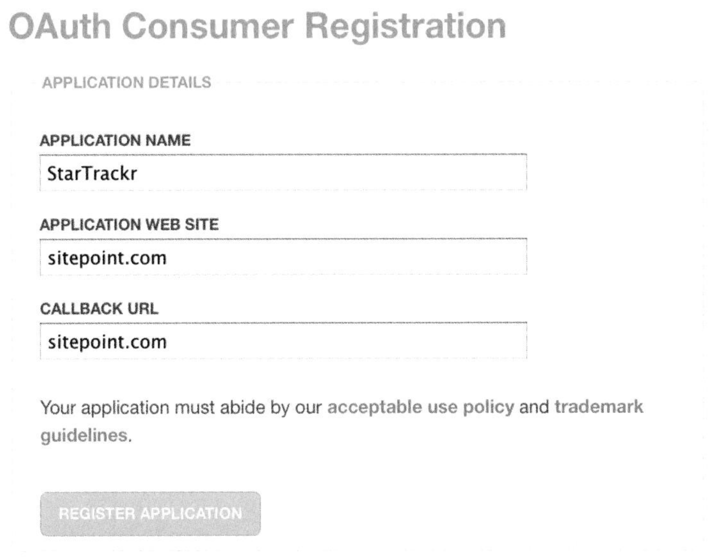

OAuth Consumer Registration

APPLICATION DETAILS

APPLICATION NAME

StarTrackr

APPLICATION WEB SITE

sitepoint.com

CALLBACK URL

sitepoint.com

Your application must abide by our acceptable use policy and trademark guidelines.

REGISTER APPLICATION

Figure 5.2. Signing up for foursquare OAuth keys

Immediately after submitting the form, you'll receive your authentication details. The client ID identifies the application that's making the call. This is public information, and it's safe to put it in your client-side app. But the client secret value is, well, *secret*—therefore, you should do your authentication and search calls on the server side and simply return the resulting data to your application. Otherwise, anyone viewing your site could access your client secret by viewing the source of your page!

PhoneGap and Keys

If you only plan on releasing your app as a native app using PhoneGap—as we'll cover in Chapter 7—and not on the Web, feel free to include your keys in your JavaScript. PhoneGap applications are compiled, so users will be unable to view the source and discover your keys.

For demonstration purposes, however, and so it's easy for you to follow along and test the code, we're going to just stick our details in on the client side. If you're following along with the code archive, remember to put in your own details—otherwise the code will fail to work.

To use the foursquare API, we need to build up a query string that contains the latitude and longitude we retrieved from the user, and the secret details for our application. Here's our `fetchLocations()` method:

javascripts/ch5/01-geolocation.js *(excerpt)*

```
function fetchLocations(lat, lng) {
  var url = "https://api.foursquare.com/v2/venues/search?",
      location = "&ll=" + lat + "," + lng,
      secrets = "&client_id=CLIENT&client_secret=SECRET";

  $.ajax({
    url: url + location + secrets + "&callback=",
    type: "GET",
    dataType: "JSON",
    success: function(data) {
      displayLocations(data.response.groups);
    },
    error: function() {
      alert("Error fetching locations.");
    }
  });
}
```

The structure of the query URL is fairly straightforward. All it requires is an *`ll`* parameter with our latitude and longitude, separated by a comma, *`client_id`* and *`client_secret`* parameters with our details, and finally the usual *`callback`* parameter to retrieve JSONP. We then make a `GET` request to that URL using jQuery's `$.ajax()` method.

If successful, foursquare will give us some data about locations in the user's city. The full format of the data is listed in the documentation at https://developer.foursquare.com/docs/, but we only care about the field `data.response.groups`, which contains a list of venues near the user.

We pass the data to a `displayLocations()` function, which will take that data and display it in a form useful to our users. Its first task is to remove any current venues in our display list, to make room for the new location-based list:

javascripts/ch5/01-geolocation.js *(excerpt)*

```
function displayLocations(groups) {
  $("#spots-list").children().remove();
  ⋮
}
```

Now we can add the new results. The venues we retrieved from foursquare are organized into groups, such as nearby venues, trending venues, or even time-sensitive venues like polling places if an election is underway! As these groups can vary over time, it's up to us to pick out which groups we're interested in. The one that will be most useful to us is the `nearby` group! When we find this one, we'll add all the elements to the list:

javascripts/ch5/01-geolocation.js *(excerpt)*

```
for(var i = 0; i < groups.length; i++) {
  if(groups[i].type === 'nearby') {
    $("#tmpl-4sq")
      .tmpl(groups[i].items)
      .appendTo("#spots-list");
  }
}
```

The `items` object has the real goodies. We'll use the templating technique from the last chapter to format the output. The template we're using looks like this:

ch5/01-geolocation.html *(excerpt)*

```
<script id="tmpl-4sq" type="text/x-jquery-tmpl">
  <li>
    <a href="spot.html">
      <h2>${name}</h2>
      <span class="relative-distance">${location.distance}m away</span>
      <span class="sightings">${hereNow.count}</span>
    </a>
  </li>
</script>
```

With all this code in place, the final step is to fire the `fetchGeo()` function to start the ball rolling—which we'll do when the user presses the crosshairs "locate me" button in the Spots search field:

javascripts/ch5/01-geolocation.js *(excerpt)*

```
$(".locate-me").click(function(e){
  e.preventDefault();
  fetchGeo();
});
```

Now, when you hit the button, after allowing geolocation in your browser, you'll be presented with a list of nearby places, nicely formatted in our app's layout, as Figure 5.3 shows.

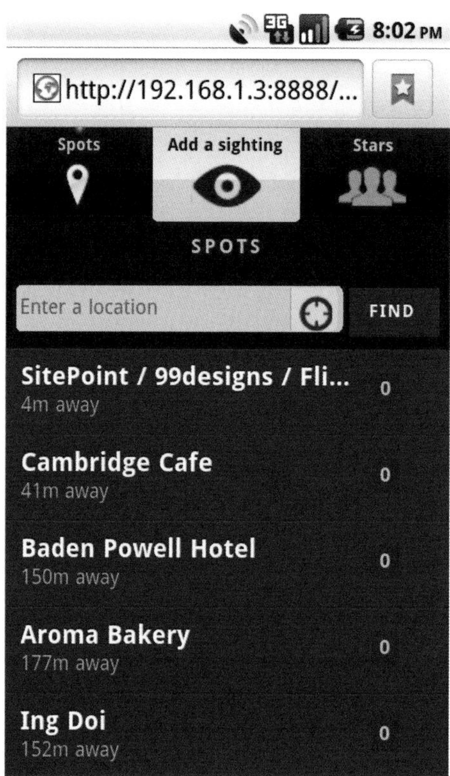

Figure 5.3. Nearby venues displayed in our app, thanks to the foursquare API

We also have the option to specify some keywords with the latitude and longitude, so we might as well use the text box that's already there, and allow the user to refine their search. The keywords need to be added to the query string in the `fetchLocations()` function:

javascripts/ch5/01-geolocation.js *(excerpt)*

```
var keywords = $("#address").val(),
    query = keywords ? "&query=" + keywords : "";
⋮
$.ajax({
  url: url + location + query + secrets + "&callback=",
  ⋮
});
```

Foursquare is certainly not alone in its ability to handle geolocation data; there are a myriad of startups and services that can add real-world, real-time data to your applications.

Handling Errors

Geolocation is quite magical in its own way, so it's no surprise that we don't always get the results we're after. Because of this, we need to be thorough about how our application reacts to errors. We've been supplying an error callback in our code, but we've yet to actually do anything useful with it.

The error callback is passed a `PositionError` object. This consists of two attributes—one for the error code, and one for the error message. The error code points to one of the three constants:

- `error.PERMISSION_DENIED`
- `error.POSITION_UNAVAILABLE`
- `error.TIMEOUT`

You'll receive the `PERMISSION_DENIED` error if the user said "no" to your request to be geolocated. This will be common (especially if geo isn't integral to your application), so make sure you have a good fallback and user experience if you find yourself with this error. As we noted earlier, the request to allow the app will never appear again for the user (unless they reset their browser settings), so you'll always end up here if they've blocked you.

The other two errors result from problems fetching the location: `POSITION_UNAVAILABLE` is a more generic "something went wrong" error, and `TIMEOUT` will occur if it takes too long (longer than you specified in the options) for a request to return.

The `error.message` property is more verbose than the error code. For example, Chrome reports "User denied Geolocation" as the message for a permission denied error. However, the messages vary from device to device, so it's recommended that you don't use these in your application. Instead, you could create your own messages like this:

```
// Failed to get location
var msg = "";
switch(error.code) {
```

```
    case error.PERMISSION_DENIED:
      msg = "Ooops. You have disallowed our app!";
      break;
    case error.POSITION_UNAVAILABLE:
      msg = "Sorry, we couldn't get your location.";
      break;
    case error.TIMEOUT:
      msg = "Sorry, fetch timeout expired.";
      break;
  }
```

As we've seen, it's incredibly simple to add basic geolocation features to a mobile application, and the sky's the limit when it comes to the functionality you can dream up with location data. That's a lot of power, so be sure you keep your users in mind and use this information responsibly.

Device Rotation

At the moment (and, it's probably fair to say, for the foreseeable future), mobile devices are rectangular. This means that the device's display can be oriented in one of two ways: portrait, or landscape.

The ratio difference between portrait and landscape is massive, and will have a huge impact on your designs, so you have to consider carefully the user experience you want to create. In our case, because we've built our layout using relative units like percentages and ems, our design will flow effortlessly into whatever screen dimensions we throw at it. Sometimes, however, you might want your application to provide an entirely different layout—or different features—to different screen orientations. For example, while portrait mode might show a simple list of items, landscape mode might show a two-panel display with a list on the left and details for each item on the right.

One way of adapting your layouts is to use media queries, which we discussed way back in Chapter 1. You could use `min-width` to target styles to viewports of a certain minimum width:

```
@media only screen and (min-width: 480px) {
  /* Styles here will only be applied when the viewport is wider than 480px */s
}
```

This way, if an orientation change causes the viewport's width to jump above (in this case) 480px, our alternate styles will kick in.

Even more interesting, though, is a media query specifically targeting the device's orientation:

```
@media screen and (orientation:portrait) {
  /* Portrait styles go here */
}
```

```
@media screen and (orientation:landscape) {
  /* Landscape styles go here */
}
```

The above code will apply the first block of styles when the device is in portrait orientation, and the second when it's in landscape mode.

But what if you'd like to have your app react to a change in orientation? Fortunately, there's a JavaScript API just for that! It's very simple, and relies on the `orientation` property and the `OrientationChange` event on the `window` object.

To show off the capabilities, we'll need a use case. So far our application lacks an "About" page, and the team is eager to have their names in there somewhere so they can show off to their friends. Let's give them an entire screen that kicks in when users rotate their device. This is going to require an element we can position absolutely. It should go outside the main page's container, in order for it not to be styled as a regular page:

ch5/02-orientation.html *(excerpt)*

```
<div id="about">
  <div id="header">
    <h1>About Us!</h1>
  </div>
</div>
```

Then we'll hide it by default, and stretch it over the entire screen by setting all its edges to `0`. You may need to also adjust the `z-index` if it's getting lost behind your pages:

ch5/02-orientation.html *(excerpt)*

```
#about {
  display:none;
  position: absolute;
  top:0;
  left:0;
  right:0;
  bottom:0;
  background-color: #400;
  z-index: 250;
}
```

Now we're ready to use the `orientation` property and the `orientationchange` event. Let's start by checking that we have access to the property, by adding a quick alert to our page and loading it on a phone:

```
alert(window.orientation);
```

Depending on how you're holding your phone, you'll receive a different response each time you refresh the page: portrait mode will return 0, landscape mode tilted counter-clockwise will return 90, and landscape mode tilted clockwise will return -90.

You don't want to have to keep checking if the user is flinging their phone around, so now the second part of the orientation team steps in to save the day: the `orientationchange` event. This fires whenever the orientation value changes. We can use this to activate our About page by showing it when we're in landscape mode, and hiding it when in portrait mode.

javascripts/ch5/02-orientation.js *(excerpt)*

```
$(window).bind("orientationchange", function(){
  switch(window.orientation) {
    case 0:
      $("#about").hide();
      break;
    case 90:
    case -90:
      $("#about").show();
      break;
  }
});
```

Accelerometers: Device Orientation

It's taken a while, but the W3C is now churning out draft APIs for all the most common mobile device features. It takes even longer for these to trickle down into widespread adoption, but it is happening! One example is the DeviceOrientation Event Specification.[4] It's different from the orientation events we just looked at. This spec defines an interface to the device's accelerometer, magnetometer, and gyroscope, supplying us with fine-grained information about the angle of orientation and motion; so rather than just "portrait" or "landscape," we can get "68.5 degrees in the Z plane, and falling fast"!

Support for these APIs is still limited—so proceed with caution and keep the principle of progressive enhancement in mind. There's some good news though: while the API is yet to be widely available in the browser, most devices do have this functionality on a hardware level. In later chapters, when we look at using PhoneGap to turn our web app into a native app, any work we've done with the DeviceOrientation API will carry over without needing any modification, and will work on a broader range of devices.

[4] http://dev.w3.org/geo/api/spec-source-orientation.html

Accelerometers

How accelerometers work is best left explained by Wikipedia,[5] but it's probably more fun to see them in action first, and read the theory later. Whichever way you want to do it, it's helpful to know if your device even supports the accelerometer API. If your browser window indicates the existence of the `DeviceMotionEvent` object, you're in luck:

```
var hasMotion = window.DeviceMotionEvent;
if(hasMotion) {
  alert("We got one!");
}
```

The `DeviceMotionEvent` object exposes an event called `devicemotion`. It's targeted at the `window`, so that's where we'll need to attach our event listener:

javascripts/ch5/03-accelerometer.js *(excerpt)*

```
$("window").bind("devicemotion", function( e ) {
  // Something moved
});
```

The event object is filled with a bunch of goodies about the acceleration and orientation of the device. The most interesting parts for us are `acceleration`, `accelerationIncludingGravity`, and `rotationRate`.

The acceleration properties are instances of `Acceleration`, and they contain properties for the X, Y, and Z axes. The `rotationRate` is only available if your device has a gyroscope in it, which is less common, so for now we'll concentrate on the accelerometer. Remember that jQuery has normalized the event, so to get at the good bits we need to examine the `originalEvent` property.

javascripts/ch5/03-accelerometer.js *(excerpt)*

```
$("window").bind("devicemotion", function( e ) {
  // Something moved
  var motionEvent = e.originalEvent,
      accel = motionEvent.accelerationIncludingGravity,
      x = accel.x,
      y = accel.y,
      z =  accel.z
});
```

We can't just alert these values to see what's going on—because the events are fired a *lot*—around 50 times a second. We'll just print them on the screen for now:

---

[5] www.wikipedia.org/wiki/Accelerometer

javascripts/ch5/03-accelerometer.js *(excerpt)*

```
$("body").html(
  "x:" + x + "<br/>" +
  "y:" + y + "<br/>" +
  "z:" + z
);
```

That's fairly exciting—some crazy numbers appearing on the screen! Analyzing the data will inform you how the user is moving their phone around. This information would usually be used for games, or tools like spirit levels. We want to avoid getting too bogged down with the math, so we'll only use the accelerometer in a simple way for our app.

Graphing the Numbers

It's hard to appreciate what an endless stream of numbers represents. If you want a more visual indication of what's going on, have a look at http://mrspeaker.net/dev/js-accel/. There you'll find a web app that graphs the X, Y, and Z axes over time—so you can see what happens as you rotate your device.

Shake Gesture

A novel use for the accelerometer is the shake gesture—performed by simply shaking your phone. It's sometimes used to trigger an undo or page refresh. There's no built-in "onShake" event we can target—so it's time to put on the thinking cap and figure out how to do it ourselves. The DeviceOrientation API shows us how far the device has moved since the previous interval. If the difference between two sample points is large, we can infer that the device is being shaken.

We need some variables to track the two sample points, and to store when the last shake event happened. We'll call these `lastX`, `lastY`, `lastZ`, and `lastShake`. Finally, we also want a constant that defines how big a shake needs to be for us to call it a shake, which we'll call `threshold`:

javascripts/ch5/04-shake.js *(excerpt)*

```
var lastX,
  lastY,
  lastZ,
  lastShake = new Date().getTime(),
  threshold = 10;

$(window).bind("devicemotion", function(e){
  var motionEvent = e.originalEvent,
      accel = motionEvent.accelerationIncludingGravity,
      x = accel.x,
      y = accel.y,
```

```
        z =  accel.z;
    ⋮
});
```

Now that we have the X, Y, and Z accelerations, we can compare them to the last time. If the variables are `null`, it means it's the first time through, so we won't do anything. But if they have values, we calculate the difference between this time and last time:

javascripts/ch5/04-shake.js *(excerpt)*

```
if(lastX !== null && lastY !== null &&  lastZ !== null) {
  // Get the distance moved
  var diffX = Math.abs(x - lastX),
      diffY = Math.abs(y - lastY),
      diffZ = Math.abs(z – lastZ);
  // Shake detection code will go here
}
lastX = x;
lastY = y;
lastZ = z;
```

After the main shake-detection code is complete, we store the new X, Y, and Z variables for the next run.

For a shake to be a shake (and not, say, a drop) we need to check the phone has moved a fair amount on two of its axes—either the X and the Y, X and Z, or Y and Z:

javascripts/ch5/04-shake.js *(excerpt)*

```
if (diffX > threshold && diffY > threshold ||
    diffX > threshold && diffZ > threshold ||
    diffY > threshold && diffZ > threshold) {
      // It was a big difference!
      ⋮
}
```

With that, we're almost done. But if we stopped there, we'd have a slight bug: if the user is shaking madly, then the above check will still be true on the next, and subsequent, iterations. So instead of detecting one shake, we'd be detecting many. To work around this, we'll timestamp the shake, and make sure we don't check again for half a second.

javascripts/ch5/04-shake.js *(excerpt)*

```
if (diffX > threshold && diffY > threshold ||
    diffX > threshold && diffZ > threshold ||
    diffY > threshold && diffZ > threshold) {
```

```
  var now = new Date().getTime(),
      diffTime = now - lastShake;

  if (diffTime > 500) {
    alert("Shaken!");
    lastShake = now;
  }
}
```

Having passed all our tests, we now conclude that the user is shaking. Here's where we can run our code to undo, or refresh, or pop up a message saying "Please don't shake me." We'll also finish up by storing the `lastShake` time, so we can check against it next time.

Touch Gestures

Touch screens turn out to be a very natural way of interacting with our portable devices—so much so, that playing with a gadget that has a screen you *can't* control via touch now seems foreign! But the downside to the simplicity of the touch interface is the loss of the flexibility and precision that's achieved with a mouse or stylus. There's no hovering, no right-clicking—and even the smallest target needs to be big enough for a finger to find it.

However, there's one area where touch screens have the edge over other input methods: gestures. Rather than be limited to simple taps and drags, gestures let us track and respond to more complex finger movements, augmenting our basic palette of input interactions. Most of the devices we target won't tell us when specific gestures occur; rather, they provide a handful of basic events for us to track. It's then up to us to turn these streams of event data into something meaningful.

In the last chapter, we grew familiar with touch events when we looked at simple tapping, but today's sensitive touch—and multi-touch—screens are capable of much more. Thanks to some well-designed software, combined with a healthy dose of user training, there are now a few common gestures we can use to assist navigation in our apps.

Before we start, though, it's worth noting that touch events are only supported on iOS and Android, and even multi-touch Android devices only give you information about one touch at a time in the browser. We recommend having a quick read through PPK's Touch Table for more in-depth compatibility information about touch events.[6]

To do something interesting with touch events, we need to examine some of the key properties they provide us. Although touch events are similar to mouse events, the differences are important and potentially confusing. Mouse events can be nice and simple, because we can only have one mouse pointer on the screen at a time, but touch events need to provide us with a bit more context in relation

[6] http://www.quirksmode.org/mobile/tableTouch.html

to what other touches are happening. This context is provided in the form of the `touches`, `targetTouches`, and `changedTouches` collections that are provided for each touch event.

The `touches` collection contains a list of all touches that are currently happening on the screen (for most devices, this can only be one touch at a time, remember). The next collection is `targetTouches`, which is concerned with the specific element you bound the event listener to. In other words, if you attached the event listener to, say, a `div` element, the `targetTouches` collection would contain only the touch events occurring on that particular `div`. Finally, `changedTouches` is a list of events that have changed. If you lift a finger off the `div`, for example, the event would have changed—so it will be listed here, but it will no longer be in the `touches` or `targetTouches` collections.

This set of events and properties can seem fairly complex, so let's dive right into some code, in order for you to get a feel for how they work.

Swiping Photo Gallery

A swipe is a short, quick drag. It's used in a bunch of situations; for example, in unlocking your device, or marking a list item for deletion. Yet it maps most elegantly when navigating through a collection of items, where dragging to the left moves to the next item, and dragging to the right moves to the previous one—as if flipping through the pages of a book.

No devices currently provide an "onSwipe" event—so we need to build our own. Let's consider how we might go about it. We need to wait until the user touches our swipe target—but we don't want them to just tap it, so we need to track any drag movements. If they drag a certain horizontal distance in a short period of time before lifting their finger, we'll call that a swipe.

Before we worry about the details, let's set up something to swipe. Our "Recent sightings" page has a bunch of photos associated with it, but no way to view them. A simple gallery could be fun: we'll just dump a stack of (same-sized) images into our container, and then move to and fro as the user swipes away. Let's start with some basic markup:

ch5/05-swipe.html *(excerpt)*

```
<div id="gallery">
  <img src="img1.jpg" class="current" />
  <img src="img2.jpg" />
  <img src="img3.jpg" />
  <img src="img4.jpg" />
  <img src="img5.jpg" />
</div>
```

Our images are going to take up 100% of the width of the screen. It's not important that they be images, though, so if you have smaller elements, you could place them inside `div` containers and scroll those instead.

To do the actual scrolling, we're going to use a modified version of our `transition()` function from the last chapter. We'll treat the images as if they were pages, and transition between them. First, we need to position them absolutely, and label one of the images the current one:

ch5/05-swipe.html *(excerpt)*

```
#gallery img {
  position:absolute;
  top: 0;
  left: 0;
  display: none;
  width: 100%;
}
#gallery img.current {
  display: block;
}
```

Next, we'll set up our swipe framework, which involves attaching all the touch handlers to our gallery container. We've also defined a variable called `xStart`. This is what we'll use to test if the user has moved their finger far enough for a swipe:

javascripts/ch5/05-swipe.js *(excerpt)*

```
// Swipe left & right
var xStart;
$("#gallery").bind({
  "touchstart mousedown": function(e) {
    e.preventDefault();
    // Handle the start
  },
  "touchend mouseup": function(e) {
    // Handle the end
  },
  "touchmove": function(e) {
    e.preventDefault();
  }
});
```

So that we can test on the desktop—and provide support to older mobile devices—we're also binding to the regular mouse events. It complicates our code a little bit, but it's a lifesaver in terms of testing time, as it's a lot easier to prototype on the desktop! To make both mobile and desktop happy, we fetch the original event from jQuery and test to see if it contains the `targetTouches` object. If it does, we use this as our touch object. If it doesn't, we're on the desktop (or a non-touch mobile device), so we just use the event itself (as this has the `pageX` property that we need):

javascripts/ch5/05-swipe.js *(excerpt)*

```
// Handle the start
var event = e.originalEvent,
    touch = event.targetTouches ? event.targetTouches[0] : e;
xStart = touch.pageX;
```

Actually, the only bit of work we need to do in the `touchstart` handler is to store the `pageX` position (the position of the user's finger) in our `xStart` variable. Then we can forget about it until the user finishes their gesture. We've decided to go with `targetTouches`, so we can be sure we're dealing with an event that's targeted at our gallery. However, we can't use `targetTouches` for the `touchend` event—because as soon as the user lifts their finger, the event is removed from the `touchTarget` (and `touches`) list. The only place we can find the end event is in the `changedTouches` list:

javascripts/ch5/05-swipe.js *(excerpt)*

```
// Handle the end
var event = e.originalEvent,
  touch = event.changedTouches ? event.changedTouches[0] : e,
  diffX = touch.pageX - xStart;

// See if we swiped!
if(Math.abs(diffX) > 30) {
  if( diffX > 0 ){
    alert("Swiped right");
  }
  else {
    alert("Swiped left");
  }
}
```

The code for detecting swipes is quite similar to the code we used for detecting shakes earlier: we subtract the current position from the original position, and if it's a big difference, it's a swipe. The difference also tells us if it's a left or a right swipe: a positive difference means the user is moving to the right, while negative means to the left.

Before we attach the swipe gesture to the gallery, we need to make a change to the `transition()` function. Originally, we assumed that our function was only swapping between pages, so we hardcoded the `fromPage`:

javascripts/ch5/05-swipe.js *(excerpt)*

```
function transition(toPage, type, reverse) {
  var toPage = $(toPage),
      fromPage = $("#pages .current"),
      ⋮
}
```

Now, seeing the error of our ways, we want to be able to specify a custom "from" page, so we need to pass in an extra parameter:

javascripts/ch5/05-swipe.js *(excerpt)*

```
function transition(toPage, fromPage, type, reverse) {
  var toPage = $(toPage),
      fromPage = $(fromPage),
      ⋮
```

Finally, we can move on to moving the pictures. We'll create a function called `slidePic()`, whose task is to transition the images left or right, according to the Boolean *`isLeft`* value provided. If we are swiping left, we transition from the current photo to the next photo, and if we're swiping right, we transition to the previous photo; we also pass `true` as the *`reverse`* parameter so that the photo slides back in:

javascripts/ch5/05-swipe.js *(excerpt)*

```
function slidePic(isLeft) {
  var photos = $("#gallery .photo"),
    current = photos.siblings(".current"),
    next;

  if(isLeft) {
    next = current.next();
  }
  else {
    next = current.prev();
  }
  if(next.length === 0){
    return;
  }

  transition(next, current, "push", !isLeft);a
}
```

To hook the swipe detection up to our `slidePic()` function, we just replace our alerts with function calls:

javascripts/ch5/05-swipe.js *(excerpt)*

```
if( diffX > 0 ){
  slidePic(false);
}
else {
  slidePic(true);
}
```

Be sure to play with the threshold for swiping (we've used 30 pixels), and see what feels better. A good "feel" is probably the most important part of mobile web development, and that means—as always—plenty of experimenting.

Pinch and Zoom

Another common interaction is the two-finger "pinch and zoom" gesture. It's a bit more peculiar than the swipe—achieved by placing two fingers (well, usually a thumb and forefinger) on the target, and then either sliding the fingers away from each other (zoom), or towards each other (pinch). The standard use is for zooming in and out of a web page, mapping application, or image. A slight variation on this is the rotate gesture—where moving two fingers in a twisting motion will rotate, say, an image, or a map orientation.

These gestures are far more complex than the swipe, so it's lucky for us that we receive some extra help in the form of the gesture events: `gesturestart`, `gesturechange`, and `gestureend`. They are analogous to the touch events, but will fire when multiple fingers are used at the same time. Unfortunately, they're currently only supported on iOS, so they should only be used for "nice to have" features that aren't essential to your application.

The StarTrackr application has seen heaps of fantastic celebrity photos pouring in—but a lot of them have been snapped quickly by users who may have been under the influence of the celebrity's magical aura, and so many photos are poorly cropped. To cut down the amount of in-house editing we need to do, let's add a feature where the users can rotate and zoom the images for us.

We first need a page to display the original photo in. We will create a new page and, for testing purposes, set this as our default:

ch5/06-pinchzoom.html *(excerpt)*

```
<div id="photoedit" class="current">
  <div id="cropper">
    <div id="photo"></div>
  </div>
</div>
```

Because the image will be shrinking, growing, and spinning, we need to set the containing element's `overflow` property to `hidden`, so that it doesn't go taking over our whole app:

ch5/06-pinchzoom.html *(excerpt)*

```
#photoedit {
  overflow: hidden;
}
```

Now we're ready to handle some rotating and scaling. We have to keep a couple of variables around to store the state where the last gesture ended—otherwise the photo would "reset" back to it's original position every time we started a new gesture on it:

javascripts/ch5/06-pinchzoom.js *(excerpt)*

```
var rotation = 0,
    scale = 1;
```

The rotation variable is set to 0 degrees (right side up), and the scale to 1. Rotation can move between 0 and 360 degrees, and scale gives us the ratio of the original—for example, 0.5 is half the original size, and 2 is double. And finally, the new events. We'll need to capture `gesturechange`—because that's when the user is actually moving their fingers—and `gestureend` for storing the state for next time:

javascripts/ch5/06-pinchzoom.js *(excerpt)*

```
$("#cropper").bind({
  "gesturechange": function(e){
    var gesture = e.originalEvent;
    // Update the image
  },
  "gestureend": function(e) {
    var gesture = e.originalEvent;
    // Store the details for the next gesture
  }
});
```

The gesture handlers are bound to the parent container, because if we bound them to the actual photo element, it would be hard to twist and resize if it became really small. We also have to fetch a reference to the original event, via `originalEvent`, rather than use the wrapped event object jQuery hands us. The normalized jQuery events are much nicer for most purposes, but they don't provide accessors for the gesture properties that we want to inspect.

Gesture events expose two very useful properties: `scale`, and `rotation`. We'll combine these with the existing values (multiplying the scale and adding the rotation) to arrive at the new values:

javascripts/ch5/06-pinchzoom.js *(excerpt)*

```
// Update the image
var curScale = gesture.scale * scale;
var curRotation = (gesture.rotation + rotation) % 360;
```

With the calculations all taken care of, it's time to apply them to the photo element. Using a CSS3 transform, we can scale and rotate the image in one go:

javascripts/ch5/06-pinchzoom.js *(excerpt)*

```
$("#photo").css(
  "webkitTransform",
  "scale(" + curScale + ")" + "rotate(" + curRotation + "deg)"
);
```

The photo can now be manipulated—but if we then tried to make further adjustments, it would spring back to its original state. That's because we still need to update our `scale` and `rotation` variables with the current state. We can do that in the `ongestureend` event handler:

javascripts/ch5/06-pinchzoom.js *(excerpt)*

```
// Store the details for the next gesture
scale *= gesture.scale;
rotation = (rotation + gesture.rotation) % 360;
```

That's a fairly simple implementation of pinching, zooming, and rotating. You might want to add some extra handling in there—for example, applying restrictions on the minimum and maximum scaling sizes. In addition, you can easily adapt it for situations where the user needs to rotate elements in steps of 90 degrees—for example, reorienting images.

Touch interfaces are very much still in their infancy, and browser support for these APIs has a long way to go. For most web applications, support just isn't wide enough to warrant their use for key features—but it can be fun to play with them to gain an idea of what the future holds for mobile web development. Moreover, if you plan on using PhoneGap to make your web app into a native iPhone app, these events can be relied on, making your interface that much more responsive and intuitive.

Going Offline

We're starting to see it all come together really nicely: our app has a fantastic design and some great functionality, so it's only natural that you want to play with your new creation everywhere you go. You fire it up and have a look first thing in the morning, marvel at your beautiful transitions over breakfast, work out any little UX issues as you ride the subway to work, and—hey, what's this? "Server not found: application closed."

It's only when you're underground, beyond the reach of WiFi and 3G, that it becomes painfully obvious: our application is just a web page. No network equals no app. You curse under your breath. Surely there must be something we can do about this?

The answer is the HTML5 Offline Web Applications API.[7] Offline web apps let the browser cache a local copy of your application, which means there's no reliance on the network; it will continue

[7] http://www.whatwg.org/specs/web-apps/current-work/multipage/offline.html

to work, even under the ground or on an airplane. Making the app available offline also helps complete the illusion of a native app, except that unlike native app developers, we aren't at the mercy of a proprietary app marketplace!

The Cache Manifest

The heart of the offline web application is the **cache manifest file**. This is a plain text file that lists the full path to all the resources that your application needs in order to run. It also provides instruction for different actions to take when the network is (or isn't) available. Here's an abridged version for our StarTrackr application:

ch5/cache.manifest *(excerpt)*

```
CACHE MANIFEST
# v0.1

index.html
stylesheets/screen.css
javascripts/vendor/jquery-1.6.1.min.js
images/background-body.gif
```

This is saved in the root directory of our application with the file name **cache.manifest**. Actually, the important part is the **.manifest** extension; you could call it **startrackr.manifest** if you like.

All Those Files

If you have a large number of files in your project, you won't want to type them all out. If you're on a Unix-based system, you can enter this at the prompt to spit out all the file names:

```
find . -type f -print | sed 's/.\///'
```

You can pipe the output into your text editor or to a file (for example, appending " > `cache.manifest`" to the end of the line will send the output to the **cache.manifest** file).

The closest command line option we've found for Windows is:

```
dir /A:-D /B /S - dir /s /b>FileList.txt
```

Unfortunately, this simply recurses through the directories. You'll need to do some find/replacing to remove the drive and get the slashes the right way!

The first line in the manifest file must be the text `CACHE MANIFEST`. The next line is a comment: any line that begins with a hash symbol (#) is ignored by the API—so go nuts. Our comment is simply an arbitrary version number for our manifest (it doesn't matter what number we use, but we'll see why it's important to include one soon), and after that is a list of every resource our application uses. *Every* resource. If you miss a single image or CSS file, it won't work. Once you have your manifest file ready, you have to tell the browser to read it. You do this in the opening `<html>` tag in your main page, via an attribute called `manifest`. The value of the attribute is a string that points to the manifest file:

ch5/07-cache-manifest.html *(excerpt)*

```
<!DOCTYPE html>
<html manifest="cache.manifest">
<head>
⋮
```

Now comes a hairy bit: the **cache.manifest** looks like a plain text file, but it must be served by the web server with a MIME type of `text/cache-manifest`, and not `text/plain`.

MIME Types

When a web server delivers a file to a browser, it sends along a bunch of metadata in the form of HTTP headers. One of these headers is used to indicate the file's type: `text/css` for CSS files, `image/jpeg` for JPEG images, and so on. Web servers are generally configured to serve the most common MIME types based on a file's extension, but **.manifest** is a fairly new addition to the Web, so many web servers aren't set up to deliver it with the correct type.

One way to check this is to navigate directly to the **cache.manifest** file's URL in your desktop browser, and inspect the headers using the browser's debugging tool. The information you're looking for will be in either the **Network** or **Resources** tab, as Figure 5.4 shows.

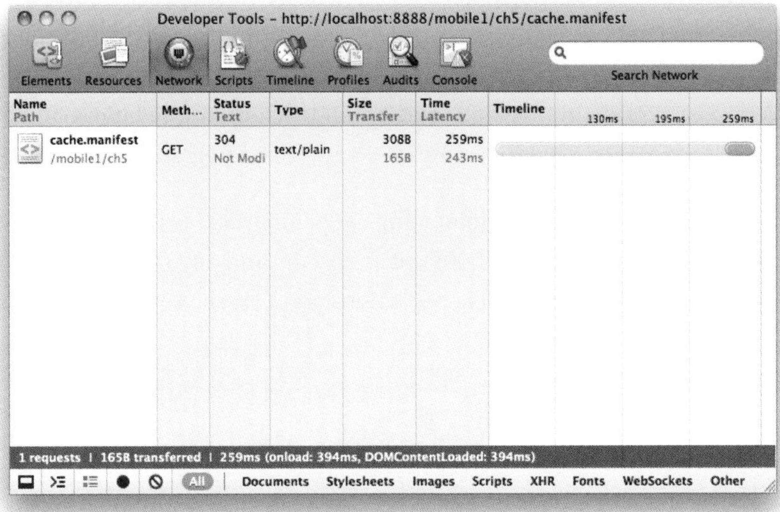

Figure 5.4. Inspecting the **cache.manifest** file's headers in Chrome's Developer Tools

If the type is incorrect, you'll need to adjust your server settings. Configuring MIME types is very simple on most web servers; if you're hosting your website with a managed hosting provider, you can check in your control panel for MIME type settings.

With all this setup done, it's time to test it out. First, add your app to the home screen (or simply bookmark it); then launch the app. This is where the magic happens: the browser will see the `manifest` attribute in your HTML file, read the manifest file, and cache all the resources. But it all happens in the background, so you have no way of knowing if it's worked.

To find out, close the app, and disable your device's network connection by switching on "airplane mode" or switching off your data capabilities. Now, hold your breath and relaunch the app. Either it launches beautifully, and your app is offline! Or … you might have a similar view to Figure 5.5.

Figure 5.5. Not much of an offline web application

The dreaded "Cannot open page" dialog of doom. Tracking down the cause of cache manifest errors can be a bit frustrating; the phone itself reveals little about what's going on, and there's no debug console to help us out.

That's why it's smart to test it on the desktop too. We've been focusing on mobile devices, but offline apps can benefit desktop users as well; for example, you could use this API (combined with some of the storage options we'll look at in the next chapter) to create a document editor that works without network access, syncing up to the cloud when the network is later available. For now, though, we just want to steal the desktop browser's superior debugging facilities.

Google Chrome is particularly useful for debugging cache manifest issues, as the JavaScript console lists all files that it tries to cache, stating whether it succeeds, and any errors that occur. The **Resources** tab also has a section for the application cache, where you can see the status of cached resources for the current page, evident in Figure 5.6.

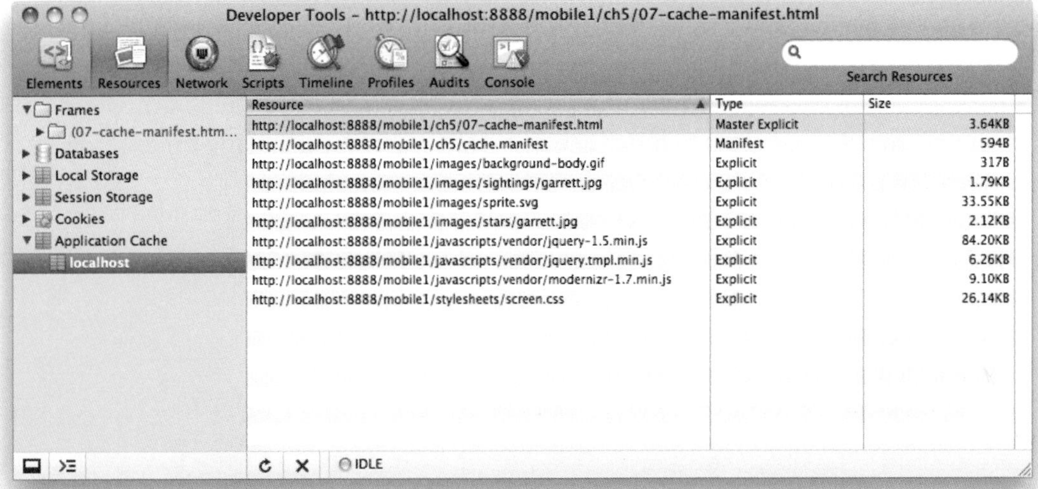

Figure 5.6. Chrome's developer tools let us inspect our application's cache

With these tools, you can track down pesky missing files. Figuring out what's being cached and what isn't can be quite a headache, so we should use all help that's available.

Cache Manifest Events

Once you've conquered storing files, you'll quickly come up against the next hurdle: how to unstore them. More specifically, how do we update the cache with newer versions of the files? Here's where that special comment line in our cache manifest file comes into play. Any time the cache manifest file is updated, the cache is considered invalid, and the browser will try and re-cache all the resources. But what if there's been no change at all to the list of files—only the contents of one or two of them?

Updating a version number inside a comment is an ideal (and easy) way to force the browser to update its cache:

```
CACHE MANIFEST
# v0.1.1
```

After updating the cache file, you can relaunch the app, and all the files will be re-cached. There is currently no way to update only particular files out of the bunch, so any changes in your app means that the user must grab them all again. The caching happens *after* your app has loaded, in the background, so those changes will only be evident the next time you launch. This is a bit annoying, but it makes sense; for instance, sometimes there will be a lot of files (or large files) cached, and you don't want your users twiddling their thumbs waiting for everything to download.

It's possible to keep track of what's occurring in the background, though, because whenever anything happens, it fires an event to tell us all about it. When the browser finds a new version of the manifest, and for every file that's cached, it generates an event. We can use these events for debugging purposes, or even to display progress reports (useful if you have a lot of files to cache). Let's set up our own DIY debugger to log all the events to the console, so that when we're having trouble, we can try to pinpoint the error:

javascripts/ch5/07-cache-manifest.js *(excerpt)*

```
var cache = window.applicationCache,
    cacheStatusValues = [
      "uncached", "idle", "checking",
      "downloading", "updateready", "obsolete"
    ];
```

First, we'll set up a shortcut to the `applicationCache` object, and an array to hold all the possible statuses that our cache can have (note, the order is important!). Then we'll bind to all the cache events that can be generated and log them to the console:

javascripts/ch5/07-cache-manifest.js *(excerpt)*

```
$(cache).bind({
  "cached checking downloading error noupdate obsolete progress updateready":
  function(e){
    var msg = "event: " + e.type + ", ";
    msg +=  "online: " + (navigator.onLine) ? "yes" : "no";
    msg += ", status: " + cacheStatusValues[cache.status];
    if (e.type == 'error' && navigator.onLine) {
        msg+= ' (probably a syntax error in manifest)';
    }
    // Print the message
    console.log(msg);
  }
});
```

Notice we're binding to eight different events using jQuery's `bind()` method. The `progress` event is the one you'll see pop up most, because it's fired once per item in your cache manifest. It's the event you'd be most interested in if you were writing a progress indicator.

We're using the value of `cache.status` as a key to retrieve the status from our array. This is why the order is important: the value of `cache.status` will be an integer from 0 to 5, with each value representing a different state. To make our lives a bit easier, we've mapped the values to an array so that we can acquire more human-friendly names for the states.

Online or Offline?

In the event code, you'll also notice a couple of references to `navigator.onLine`. This is a flag that indicates if the browser is currently online. However, you shouldn't depend entirely on the value of this property, as it will return `true` if the device is connected to a network—regardless of whether it really has access to the Internet.

One more reason to listen for events is to know when the application is finished caching. This will fire the `updateready` event, signifying that the new cache is ready to be used. If you do nothing, the new cache will be used the next time the app is loaded, but you can manually switch the caches by calling the `swapCache()` method:

```
$(cache).bind("updateready", function(){
  cache.swapCache();
});
```

Swapping the cache means that any future accessing of the cache will use the new files. This won't magically reload our images and CSS files, however, so there's barely any gain!

Network and Fallback

So now we're caching all our application's static resources, but we're also making Ajax requests to fetch application data. It would be better if attempts to access these resources could skip the cache and go looking for live data if it's available. And that when the content *isn't* available, we wouldn't receive a "Cannot open page" dialog.

You can add a `NETWORK` section header to your manifest file for that purpose. Section headers break up your cache files into different types. So far we've been adding **explicit** entries (entries that fall under no section header). To define a different type, we have to add a tag to switch sections:

```
CACHE MANIFEST
# v0.1.2

index.html
stylesheets/screen.css

NETWORK:
data/getJSON.php
```

By adding the text `NETWORK:` on its own line, we're instructing the API to add all the following files to the **online whitelist** section. Requests for these files will bypass the cache and always attempt to load the file from the server.

Whitelist items can point to your app's dynamic pages (as in the example above), or to an absolute URL on another domain. Additionally, you can provide just a prefix (for example, `data/`), which will match URLs beginning with that string. Finally, you can also specify a whitelist wildcard (`*`), which will whitelist everything that hasn't been mentioned elsewhere in the manifest file. This is most useful when we combine it with another manifest section—the fallback section.

The **fallback** section provides a mechanism for substituting resources that are unavailable because the user is offline, or that weren't successfully cached. For example, if we had a photo gallery that pulled images from a web server, we could replace the images with a generic "not available" placeholder—which is better than an error or a broken image icon.

The fallback section begins with a line that reads `FALLBACK:`. Then, to specify a fallback item, you include a line containing a URL pattern, followed by a space, followed by the path to the resource to use if the file wasn't in the cache. One novel use of the fallback section is provided in the specification:

```
CACHE MANIFEST
FALLBACK:
/ /offline.html
NETWORK:
*
```

This defines a catchall error page for any local resources not found in the cache. Unlike network items, fallback resources must come from the same domain as your app. And if an item is found in both the network and fallback sections, the online whitelist item has priority.

Offline web applications are a great way to provide your users with a seamless experience that more closely mirrors that of a native app. This is especially true when it's combined with the storage APIs we'll be looking at in the next chapter.

An Eventful Chapter

That's better—thanks to some cool event-based APIs, we've tapped into the underlying power of today's mobile devices and filled our apps with the kinds of bells and whistles that users (and clients) have come to expect. In the next chapter, we'll take this a step further, and look at some more APIs that will help us build out our app's functionality, before taking a bit of a detour to look at some good coding practices.

Chapter 6

Polishing Up Our App

With all the important components in place, it's now time to polish up our app. The mobile web world is filled with some very smart people, and they like to share their tricks. We're now starting to see some excellent libraries, frameworks, and hacks that help us complete the illusion of a native app, all the while developing and defining the character of this new breed of mobile web apps.

In this chapter, we'll look at what goodies are available for us to smooth over the inconsistencies between web and native, and see how we can tie everything together to deliver a product that holds its own in any app marketplace!

Web App Tricks

Every tech field has its secret bag of tricks, which developers collect over time as they gain experience with the quirks and foibles of the underlying technology. As mobile web developers, we've barely had any time—but we're already amassing a large bag of tricks.

Mobile Boilerplate

It's no fun trying to remember all the tricks in your head, though, so it's handy to be able to fall back on the community for help. The best and most brilliant "bag of tricks" out there is the HTML5 Mobile Boilerplate project.[1] This provides you with a fantastic baseline to commence your projects. It's designed to be very "delete-key friendly," so you can pick and choose the bits that you want.

[1] http://html5boilerplate.com/mobile/

Fixed Menus

Our application has a top navigation bar, a middle section for content, and a footer. Currently, the content expands to be as big as it needs, and when you scroll, the header disappears off the top of the screen.

One common feature of native phone applications is that headers and footers are fixed in place, always sticking to the top and bottom respectively, with the content scrolling independently. It seems like a reasonable idea, but we soon run into a problem: scrolling on mobile devices only works for the entire screen—there is no built-in way of fixing the position of elements.

Doing it manually is undesirable. The jQuery Mobile project even went so far as to invent a new interaction to work around the difficult issue: when you scroll, any fixed position elements will fade out, and the whole page moves as if there are no fixed elements. When scrolling finishes, the elements fade back in. It's a novel approach, but one that you typically won't be able to swing past a client—who'll spot it as "weird" behavior a mile away, and flippantly demand that you "just make it work."

The Fixed Scroll Problem

This issue is the bugbear of many mobile web devs. It's not an easy problem to solve, though a few people are trying. For example, one proposition is to introduce a new CSS position value, `device-fixed`, that would apply only for mobile devices.[2] Currently, though, there's no happy solution on the horizon.

So if we haven't scared you off by now, what are your options? At the time of writing, iScroll 4[3] is the best and most reliable implementation for scrolling content in a fixed-size container. To use it, you'll need to grab the library from the website, and extract the archive.

After having a quick play with the demos in the **examples** directory, look in the **dist** directory for **iscroll-min.js**. Copy this file into your project, and then link to it in your HTML files:

ch6/01-iscroll.html *(excerpt)*

```
<script src="iscroll-min.js" type="text/javascript"></script>
```

The iScroll library relies heavily on some structural conventions, and comprises three parts:

- a containing element or wrapper
- a container for the scrolling area
- scrollable content

[2] http://www.quirksmode.org/blog/archives/2010/12/the_fifth_posit.html
[3] http://cubiq.org/iscroll-4

Here's what that looks like in markup:

ch6/01-iscroll.html *(excerpt)*

```
<div id="header">Header</div>
<div id="wrapper">
  <div id="scroller">
    <ul id="contents">
      <li>Row 1</li>
      <li>Row 2</li>
      ⋮
      <li>Row 50</li>
    </ul>
  </div>
</div>
<div id="footer">Footer</footer>
```

With the skeleton in place, it's time to add some styling. The part to concentrate on is the outside wrapper; this holds everything together, and is where you set the height of the scrollable area. We're also giving the wrapper a `relative` position (though `absolute` works fine, too):

ch6/01-iscroll.html *(excerpt)*

```
#wrapper {
  height:200px;
  position:relative;
  z-index:1;
  width:100%;
  overflow:hidden;
}
```

With the wrapper in place, we can put iScroll to work. To instantiate a scroll bar, you call the `iScroll()` function, passing the `id` of the scrolling area—in our case, it's `scroller`. In response, iScroll will work with our HTML structure to add the necessary handlers, and JavaScript to create the scrollbar functionality. A JavaScript object representing the scroller is also returned, so we can programmatically interact with it later:

javascripts/ch6/01-iscroll.js *(excerpt)*

```
var scroller = new iScroll('scroller');
```

Watch Your Structure!

Notice that the `div` with `id=scroller` is *inside* the wrapper. It's easy to pass the outer `id` to the `iScroll()` function by mistake—especially if the container names are not so descriptive.

If you load this up on your mobile device, you'll have a beautiful scrolling list. But if you're running it on the desktop, you'll notice that it fails to work. That's because desktop browsers have no support for touch events. If you're using Chrome or Safari, you can fake it for testing by setting an option in the second parameter to the `iScroll()` function:

javascripts/ch6/01-iscroll.js *(excerpt)*

```
var scroller = new iScroll('scroller', { desktopCompatibility: true });
```

By setting the `desktopCompatibility` flag to `true`, we can now click and drag (and throw) the list up and down—just as you would expect it to work natively. It even has a satisfying "bounce" when it hits the edges. There are a host of other parameters you can use to customize the behavior, for example:

```
var scroller = new iScroll('scroller', {
  scrollbarColor: 'rgb(0,0,0,0.1)',
  fadeScrollbar: false,
  bounce: false
});
```

This will give us a very faint scrollbar (as we have set `scrollbarColor` to have an alpha value of 0.1) that doesn't bounce when it hits the edges (`bounce` is `false`), and won't fade in and out when it's active (`fadeScrollbar` is `false`). The entire set of options can be found on the iScroll website.

Once the scrollbar is going, we can use the object reference we saved in the `scroller` variable to control it. For example, we can programmatically move the scroller to the top of the content by using the `scrollTo()` method—which takes an X and a Y position to scroll to, and a duration:

```
scroller.scrollTo(0, 0, '500ms');
```

We can also scroll to a particular element inside the scrolling content with `scrollToElement()`, which takes a CSS selector and duration:

```
scroller.scrollToElement('#scroller > ul > li', '1s');
```

Finally, if you're transitioning between pages or changing DOM elements a lot, iScroll can lose its handle to the scroll contents, and stop working. To reattach it you can use the `refresh()` method, which updates all iScroll variables. Due to peculiar DOM timing issues, the author of iScroll recommends wrapping the call in a `setTimeout()`, if necessary:

```
setTimeout(function(){ scroller.refresh(); }, 0);
```

In most cases, iScroll will work very well—but it needs to do some fairly heavy lifting to emulate native scrolling just right, so if you're doing any heavy lifting of your own, there are chances for clashes. If you do run into problems, it is a good idea to head to the iScroll bug tracker to see if another developer has already found a workaround.[4]

iScroll Lite

You may have noticed another file in the iScroll download: **iscroll-lite.js**. Although we've only just looked at its scrolling powers, there's so much more to iScroll: pinch/zoom tracking, snapping to elements, pull to refresh, to name just a few. But if you want the scrolling, and nothing but the scrolling, the **iscroll-lite.js** file is the one you want. This contains only the bare essentials, so there's no desktop compatibility mode, which does make testing harder. A good solution is to use the full version for testing and development, and swap it out once the app is ready.

Clicking Faster

Back in Chapter 4, we started off by binding a simple `click` event, but did say that it can be faster to use the `touchend` event instead. Now we're going to have a look at the benefits and drawbacks of these approaches, and conclude with some more sophisticated techniques for providing more responsive clicks.

Yes, we're still just talking about clicks. That's as good an indicator as any that we're still working in a young field! The `click` event has a nasty 300-millisecond delay on mobile devices that occurs after you lift your finger before firing your code. This is where the device is waiting to see if you're going to double-tap instead of single-tap the screen, but the lag is quite noticeable.

We introduced a workaround by binding to the `touchend` event instead, which fires instantly as the finger is lifted:

```
$("#sightings-list li").bind("touchend": function() {
  // Do code!
});
```

This successfully does away with the delay, but has a couple of quirks of its own. The `touchend` event fires when users lift their finger, but lifting your finger from a button does not always mean you want it to be clicked. Perhaps the user started on one button, then moved their finger away from it, intending to cancel the click. They happened to land on another button before lifting their finger, and our `touchend` event fires, performing an action the user never intended.

We could be a little more clever, and add some timing to the click. On `touchstart`, we timestamp the element, and make sure the `touchend` occurs in a certain period (say, 400 milliseconds), otherwise we won't call it a click:

---

[4] https://github.com/cubiq/iscroll/issues

javascripts/ch6/02-fastclick.js *(excerpt)*

```
$("#sightings-list li").bind({
  "touchstart": function(e){
    $(this).data("clicked", new Date().getTime());
  },
  "touchend": function(e){
    var now = new Date().getTime(),
      start = $(this).data("clicked");
    if(now - start > 400) {
      return
    };
    // Do code!
  }
});
```

This will stop the dragging issue above, but it's a bit messy having to introduce timers for every click we want to handle.

The "Creating Fast Buttons for Mobile Web Applications" article by Ryan Fioravanti[5] outlines a more bulletproof approach, and provides some code you can adapt. Alternatively, there's a ready-to-use implementation of the same idea inside the HTML5 boilerplate helper file.[6]

With this code, you can use the `MBP.fastButton()` method to turn a regular button into a super-quick button. The fast button will check if the user has moved a finger a certain distance (10 pixels), and if so, the click is canceled. Just pass in the element you want to make into a fast button, and the callback code to run when it's clicked:

javascripts/ch6/03-fastbutton.js *(excerpt)*

```
$("#sightings-list li").each(function(){
  new MBP.fastButton(this, function() {
    alert("super fast click!");
  });
});
```

It might seem like a lot of work just for a click, but the click is the most basic user interaction we have, so it's important to get it right.

Loading Your Libraries

Here's a simple one that falls firmly into the "clever hack" category. So many sites and apps use libraries such as jQuery and Prototype, that the library creators make their libraries available via Content Distribution Networks (CDN) that specialize in serving lots of files, really fast. The best

[5] http://code.google.com/mobile/articles/fast_buttons.html

[6] https://github.com/shichuan/mobile-html5-boilerplate/blob/master/js/mylibs/helper.js

part is that since the library is always served from the same URL, if a browser has cached the library on one site, it will be able to used the cached version on any other sites that use the same CDN.

This is great for our mobile apps—but we don't want to rely on the CDN for our app's functionality. This is especially true if our app is running offline, either using the Offline Web Applications spec or packaged into a native app with PhoneGap, as we'll see in the next chapter. For the best of both worlds, we can try loading from a CDN first, and if that fails, we can fall back to our local version:

ch6/04-smartload.html *(excerpt)*

```
<script
    src="http://ajax.googleapis.com/ajax/libs/jquery/1.6.1/jquery.min.js"
    type="text/javascript"></script>
<script>
  if(!window.jQuery) {
    document.write("<script src='vendor/jquery-1.6.1.min.js'>\x3C/script>")
  }
</script>
```

The second script element checks to see if jQuery was loaded successfully. If it wasn't, it does a `document.write` to create a `<script>` tag to our local version. That cryptic-looking string of characters at the end is the encoded version of a "less than" symbol (<) bracket, to stop some browsers from being confused. Very nifty!

Feature Detection

Way back at the start of Chapter 4, we realized we needed to do a bit of feature detection for our app to work correctly on both desktop and mobile devices. If the browser window contained the `touchend` object, we could assume that it supported the touch events.

The idea of feature detection as a development choice and all-round "good thing" arose from the standards movement in web development. Previously, decisions about which features to enable for a given user were based on **browser sniffing**: "The user has browser X, browser X supports feature Y, therefore we'll enable feature Y." This proved to be problematic over time, as the features of browser X could change at any point.

Sniffing Is Back

Interestingly, the discussion of the merits of browser sniffing has reappeared because of the boom in mobile web and HTML5. The current landscape of devices varies so widely, and is so filled with bugs (both obscure and obvious), that simply detecting features is often no longer enough. But in the long term, feature detection will win out—so it's best to avoid filling your code with unnecessary browser sniffing if you can.

Because we'll usually end up doing the same feature detection in every project, it makes sense to collect all our detection code in one place. Then when our methods change, or we find a new test, we can add it to our library of detections. A simple way to do it is to store everything together in an object, and use that one object for all our tests:

javascripts/ch6/05-feature-detection.js *(excerpt)*

```
var $has = {
  touch: "ontouchend" in document,
  orientation: "onorientationchange" in window
};

// Use our detection object
if($has.touch) {
  alert("we've got touch!");
}
```

Our object only has two tests so far: one for touches, and one for screen orientation (which we looked at in Chapter 5). Now, let's build on this object and include anything we'd like to know about the features of our device:

javascripts/ch6/05-feature-detection.js *(excerpt)*

```
var $has = {
  touch: "ontouchend" in document,
  orientation: "onorientationchange" in window,
  geolocation: typeof navigator.geolocation != "undefined",
  transitions: "WebKitTransitionEvent" in window,
  canvas: !!document.createElement("canvas").getContext,
  audio: !!document.createElement("audio").canPlayType
};
```

For many tests, we just need to look for the existence of the feature object on the browser window, but other features are trickier, requiring us to create document fragments, and test the results of manipulating them in special ways. Examining open source projects like jQuery Mobile and Sencha Touch is a great way to spot novel and interesting feature-detection tricks. And, of course, the Modernizr library we discussed back in Chapter 3 has more than its fair share of clever detection code.

Widgets

The idea of mobile device "widgets" is a little different from the desktop; on the desktop we think of widgets as small elements of the entire page, and the emphasis is on the functionality that it provides. On the mobile device, a widget takes up a lot more room, and starts to become a major part of our app's design. Many of the big frameworks' primary focus is their built-in widgets collection—and associated look. Although that enables us to have fantastic-looking apps happening quickly, they can start to look a bit generic.

We want our apps to be stamped with our personality, so we'll build our own general-purpose elements.

Dialog Boxes

Dialog boxes are a tough one. If we wanted to pretend that we're a native app, we'd have to recreate the look of a native dialog box on every device we're targeting. This would be a lot of work, with the results probably not entirely satisfactory, so we'll take a different approach and make a box that fits our app, rather than our device.

A dialog box consists of a couple of parts; one is a mechanism to disallow other actions while the box is open. The second is a message containing at least one button (to dismiss the dialog). Our dialog will just be regular old HTML, so we can make it look and act however we want; however, users have expectations about how dialogs work, so best not to stray too far from the formula: a small window centered in the middle of the screen with a message, and one or more big buttons.

That leaves us with two problems: how to make our box "modal" (in other words, how to prevent other actions from occurring), and how to center it on the screen. The modal part we'll handle by adding a new element to our pages and using it to mask out the entire screen, like those used in "lightbox" effects on the desktop. All we need to do is give it a dark background, and set an opacity less than one to make it semitransparent. Because it stretches over the entire window, touch events won't be sent to the underlying elements:

ch6/08-dialog.html *(excerpt)*

```
#mask {
  display: none;
  position: absolute;
  background-color: #000;
  opacity: 0.6;
  z-index: 500;
  top:0;
  bottom: 0px;
  left: 0;
  right: 0;
}
```

The mask `div` can be inserted anywhere in the markup, usually toward the end:

ch6/08-dialog.html *(excerpt)*

```
<div id="mask"></div>
```

Next, outside the mask we add the layout for our dialog. We'll include a span in the middle that we'll fill with our dialog message:

ch6/08-dialog.html *(excerpt)*

```
<div id="dialog">
  <h3 class="heading"></h3>
  <span class="content"></span>
  <button id="ok">OK</button>
</div>
```

Here are a couple of styles to position our dialog:

ch6/08-dialog.html *(excerpt)*

```
#dialog {
  display: none;
  position: absolute;
  background-color: #fff;
  width: 90%;
  height: 200px;
  z-index: 600;
  -webkit-border-radius: 10px;
  -webkit-box-sizing: border-box;
}
```

Now, to show the dialog, we need to display the mask and the dialog contents. A nice and simple way is to use jQuery's `fadeIn()` and `fadeOut()` methods:

javascripts/ch6/08-dialog.js *(excerpt)*

```
$("#dialog,#mask").fadeIn();
$("#ok").one("click", function(){
  $("#dialog,#mask").fadeOut();
});
```

This dialog doesn't lend itself much to reuse, though: the text is static, and we have to write the same code over and over in our app wherever we want a dialog to appear. A cleaner approach would be to write a method to encapsulate the functionality; we'll call the function `showDialog()`. For the sake of illustration, it will be reliant on the markup we provided, but if you were making a standalone dialog class, you'd want the DOM elements to be referenced from the outside application, rather than hardcoded in:

javascripts/ch6/08-dialog.js *(excerpt)*

```
function showDialog(options, OKCallback, CancelCallback) {
  var dialog = $("#dialog");
  ⋮
}
```

The parameters we'll accept are an object containing all the options for the dialog: heading text, body content, and a Boolean value to say if the cancel button should be displayed. We'll also have two callback functions: one for code to run if the user clicks **OK**, and one to run if the user clicks **Cancel**.

We set up some defaults using jQuery's `extend()` method, and then fill in the fields of the dialog using a simple templating technique:

javascripts/ch6/08-dialog.js *(excerpt)*

```
// Set defaults.
var settings = $.extend({
      heading: "Notice",
      content: "",
      cancel: false
    }, options);

// Set the text
dialog.find(".heading").text(settings.heading);
dialog.find(".content").text(settings.content);
```

Next, we set up a click handler on our **OK** button, hiding the dialog and firing the callback:

javascripts/ch6/08-dialog.js *(excerpt)*

```
dialog.find("#ok").one("click", function() {
  $("#dialog,#mask").fadeOut();
  OKCallback && OKCallback();
});
```

If the dialog has a cancel option, we'll do the same for it.

Single-line Duck-type Checking

To check for the `OKCallback()` function's existence and run the function in a single line, we use the "logical and" trick: `OKCallback && OKCallback();`. This works as a Boolean expression that first detects if the function exists; if it doesn't, the first part of our statement will be `false`, and the statement will terminate. But if the function *does* exist, the second part of the expression (the actual function call) will be evaluated, causing the function to be run. It's a nice trick for writing concise code, but some people avoid it due to its cryptic notation, and because it will attempt to execute any value that evaluates to `true`, even if it's just a number!

We'll also use the same block to show or hide the button initially:

javascripts/ch6/08-dialog.js *(excerpt)*

```
if(options.cancel) {
  dialog.find("#cancel")
    .one("click", function(){
      $("#dialog,#mask").fadeOut();
      CancelCallback && CancelCallback();
    })
    .show();
}
else {
  dialog.find("#cancel").hide();
}
```

Then, to kick it all off, we fade in the dialog:

javascripts/ch6/08-dialog.js *(excerpt)*

```
$("#dialog,#mask").fadeIn();
```

Spinners

Just like on a desktop, it's important to give a visual indication to the user when our application is off fetching data. The perceived "snappiness" of an app is crucial to a good user experience, and a nice spinner (sometimes called a "loader" or "activity indicator") is a fine way to assist that perception.

We'll take the mask with us—that way no one can start hitting buttons while our Ajax request is happening—but we'll replace our dialog with a spinning icon. Let's start with the markup for the spinner:

ch6/09-spinner.html *(excerpt)*

```
<div id="spinner">
  <img src="images/spinner.gif" />
</div>
```

The functionality is fantastically simple, consisting of two states: visible or hidden. We'll make a function to set which state we'd like, passing in `true` to show it, or `false` to hide it:

javascripts/ch6/09-spinner.js *(excerpt)*

```
function spinner(blnShow) {
  var elements = $("#spinner,#mask");
  if(blnShow) {
    elements.fadeIn();
  }
  else {
    elements.fadeOut();
  }
}
```

No need to overcomplicate the situation—fade in, or fade out. And using it is just as simple; show it when we commence a request, and remove it when it concludes:

javascripts/ch6/09-spinner.js *(excerpt)*

```
spinner(true);
$.ajax({
  url: "http://search.twitter.com/search.json?q=stars&callback=?",
  success: function(data){
    // Do something with the data
  },
  complete: function(){
    spinner(false);
  }
});
```

That's all there is to it!

Storing Data on the Client

Even before the days of web applications and Ajax, when the browser's only job was to display HTML, there was a need for a local storage mechanism. Originally, cookies served that role—enabling websites to store personal preferences to help maintain a consistent experience across otherwise stateless visits. Although useful, cookies are extremely limited in the amount of data that can be stored.

Local Storage

Enter HTML5's local storage. Local storage provides a mechanism for storing larger amounts of key/value data on the client. How much larger? It's still fairly little—around 5MB—but far more than the few kilobytes we get with cookies. Why would we want so much storage? Here's the use case provided in the specification:

> Web applications may wish to store megabytes of user data, such as entire user-authored documents or a user's mailbox, on the client side for performance reasons.

So local storage is like a mega-cookie—but even better, because the data isn't passed between the client and the server with every request, so there's no bandwidth wastage or slowed-down pageload times. The interface for interacting with local storage is a lot more enjoyable than dealing with cookies, too.

Before we start using it, we should test to see if the device supports it. This check should be fairly familiar to you by now—and you can add it to the feature-detection object we made earlier, if you like:

javascripts/ch6/10-storage.js *(excerpt)*

```
var hasStorage = "localStorage" in window;
```

If the result is `true`, we're ready to store. Local storage is a key/value pair system. You can only store strings—so if you wanted to store a JavaScript object, for example, you'd need to serialize it first.

There are two ways to fetch and set data, and the one you use will depend entirely on your coding preference. You can use the `setItem()` and `getItem()` methods:

javascripts/ch6/10-storage.js *(excerpt)*

```
var store = window.localStorage;
store.setItem("fav-celeb", "Johnny Deep");
var fav = store.getItem("fav-celeb");
```

We start by making a shortcut to the `window.localStorage` object—this just helps keep our code a bit shorter, and saves us from having to type too much. Then we store data using the `setItem()` method, which accepts two parameters: a key (`"fav-celeb"`), and a value (`"Johnny Deep"`). That's all we have to do to store the value permanently (or until the user clears their storage cache). To retrieve it, we use `getItem()`. This takes a single parameter—the key name—and returns the string associated with it. If there's currently no key with that name, it returns `null`.

Windows

Local storage, unlike cookies, spans over multiple windows. This isn't so interesting for our mobile apps (yet), but if you have two windows open in your desktop browser, you can set and retrieve values instantly on both.

The specification defines the `getItem()` and `setItem()` methods, but all current implementations of local storage also allow you to get and set values using brackets or dot notation:

javascripts/ch6/10-storage.js *(excerpt)*

```
// Set values
store["lastSpot"] = new Date();
store.lastLocation = "Hollywood";

// Retrieve values
var spotTime = new Date(store["lastSpot"]),
    spotPlace = store.lastLocation;
```

There is no explicit way to update values. If you want to modify some data, you just set it again with the same name, and it'll overwrite the last value. It's fantastically simple! If you want to remove an existing value, you can either set it to `null`, or use the `removeItem()` method, passing in the key to delete. And if you want to remove all the keys (and all the values) that have been set by your domain in one fell swoop, you can make a call to `clear()`:

javascripts/ch6/10-storage.js *(excerpt)*

```
// Unset the favorite celebrity
store.removeItem("fav-celeb");
// Reset everything!
store.clear();
```

What about values that aren't strings? In an earlier example, we tried to store a `Date` object directly. But under the covers, the API calls the `toString()` method and converts it to a string before storing it. That's why we had to convert it back to a date object when we retrieved it. You'll need to do the same if you're storing numbers:

javascripts/ch6/10-storage.js *(excerpt)*

```
// Get the visits
var hits = store["hitCount"];
if( hits == null) {
  hits = 0;
} else {
  hits = parseInt(hits, 10);
}
```

```
// Update the visit count
store["hitCount"] = hits + 1;
```

In this example, we keep a running count of page hits by the user. Every time they return, we parse the number of current hits, and then update the new count back into local storage. It's a very simple, but flexible, system.

Having figured out all the fiddly bits, let's do something practical with them. Back in Chapter 3, we looked at providing a prompt for the user to let them know that they can add our app to their home screen. But we want to avoid annoying them with the message every time they visit our site, so we'll use local storage to remember that they've already seen the prompt.

Our original code checked to see if the browser supported standalone mode, and if standalone mode was currently active—no point showing a prompt if the user's already added us to their home screen.

We'll add in one more check, for a `seen` variable that we'll set according to a local storage value, also called `seen`:

javascripts/ch6/10-storage.js *(excerpt)*

```
var seen = false;
if($has.localStorage) {
  seen = window.localStorage["seen"] || false;
  window.localStorage["seen"] = "seen";
}
if(navigator.standalone != undefined && !!!navigator.standalone && !seen) {
  $("#addToHome").show();
}
```

We begin by checking the browser for local storage support, and defaulting our `seen` variable to `false`. Then we look in local storage for our `seen` key. If it's yet to be saved, it will be `undefined`, which will cause our code to fall through and receive the `false` value instead. If it has been set, the variable will take on the value that was set there.

Now that we've looked in local storage, we'll store a new value to indicate that the user has seen the prompt. Finally, we look to see if we need to display the prompt. Because `seen` defaults to `false`, and we only change it if the browser supports local storage, we'll simply display the prompt every time if there's no storage.

Note that we're saving the string `"seen"` rather than the value `true`—remember that local storage can only accept strings. Fortunately, JavaScript evaluates non-empty strings as `true`, so it works fine.

Web SQL Database

Local storage is a simple and flexible way to keep track of information on the client side—but what if you need a more sophisticated tool than simple key/value storage? There are times when you really need to store more than a few strings. For web developers accustomed to building server-side applications, that means one thing: a database. The good news is that there's an excellent, simple, and useful database API available on most of the devices you'll want to target. The bad news is that it might not be around forever.

If you visit the W3C specification for the Web SQL Database,[7] you'll be greeted with a huge yellow-on-black warning saying that development of the spec has ceased. The reason stated is that the committee is at an impasse: all the browser-makers implemented the same database back end (SQLite), and they're unable to make a specification based on one implementation. Weird, but that's the rules.

The implementation is widespread, though, so for the time being it's the best we have. And what we have is a set of APIs for manipulating a client-side database through SQL. We're going to use these to add a feature that lets users store random notes about stars they're currently tracking.

SQL

Web SQL, as the name implies, is based on SQL—a query language for interacting with relational databases. A crash course on SQL could easily fill a book this size on its own,[8] so in this section we'll be assuming you're already familiar with the rudiments of the language. If you don't know your `SELECT`s from your `JOIN`s from your `INSERT`s, feel free to skip ahead to the next section. Or alternatively, you can look up any number of great SQL tutorials available on the Web—an extra skill never hurt anyone!

We can check for the existence of the Web database by seeing if the main method `openDatabase()` exists:

javascripts/ch6/11-websql.js *(excerpt)*

```
var hasWebDB = "openDatabase" in window;
```

The `openDatabase()` method takes a handful of parameters and returns a newly constructed database object that we can work with. The required parameters are the name, version, and display name for the database—these are all string values. The last required value is a number that represents the estimated size of the database in bytes:

---

[7] http://www.w3.org/TR/webdatabase/

[8] In fact, SitePoint has published such a book: *Simply SQL*. [http://www.sitepoint.com/books/sql1/]

javascripts/ch6/11-websql.js *(excerpt)*

```
var db = window.openDatabase(
  "celeb-notes",
  "1.0",
  "Celeb Notes",
  4 * 1024 * 1024
);
```

We've declared a database called `celeb-notes` and estimated its size at 4MB (or 4×4×1024 bytes). The display name and the size are there to act as hints for the browser. The idea for the estimated size is that if your application has huge space requirements, you can let the user know up front, so they can agree to it.

Once the database is created, everything else is just standard SQL statements: we can create tables, insert and delete rows, and select data. There are two components required to run our statements: a `transaction` object, and its `executeSql()` method. To start a transaction, we call the `transaction()` method on the database we opened, and provide a callback that takes one parameter—the transaction itself. The transaction's `executeSql()` method takes our SQL string, runs it, and then calls either our success callback (the second parameter) or the error callback (the third):

javascripts/ch6/11-websql.js *(excerpt)*

```
// Create the table
db.transaction(function(t) {
  var sql = "CREATE TABLE IF NOT EXISTS notes ";
  sql += "(id INTEGER PRIMARY KEY ASC, celeb, note)";

  t.executeSql(sql, function(){
    selectNotes();
  }, function(){
    selectNotes();
  });
});
```

We've created a new table called `notes` that contains three columns: `id` (a number), `celeb` (a string), and `note` (also a string). If the table does not exist when we run this transaction, it will create it and call our success callback. If the table *does* exist, it throws to our error callback. In either case, we then want to move on to selecting the existing notes from the database and displaying them in a list:

javascripts/ch6/11-websql.js *(excerpt)*

```
function selectNotes() {
  db.transaction(function(t){
    t.executeSql('SELECT * FROM notes', [], function (t, data) {
```

```
      // Display the data
    });
  });
}
```

This snippet of code is very similar to the previous one, except that instead of running a `CREATE` query, we're running a `SELECT`. For this command, we also need to pass any arguments as an array; we don't have any, so we just pass an empty list. The success callback returns the transaction object, as well as an object containing the selected rows. Now we can inject them into our page:

javascripts/ch6/11-websql.js *(excerpt)*

```
// Display the data
for (var i = 0; i < data.rows.length; i++) {
  var item = data.rows.item(i);
  $("<li></li>")
    .append("<span>" + item.celeb + "</span>")
    .append("<span>" + item.note + "</span>")
    .appendTo("#notes-list")
}
```

The returned data is an object of type `SQLResultSet`, which has a property called `rows`. To target the rows, we use the method `rows.item()` and pass in an integer for the row we're looking for.

The first time you run the code, you won't have any notes to display, so let's add a button to the page, and prompt the user to enter in some new note data:

javascripts/ch6/11-websql.js *(excerpt)*

```
$("#addNote").click(function(){
  var celeb = prompt("Celeb's name"),
      note = prompt("Note contents");
  if(celeb && note) {
    insertNote(celeb, note);
  }
});
```

The final step is to insert the data into the database. Again, this is very similar to our other calls—though this time we're passing the `celeb` and `note` variables in via an array. This is preferable to merely building the entire string manually, because it allows the browser to take actions that prevent SQL injection attacks, which could occur if the user entered malicious data in one of our fields:

javascripts/ch6/11-websql.js *(excerpt)*

```
function insertNote(celeb, note) {
  db.transaction(function(t) {
    var sql = "INSERT INTO notes (celeb, note) VALUES (?, ?)";
    t.executeSql(sql, [celeb, note], function(){
      alert('Saved!');
    });
  });
}
```

If you refresh the page, your new note will be saved. Of course, this is just the skeleton of our notes feature—but you can see how having a fully-fledged SQL database on hand really emphasizes the potential of mobile apps to rival their desktop counterparts.

Tying Everything Together

We now have all the ingredients for almost any application we can imagine. We can show and transition pages, load data via Ajax, and store information in databases. As our abilities and capabilities grow, it becomes more likely that our code base will degenerate into a huge mess of unmaintainable spaghetti code. To combat this, we need to make use of some abstraction—to encapsulate our code into logical components, with minimal dependencies on each other. In this section, we'll take a quick whirlwind tour of possible methods to achieve this, and then have a look at some third-party frameworks that can help us out.

Modules

Throughout the book, many of the examples have used global variables to keep track of a widget or interaction's state. This made it easy to understand the purpose of the code, but in a real system it quickly leads to name conflicts and bugs that are hard to find. It's also considered very "old school"—and we don't want our code to be called that.

We're now moving into the area of application architecture, and, thanks to the flexibility of JavaScript, there are many approaches you can take: from our dumping everything in the global scope, as we've been doing so far, to creating an over-the-top, full-stack framework that also makes you coffee. As well, there are third-party projects out there that handle various aspects of your application architecture, and we'll talk about them in the next section.

For our app, however, we'll take the simple approach of namespacing and encapsulating related functionality with JavaScript object literals. Rather than have our state variables and functions floating around in the global namespace, we shove them inside an object:

javascripts/ch6/12-module.js *(excerpt)*

```
var startrackr = {
  init: function(){
    alert("Ready for action");
  }
};
```

Now we have a container to hold all our application functionality. It's a mini-controller that will be responsible for keeping track of the state of the app, and instructing pages in our app to load and transition.

The pages themselves will also be objects. Each of our pages will include at least two methods: `init()` and `load()`. The `init()` function will run when the application starts, and will be responsible for binding event handlers and setting any initial values. The `load()` function will be called when we want the page to load its data and display itself:

javascripts/ch6/12-module.js *(excerpt)*

```
var spots = {
  init: function(){
    // Do DOM binding on ready
  },
  load: function(){
    // Logic to load and show page
  }
};

// Another page...
var spot = {
  init: function(){},
  load: function(){}
};
```

Our `startrackr` object can now help us control the pages. We'll tell the object about each of the pages so that we can initialize them and load the first page. The `startrackr.init()` method loops through each added page, and checks if the page has an `init()` method to run using the single-line, check-and-execute trick we saw earlier.

The `loadPage()` function just calls `load()` on the next page. Moving this up to our controller object will make it easier to later extend it to include history tracking, or other functionality:

javascripts/ch6/12-module.js *(excerpt)*

```
var startrackr = {
  pages: [],
  init: function(){
```

```
    $.each(this.pages, function(){
      this.init && this.init();
    });

    if(this.pages.length){
      this.pages[0].load();
    }
  },
  addPage: function(page) {
    this.pages.push(page);
  },
  loadPage: function(page, data) {
    page.load(data);
  }
};
```

The `startrackr` controller also has a function to add pages we want to keep track of. We'll add the `spot` and `spots` pages we created above:

javascripts/ch6/12-module.js *(excerpt)*

```
startrackr.addPage(spots);
startrackr.addPage(spot);
```

Finally, we can kick it off by calling the main object's `init()` function when the DOM is ready. This will loop through all the pages we added, call their `init()` functions in turn, and then load up the first page:

javascripts/ch6/12-module.js *(excerpt)*

```
$(document).ready(function() {
  startrackr.init();
});
```

So far, we have a structure, but no functionality. Now we have to actually do some work on the pages. We'll bind some UI elements in `init()`, and load some data via Ajax in the `load()` function:

javascripts/ch6/12-module.js *(excerpt)*

```
var spots = {
  init: function(){
    // add handlers;
    $("#spots li a").live("click", function(e){
      e.preventDefault();
      spot.load($(e.target).attr("data-id"));
    });
  },
  load: function(){
```

```
    showSpinner();
    $.ajax({
      url: "/spots/",
      complete: function(){
        hideSpinner();
        transition("#spots", "fade");
      }
    });
  }
};
```

Similarly, we have to set up the Spot detail page. It's almost identical, except we also set up the Back button to transition back:

javascripts/ch6/12-module.js *(excerpt)*

```
var spot = {
  init: function() {
    $("#spot-back").click(function(){
      transition("#spots", "push", true);
    })
  },
  load: function(id) {
    $.ajax({
      url: "/spot/" + id,
      complete: function(){
        // Set the header
        $("#spot .page-header h1").text(id);
        transition("#spot", "push");
      }
    });
  }
};
```

This is just for the sake of example—you'd probably want to use the history functionality we created in Chapter 5 instead. If so, you could then move the history handling out of the `transition()` function and into the controller object.

Even though this controller-with-pages model is very simple, the difference it makes as your application grows is impressive. Each page is now a bundled-up, self-contained entity, so maintaining and extending the application becomes a lot easier.

Custom Events

A popular technique for decoupling components and coordinating communication between isolated entities in your application is through events. We're no strangers to the event-driven programming model: clicks, page loads, geolocation changes, and so on. So far, we've only been listening for events—but we can take it further: we have the ability to create our own custom events that can be triggered by our app.

By creating our own custom events, we can decouple parts of the system that don't really need to know about each other. For example, say we have a common header component in our application, which is updated any time a page changes. Wherever a page change occurs, we have to update the header with the new text. Likewise, when a page changes, we want to transition to the new page.

We could lump all the functionality together—but if a lot of things happen when a page changes, we'll wind up with a big list of function calls that need to be reproduced for every change. Instead, what if we created a custom `page-change` event that any parts of our code could listen out for—just like any other event? This kind of system is known as the **publish/subscribe** (or pub/sub) pattern.

To publish our `page-change` event, we'll use the jQuery `trigger()` method. The event will be fired from the callback of our Ajax calls, after we've acquired the necessary data for the page:

javascripts/ch6/13-custom-events.js *(excerpt)*

```
$(document).trigger("page-change", {
  $el: $("#spot"),
  name: "Spot " + id,
  transition: "push"
});
```

The event is triggered on the `document` object, and takes an event name plus an object containing any data we want to pass to the event handlers.

To subscribe to the published events, we use the familiar `bind()` method—just as we would for any other event. The data that we passed from the publisher will be available as the second parameter in the handler callback:

javascripts/ch6/13-custom-events.js *(excerpt)*

```
$(document).bind("page-change", function(e, data){
  data.$el
    .find(".page-header")
    .text(data.name);
});
```

Here, we've subscribed to the `page-change` event, and set the page title to the correct value.

Another part of our code is responsible for performing the page transition. We can separate this from the title logic above by attaching another event handler:

javascripts/ch6/13-custom-events.js *(excerpt)*

```
$(document).bind("page-change", function(e, data){
  transition(data.$el, data.transition);
});
```

The primary advantage of the pub/sub model is allowing our components to be loosely coupled: the transition module doesn't know or care about the templating module, and can react to changes entirely independently. Combined with a good modular architecture, a well-designed event system can make even a large, complex JavaScript application fairly simple to update and maintain.

Other Frameworks

There are a lot of developers out there working on the problem of managing complexity in large JavaScript applications, and many of the solutions are applicable to our mobile apps too. We've already talked about the pros and cons of using a monolithic framework like Sencha or jQuery Mobile, but recently there's been a shift to small, self-contained libraries that "do one thing, and do it well."

That's not to say that those frameworks won't help you structure your app—far from it. Sencha Touch, to pick just one, includes a comprehensive MVC framework! However, some great little libraries are springing up that let you keep your own coding style, while providing a helping hand with the app skeleton.

Sammy.js[9] is a small routing and event framework that maps URL hash values to functions. When a given URL is entered, it will route the request to the correct code. In the example below, the URL #/stars will load our Stars page. This way, all navigation is maintained through regular URLs:

```
Sammy("#page-stars", function() {
  // triggered by URL "#/stars"
  this.get("#/stars", function() {
    this.$element() // this will be #page-stars
        .html("The stars!");
  });
}).run();
```

If Sammy isn't enough for you, then maybe you need some Backbone. The Backbone project[10] is a bit more heavy duty, providing a framework for organizing your application through models, collections (of models), and views. It's easy to bind UI changes to your model changes (and vice versa), and send the changes to the server via Ajax.

[9] http://sammyjs.org/

[10] http://documentcloud.github.com/backbone/

Backbone also includes an event system to bind everything together, similar to the custom event system we built in the last section. Like Sammy, it can also watch the URL bar and route requests accordingly.

It's important to remember that there are many paths you can take for structuring your application, and the kind of abstraction and encapsulation you use will ultimately .depend on your own style and preferences.

Conclusion

A couple of powerful HTML5 APIs for saving data on the client device, some custom user-interface components, and a modular, event-driven application architecture—all in a day's work! You might be starting to feel as if you're building a real client-side application, rather than a simple website or even web-based application, and that's exactly what we've been building. We have an app that (at least on some platforms) runs full screen with no browser chrome, works when offline, takes advantage of the device's hardware features, and can store data locally and send it up to a server asynchronously.

For a lot of developers, that's good enough—and for a lot of users and clients as well. But there are still a few stubborn strongholds where the native app holds dominion: the app marketplaces, and some more elusive device functionality like cameras and contact lists. For the rest of this book, we'll look at a cool new way of taking all the work we've put into making our web app the best it can be, and carrying it over with a minimum of hassle into the world of the native app.

Chapter 7

Introducing PhoneGap

The client is over the moon with the progress of the Startrackr mobile app, but they've just called with an additional request. They've read on a blog that selling mobile apps is an awesome way to bring in additional revenue. Indeed, while web apps—like the one we've built so far—are easy to deploy and access via the Web, the downside is there's no one simple way to charge for access to them.

The client has also told us that they really want stalkers—er—*fans* to be able to take pictures of their favorite stars if they see them in the street, and upload them directly to the site. So far, we've managed to convince them that this feature isn't essential—mainly because it's impossible on today's mobile browsers.

Impossible?

Actually, that isn't quite true. Android 3.0 has one of the first browsers to implement the W3C's Media Capture API,[1] which allows the browser to access video or images from the device's camera, or audio from the microphone. Alas, Honeycomb's current market share isn't quite large enough to appease the client.

To gain real access to all of a device's functionality—like the camera, file system, and contacts list, for example—as well as be able to sell the app via the device platform's app marketplace: sounds like the province of the native application.

[1] http://www.w3.org/TR/2010/WD-media-capture-api-20100928/

The client wants to make their app available on as many smartphone devices as possible—this is one of the reasons we opted for building a web application rather than a native one in the first place. But now that we've bumped up against some of the limitations of mobile web apps, we're faced with an interesting problem: how are we going to build native apps for a number of platforms in different programming languages that we're unfamiliar with? And, as if that wasn't a big enough problem, the budget for the project is certainly no open checkbook, so we need to make sure we can build these apps within a reasonable time frame.

Embedding Web Pages in Native Apps

There are a number of ways we can take our application native. The most obvious solution would be to rewrite the application for each target platform using whatever language that platform supports. We know that would mean learning a number of new programming languages, but we'd also need to test and maintain multiple versions of our application; furthermore, every new feature or bug fix would need to be implemented multiple times—once for each target platform.

Fortunately, there's a better way. All the major smartphone platforms—from iOS to Android to BlackBerry to webOS—support embedding HTML views in native applications. This means that a native app developer can include web pages in their apps—whether it be for a login form, or maybe to reuse parts of their existing websites that don't need to be reimplemented natively.

This opens up an interesting possibility: what if it were possible to take our existing web application and include it in native applications by means of these "web view" components?[2] We'd still need to write some platform-specific code to create the web view and load up our HTML, but all the core application logic would be cross-platform JavaScript—much of it already written.

Of course, we'd still need to add *some* native code in order to access the hardware that we were unable to access—remember that mobile browsers have restricted access to device functionality like contacts or files. We'd need to create what is called a bridge.

Bridge Over Troubled Water

A **bridge** is a way of exposing a set of methods that are written in one language to another language. For example, if you have used ImageMagick in PHP, you've used a bridge that converts the ImageMagick library (written in C/C++) into PHP functions that you can call. From your perspective as a developer, ImageMagick appears just like any other PHP library. Behind the scenes, though, every function you call is calling some C code in the core ImageMagick library, and the return values are being converted back into PHP variables for you.

[2] The exact name of the component varies from platform to platform: on Android it's called a WebView; on iOS, it's UIWebView. BlackBerry's is called a BrowserField. We'll be referring to them generically as web views or embedded browsers.

What we'd like is a set of bridges that provide us with a consistent set of JavaScript APIs; these then map onto the native functionality made available by each different smartphone platform.

We'd also prefer to avoid having to write and maintain all these bridges ourselves. It sounds like a lot of work, after all.

Say hello to our new friend: PhoneGap.

PhoneGap

PhoneGap is an open source project that does precisely what we need, with a few useful extras. It provides us with a JavaScript bridge API to underlying hardware, such as the camera, GPS, and accelerometer, as well as the file system. It also supports a number of different platforms such as Apple iOS, Google Android, RIM's BlackBerry, Palm's webOS, and soon, Windows Phone 7. That's quite a list, covering a sizable portion of the smartphone market.

By dropping our existing web application into PhoneGap, and making a few small tweaks, we'll be able to convert the StarTrackr mobile site into a bona fide native app without having to learn any new languages or maintain too much extra code. Sounds like a winner!

PhoneGap Features

PhoneGap supports the majority of device functionality on the majority of platforms—but there are some, ahem, *gaps*. Check out http://www.phonegap.com/features/ for the latest feature matrix—and make sure any features you plan on including are supported on your target platforms.

PhoneGap is remarkably easy to use. You first need to install the development environments for each of the platforms you want to target (we'll be doing this next). In each one, you create a new app, then put your HTML, CSS, and JavaScript into a specific folder inside the project. PhoneGap will then load it off the file system and into the embedded browser.

In theory, we could just point the embedded browser at the mobile site on the Web, but it's not ideal, for a number of reasons. First of all, the app would fail if the user's network connectivity were to be interrupted; however, this can be remedied with the offline functionality we looked at in Chapter 6. Furthermore, you might argue that with an application like StarTrackr, which relies on data from the network for all of its functionality, there's little point in having it work offline anyway. You'd be right, but by loading the application files from the device rather than the network, your users will at least be able to see the shell of your application instead of a blank page.

Beyond the ability to function offline, there's another good reason to load your HTML from the file system. Some app marketplaces—especially those that have to approve your application before they start selling it—frown on apps that can self-update, because they could circumvent the approval process. If you're loading all the HTML for your app from a remote site, you can update it and change its behavior at will, so chances are the app will be rejected.

Considerations

Sounds like a nice solution, eh? Well, it is! But you should be aware that there are a few potential downsides to PhoneGap, and some considerations you'll need to keep in mind if you do choose to go down this road.

Learn to Love Callbacks

As we've mentioned, PhoneGap's APIs provide you with a bridge to the native functionality of the device. But interfacing between a single-threaded JavaScript engine running in a browser and the native hardware of the device can be tricky. In order to prevent scripts from locking up, the PhoneGap API uses callbacks to return values from native calls.

Web developers will be accustomed to this way of working when it comes to asynchronous actions like Ajax calls, but it can get quite painful when performing actions like testing for the existence of a file. Normally, you'd do something like this:

```
if(File.exists('/tmp/filename.txt')) {
  // Do something
}
```

But PhoneGap works differently. You need to treat every call to a piece of device functionality the same way you would an Ajax request:

```
navigator.fileMgr.testFileExists('/tmp/filename.txt', function(exists) {
  if(exists) {
    // Do something
  }
});
```

Depending on your background (especially if you come from server-side programming), this can take some adapting to.

Debugging Is Painful

On the Web, we have Firebug. Native app developers have access to step-through debuggers and inspectors. PhoneGap has neither. All you really have to work with is `debug.log()`, a simple console logger. Couple that with the need to compile and reload the application in a simulator or real device, and testing a change can take a bit of time. It's definitely slower than the change/refresh test cycles you may be used to when working on the Web, so we need to be a bit smarter about how we change code and test it.

Generally, it's a good idea to start off testing in Firefox under Firebug, to achieve as much of the business logic as possible. Then, move to a WebKit-based desktop browser, and eventually a mobile browser, to debug any crazy CSS3 attributes and animations.

Finally, at the latest point possible, load it into PhoneGap and test it there. Unfortunately, your hands are kind of tied if you're using the built-in PhoneGap APIs, as the desktop and mobile browsers lack support for them. Hence, you'll need to test in PhoneGap from the get-go.

The Uncanny Valley

In robotics, researchers talk about the uncanny valley—and we mentioned it briefly back in Chapter 2. The idea is that, as they become more and more like humans, robots generally become more likeable to humans—up to a point. When they become very similar to humans, as close as they can be while still distinctly robot-like, they provoke a reaction of revulsion instead.

You can have a similar situation with browser-wrapped applications. Because it's up to the developer to emulate the styles of native widgets in CSS, it's entirely possible that it won't seem quite right, which users will notice. A perfect example is faking scroll bars in iOS and Android. Libraries like iScroll do an amazing job emulating the native scrollbars, but they're *not* the native scrollbars.

One way around this is to move away from copying native widgets, and simply build your own UI. You need to be careful, though: many of the UI paradigms in the native widget sets are there for a reason.

App Marketplaces Can Be Complicated

Deploying stuff on the Web is easy—you upload it to the server, and you're at the bar before you know it. Distributing applications via an app marketplace is more involved, especially if the app marketplace you're targeting needs to approve applications first.

First of all, you'll have to acquire a developer license, which will cost real money. They range from cheap to not-so-cheap, depending on the platform, and they'll most likely need to be renewed on a yearly basis. Next, you may have to sign the code that you submit, which requires you to mess around with certificates and keychains, and provisioning profiles.

Then, once the app has been uploaded, you have to play the waiting game (which, as we know, is infinitely less fun than Hungry Hungry Hippos) until your app is accepted or rejected. If it's the latter, you rinse and repeat. This approval process can also wreak havoc if you discover a major bug that needs fixing urgently; updates will need to be approved too.

Alternatives

It's worth mentioning that there are other systems that allow you to create native apps in a cross-platform way, without having to learn Java, C++, or Objective-C. We'll avoid going into great detail about them, as they generally just leverage JavaScript rather than being based on HTML and CSS, but they do offer a number of features that are unavailable in a web view.

One such system is Titanium,[3] which calls native functions via a JavaScript bridge. Rather than building a website, Titanium allows you to use native UI widgets, and is only marginally slower than writing apps in Objective-C or Java. At the moment, it only supports iOS and Android, although BlackBerry support is coming soon.

The advantage of such a system is that the user interface is native, so it will perform just like a real native application. It is also threaded, so you don't have to worry so much about callbacks, as methods can block execution. It has a similar problem to PhoneGap, though, in that debugging is very hard—even harder, actually. Because your code is run inside a JavaScript context, you lose the power of the step-by-step debugger, and you're without the ability to run your code in a desktop browser first.

Installing the SDKs

Before we can start using PhoneGap to build platform-native apps from our web app, we'll need to install all the development tools for those platforms. Remember that PhoneGap is essentially just a bridge; you still need to create the native app before you can plug your HTML and JavaScript into it.

If you're new to developing for platforms other than the Web, you might be familiar with the term **Software Development Kit** (usually abbreviated to SDK). An SDK is basically a set of libraries, compilers, simulators, and everything else you need to develop for a given platform.

Because PhoneGap applications run in a browser embedded in a native application, we'll still need to install the respective SDKs for each platform that we want to target. Before we start installing the SDKs, we need to ensure that the necessary development tools have been installed.

Operating Systems

While users of any operating system can easily build and deploy mobile websites or apps, native apps are a different story. Even though the code you'll be writing is still just HTML, CSS, and JavaScript, the need to install each platform's SDK can be limited by your operating system. Most notably, the iOS SDK is only available for Mac OS X. This means that if you're a Linux or Windows user, you'll be unable to develop native iPhone or iPad apps. In addition, the BlackBerry SDK is only available for Windows.

Fortunately, the Android and webOS SDKs are available for Windows, OS X, and Linux.

[3] http://www.appcelerator.com/

To install all the required software, we'll be using MacPorts on OS X and APT on Linux (though you're free to use any other package manager you're more comfortable with). There's really no equivalent to MacPorts or APT on Windows, so we'll have to scour the Internet for the extra pieces that we'll need.

For Linux users, you should start by installing the `build-essentials` package:

```
sudo apt-get install build-essential
```

The next two steps are specific to Mac OS X, so if you're a Windows or Linux user, skip ahead to the section called "Git". It's also worth noting here that you only need a platform's SDK if you plan to release your app on that platform. If all you want is an iOS and an Android app, for example, you can skip all the steps pertaining to installing the BlackBerry and webOS SDKs. Of course, the beauty of PhoneGap is that developing for these additional platforms will take up little extra work, so there's really no harm in giving them all a go.

Xcode (OS X)

The first step for OS X is to install Xcode. Xcode is Apple's tool set for building applications, both for the Mac desktop and for the iOS platform. It comes with a number of the tools we'll be needing, including the iOS SDK.

Before you can download it, though, you'll need to register as an Apple developer; fortunately, this is free. Head over to http://developer.apple.com/programs/register and click the **Get Started** button. If you already have an Apple ID (either from iTunes, MobileMe, or from making a purchase on the Apple Online Store), you can use that. However, if you plan on releasing the apps you build later on, you might want to create a new Apple ID anyway, just to separate your personal account from your business account.

When you've signed up and signed in, click on the **iOS** link under **Dev Centers**; then find the link to download the latest version of Xcode and the iOS SDK, towards the bottom of the page. It's a big download (over 4GB), so grab yourself a beverage while you wait.

Once it is done, open the **.dmg** file, and double-click the **Xcode and iOS SDK** file. Then click through the wizard—the defaults will be fine.

MacPorts (OS X)

One you've installed Xcode, you can install MacPorts, a great package manager for OS X. With MacPorts, it's easy to install UNIX utilities on OS X without having to scour the Internet for prebuilt packages.

Go to http://www.macports.org/ and hit the **Download** link. On the download page, grab the disk image (**.dmg**) for your version of OS X. As you did for Xcode, double-click the DMG file to open it, then double-click on the package file inside it. Click through the wizard—again, you can stick with the defaults.

Finally, open up a Terminal window, and run:

```
sudo port sync
```

This will download the latest package definitions from the Internet. It ensures that when you install a program via ports, it will be the latest and greatest. It's a good idea to run that command regularly (and when you know there's a new version of a package you're using).

Git

Git is a **revision control system** that was originally developed by the team that builds the Linux kernel. It has become particularly popular in the last few years.

If you are yet to become familiar with revision control systems, they consist of software that aims to simplify managing versions of the code you write. If you've ever made a copy of a directory and appended a number to it so you can make changes, you've essentially implemented your own very rudimentary revision control system. Of course, software systems like Git give you a lot more power and flexibility to keep track of files as they change, as well as be able to share those changes with your colleagues.

Another common revision control system is Subversion. We've chosen Git because several PhoneGap plugins (which enable support for other platforms) as well as the core PhoneGap source code use Git and are hosted on GitHub—a site that provides free hosting to open source Git repositories.

This step isn't strictly required, but it's easy enough so we'll do it anyway. We'll avoid touching on it much further, but it's worth taking the time to learn Git and using it to track changes to your projects.

Linux

To install Git on Linux, run this code in a terminal window:

```
sudo apt-get install git-core
```

OS X

On OS X, we can use MacPorts:

```
sudo port install git-core
```

Windows

Go to http://code.google.com/p/msysgit/downloads/list/ and download the latest version; then run the installer. When asked about "Adjusting your PATH environment," there are two options to pick from. You can either select "Git Bash only," which means you'll need to use the Git shell whenever you want to use Git, or pick "Run Git from the Windows Command Prompt." The latter is a better option for most people, as it means you can use Git from any shell system.

When asked about line endings, select "Checkout Windows-style, commit Unix-style line endings."

The Java Development Kit

A number of mobile platforms run Java applications, including Android and BlackBerry. As a result, if you want to build apps for these platforms, you will need a Java Development Kit (JDK), which you can download from http://java.oracle.com/. Find the Java SE Development Kit for your operating system, download, and run the executable. The default settings should be fine for what we need.

Eclipse

Setting up mobile projects in Java can be complicated, so to make life easier, let's install and set up Eclipse. Eclipse is a Java-based Integrated Development Environment (IDE) that hides away much of the XML and command-line wrangling that's required when you create, configure, and build programs in Java.

While it's certainly possible to do all this stuff by hand, it will take a lot longer—especially if you're new to Java. We'll be using Eclipse for the sole purpose of setting up and configuring our projects—just enough to get going—so you can still develop your app in whatever environment you're most comfortable with.

OS X and Windows users can get Eclipse at http://www.eclipse.org/downloads/, downloading Eclipse IDE for Java Developers.

Linux

Eclipse is available via `apt-get`:

```
sudo apt-get install eclipse
```

OS X

Extract the archive you downloaded into the **/eclipse** directory, and run it by double-clicking the Eclipse icon.

Windows

Unzip the ZIP file to **C:\Eclipse**, and add `C:\Eclipse` to your Path environment variable.

Editing the Windows PATH

To edit the PATH variable on Windows 7, open up the Control Panel. Select **System and Security**, then **System**; then click **Advanced system settings**. Finally, click the **Environment Variables...** button. Find the PATH variable in the **System variables** section, and hit **Edit**. Add your new paths to the end of the variable, preceding each one with a semi-colon (;).

To test that this has worked, open **cmd.exe** (just search for it from the Start menu) and type:

```
set path
```

Hit **Return**, and your full PATH variable will be output to the terminal.

Apache Ant

Ant is a Java-based **build tool**. A build tool is a way of creating tasks that we need to repeat. Generally, these tasks are centered around building our project; in languages like Java and Objective-C, the code is compiled (or built) into a form that the device can read before it's installed.

Generally these tasks are monotonous and error-prone, so using a build system takes away some of the pain. While Xcode includes build tools for Objective-C-based iOS development, for the Java-based platforms you'll want to have Ant installed.

Linux

Linux users can install Ant via `apt-get`:

```
sudo apt-get install ant
```

OS X

OS X users should already have Ant by this point, as it comes bundled with Xcode.

Windows

Go to http://ant.apache.org/ and select **Binary Distributions** under the **Download** section, and download the latest ZIP file. Unzip it somewhere easy (and without spaces), such as **C:\Ant**. Add that directory to your PATH, as described earlier.

Apple iOS SDK

The Apple iOS SDK comes with Xcode, so if you've installed that, you're ready to go! As we mentioned earlier, the iOS SDK is only available for OS X, so the only way to develop iPhone or iPad apps is to use a Mac.

Android SDK

Native apps for the Android platform are written in Java; as a result, the SDK will run on Windows, OSX, and Linux. You'll need Java Development Kit and Apache Ant installed, as described earlier.

Installing the Android SDK

Head over to the Android SDK page,[4] and select the installer relevant to your operating system. On Windows, you'll be provided with an **.exe** file that takes care of the installation; on OS X and Linux, all you need to do is download an archive, and extract it to a memorable location.

Unable to locate the Java SE Development Kit?

When running the Android SDK installer on Windows, you might run into an issue where it says it's unable to locate the JDK. If you've already installed the JDK, press **Back** and then **Next** again, and it should work.

Next, you'll want to add the **platform-tools** directory inside the SDK folder to your system path. On Windows, just follow the same method we used earlier.

On OS X and Linux, this can be done by adding a line to your shell profile (replacing the directory with the one where you extracted the SDK):

```
export PATH=$PATH:/home/user/android-sdk/platform-tools
```

Using the SDK Manager

The download from the Android website is just a skeleton of an SDK; it doesn't contain the actual SDK files, because we've yet to tell it which versions of the Android platform we want.

However, the download comes with a tool called the Android SDK and AVD Manager, which lets you manage the platform versions and install them from a simple interface.

On Windows, you'll be prompted to launch the Manager as soon as the SDK installation completes. By default, all the Android packages will be selected, so you can just accept them and the Manager will download and install everything you need.

On OS X and Linux, you can start the Manager by typing the `android` command into your terminal (assuming you added the SDK **tools** directory to your path.) Select **Available Packages** from the left panel, then open up **Android Repository** and tick all the platform versions you want to be able to test your app on. As you can see in Figure 7.1, we're installing all versions from 2.1 upwards. Click **Install Selected** to continue.

---

[4] http://developer.android.com/sdk/

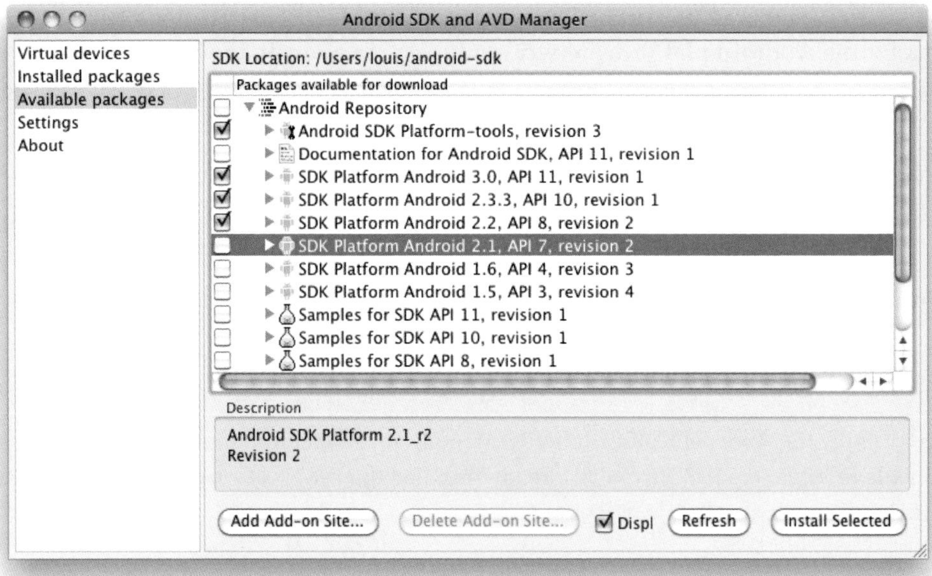

Figure 7.1. Installing various SDK versions using the Android SDK and AVD Manager

Installing the Eclipse Plugin

We're almost done now! The final step of our Android setup is to install an Eclipse plugin specifically made for creating Android applications. This part needs to be done across all operating systems. Fire up Eclipse, and click **Install New Software** in the **Help** menu.

By default, Eclipse is set up to check the Eclipse repositories for official plugins. We want to tell it to also look in a repository Google has provided in order to distribute the Android plugin. Add https://dl-ssl.google.com/android/eclipse/ in the **Work with** text field, hit **Add...**; then in the **Add Repository** dialog, give the repository a name (say, "Android"), and hit **OK**.

Check the box next to **Developer Tools**, and hit **Next**. Click **Next** again to confirm the selection. Select the option to accept the license agreement, and then press **Finish**. If you receive a warning about unsigned content, just hit **OK**. Remember to restart Eclipse when asked.

Now, we need to tell Eclipse where the Android SDK that we installed earlier lives, so select **Preferences** (on OS X this is in the **Eclipse** menu; on other platforms it will be under **Window**). Click on **Android** in the left panel, enter the path to your Android SDK, and click **Apply**. If all goes well, it should list all the Android platforms you can target.

Creating an Android Virtual Device

Finally, we need to create an Android Virtual Device (AVD). This is essentially an emulator that mimics the behavior of a set of hardware parameters combined with a specific version of the Android operating system. You can, and probably should, create a variety of emulators, each with a different screen size, resolution, layout, and configuration.

Don't Rely on Emulators

Running your app in an emulator will never be a substitute for installing it on real hardware. Emulators are just that: they *emulate* the behavior of a device as best they can, given they're running on a desktop with very different hardware. While the emulators allow you to simulate device features and events like orientation changes, geolocation, and even incoming calls, you should still test your apps on physical devices before releasing them to the public. Consider yourself warned!

You can create an AVD using the Android SDK and AVD Manager we used earlier. Instead of running it from the terminal, though, we can now run it directly from within Eclipse, as the Android plugin has added a shortcut to Eclipse's menu. Select **Android SDK and AVD Manager** from the **Window** menu. **Virtual Devices** should be selected, so hit the **New** button. Give the virtual device a name that you'll be able to recognize later, maybe using the version number such as "Android_2_3_2." You'll need to select which version of the Android platform you want to use; it makes sense to choose the lowest version you'll support first, and then test on higher versions once you know that it works.

There are a number of options for the specific hardware capabilities of the virtual device, but for most purposes the defaults are fine. Select a size for the SD Card (32MB will be more than enough for our purposes) and hit **Create AVD**.

That's it, you're now ready to develop for Android! You can see your AVD in operation by selecting it in the list and pressing **Start**. Be aware that the emulator takes a bit of time to start up, but once it's running, you'll have a simulated Android device sitting on your desktop, as Figure 7.2 shows.

Figure 7.2. An AVD running in the Android emulator

BlackBerry SDK

BlackBerry apps are also Java-based, so you'll need to install the JDK and Ant. You'll also require the BlackBerry WebWorks SDK. Unfortunately, the SDK will only run on Windows.

You can download the SDK from http://us.blackberry.com/developers/browserdev/widgetsdk.jsp. Fill in the form, and once you've grabbed the installer, run it and go through the wizard. The defaults should be fine.

WebOS SDK

On webOS, native widgets are written in HTML, CSS, and JavaScript. All PhoneGap offers is an abstraction that allows you to run the same code on webOS devices as you did on the other mobile platforms. Still, this can save you quite a bit of time, so it's worth looking at. Because there's no need to compile anything, installing the SDK is easy on OS X and Linux, and only slightly harder on Windows.

The webOS emulator runs in a VirtualBox virtual machine, so we'll need to install that. Make sure that you download version 3.2, though (at the time of writing, the emulator won't run on version 4.0). The download can be found at http://www.virtualbox.org/wiki/Download_Old_Builds_3_2.

Download the VirtualBox release for your operating system. Under Windows, the webOS SDK requires Java, so make sure you've installed that first.

Go to http://developer.palm.com/ and follow the links to the SDK download. This page contains complete installation instructions for Windows, Mac, and Ubuntu Linux. Once the installer has finished downloading, run it, choosing a complete install.

Make

Building PhoneGap applications for webOS requires the `make` command (another build tool), but this is unavailable on Windows. To install it, you'll need Cygwin, which is a set of libraries that allow many UNIX applications to run under Windows. Head to http://www.cygwin.com/ and click on **Install Cygwin**; then download and run **setup.exe**. Select the defaults in the wizard, and pick a mirror site close to your physical location—this will be much faster. In the package chooser, ensure you select `make`, as it isn't selected by default. You'll need to add **C:\cygwin\bin** to your PATH.

Cygwin

The Cygwin shell uses Unix-style directories, so the layout is a bit different from what you might expect. You can access the contents of your **C:** drive in the **/cygdrives/c** directory in Cygwin, so if you saved your PhoneGap directory in **C:\phonegap**, you'd access it with:

```
cd /cygdrives/c/phonegap
```

Installing PhoneGap

Whew! We've made it this far; now there's just a bit further to go. With the SDKs installed, we can set up PhoneGap itself. The first step for all platforms is to download the latest version of PhoneGap from http:/www.phonegap.com/, and unzip the file.

Xcode

In the PhoneGap folder that you just unzipped, open the **iOS** directory. Double-click **PhoneGapLibInstaller.pkg**, run through the wizard, and you're done! PhoneGap on Xcode is a little bit different from the other platforms, because it appears as a project type; this means you can start a new PhoneGap project with just one click.

Open up Xcode, and click **Create a new Xcode Project**. If the installation was successful, you should see **PhoneGap** under the **User Templates** section, as in Figure 7.3.

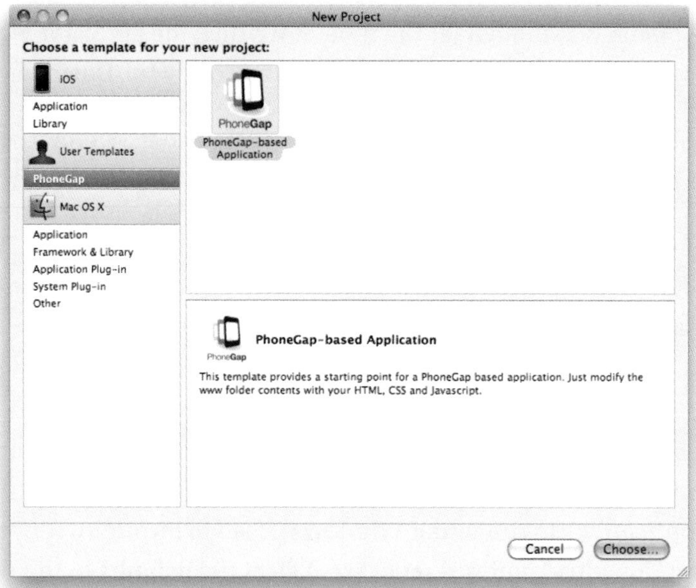

Figure 7.3. Once PhoneGap is installed, there will be a PhoneGap project available in Xcode

After selecting it, you'll be asked to create a project folder—we'll go with **startrackr**. PhoneGap creates a placeholder app for us, which we can run even though we're yet to add any code. Click **Build and Run**, and watch it load up in the simulator!

Error Running the Project

If clicking **Build and Run** fails to launch the simulator, check the drop-down menu in the top left of Xcode. If it says "Base SDK missing," choose **Edit Project Settings** from the **Project** menu; then select the **General** tab. Under **Base SDK for All Configurations**, select iOS Device 4.1 (or the latest version). Restart Xcode and your project should build and run successfully.

Android

The process of creating PhoneGap projects is a little less streamlined in Eclipse than in Xcode. You'll need to first create a new Android project, and then manually copy the relevant files across. To do this, start up Eclipse and select **New** > **Projects** from the **File** menu. Select **Android Project** from the wizard selector.

Give the project a name—let's call it StarTrackr—then select a build target. Pick the lowest version you want your app to be compatible with (we'll go with 2.1). Fill in the **Properties** section, by entering the application name and a package name. The package name must be unique, so the convention is to use a backwards domain name, such as `com.sitepoint.startrackr`. Finally, enter a value in **Create Activity**. Native Android apps are made up of activities, which are essentially just screens, or behaviors, of the app. In our case, everything is being handled in JavaScript, so we just need one activity to contain all our functionality. We can simply call it "App."

Click **Finish**. This will have created a new project in your workspace. Now to install PhoneGap, make two new directories in the project folder: **libs** and **assets/www**. This can be done directly from Eclipse's project explorer: right-click on the project, select **New** > **Folder**, and type the name of the folder.

Now, from the PhoneGap download's **Android** folder, copy **phonegap.jar** to the **libs** directory and **phonegap.js** into the **assets/www** directory. Refresh the Eclipse project (press **F5**) and the two files should appear in the project explorer.

For the moment, in order to prove that we have everything hooked up correctly, let's just drop a skeleton **index.html** into **assets/www**:

(excerpt)

```
<!doctype html>
<html>
  <head>
    <title>StarTrackr</title>
  </head>
<body>
<h1>It Works!</h1>
</body>
</html>
```

Next, open up **App.java** in the **src** directory and add `import com.phone.*;` under the other imports. Change the base class (right after `extends`) from `Activity` to `DroidGap` and replace `setContentView();` with `super.loadUrl("file:///android_asset/www/index.html");`, so your file looks like this:

(excerpt)

```
package com.sitepoint.startrackr;

import android.app.Activity;
import android.os.Bundle;
import com.phone.*;

public class App extends DroidGap {
  /** Called when the activity is first created. */
  @Override
  public void onCreate(Bundle savedInstanceState) {
    super.onCreate(savedInstanceState);
```

```
        super.loadUrl("file:///android_asset/www/index.html");
    }
}
```

Where's PhoneGap?

If Eclipse shows red squiggly lines under the `import` statement, you may have to manually tell Eclipse about the JAR file. To do this, right-click on the **libs** directory in the project explorer and select **Build Path** > **Configure Build Path…**. In the **Libraries** tab, click **Add JARs** and add **phonegap.jar** from the **libs** directory.

We're nearly there. The last step is to set permissions in the **AndroidManifest.xml** file. Open the file and insert the following code somewhere inside the `<manifest>` tags:

```
<supports-screens
  android:largeScreens="true"
  android:normalScreens="true"
  android:smallScreens="true"
  android:resizeable="true"
  android:anyDensity="true"
/>
<uses-permission android:name="android.permission.CAMERA" />
<uses-permission android:name="android.permission.VIBRATE" />
<uses-permission android:name="android.permission.ACCESS_COARSE_LOCATION" />
<uses-permission android:name="android.permission.ACCESS_FINE_LOCATION" />
<uses-permission android:name="android.permission.ACCESS_LOCATION_EXTRA_COMMANDS"
➥/>
<uses-permission android:name="android.permission.READ_PHONE_STATE" />
<uses-permission android:name="android.permission.INTERNET" />
<uses-permission android:name="android.permission.RECEIVE_SMS" />
<uses-permission android:name="android.permission.RECORD_AUDIO" />
<uses-permission android:name="android.permission.MODIFY_AUDIO_SETTINGS" />
<uses-permission android:name="android.permission.READ_CONTACTS" />
<uses-permission android:name="android.permission.WRITE_CONTACTS" />
<uses-permission android:name="android.permission.WRITE_EXTERNAL_STORAGE" />
<uses-permission android:name="android.permission.ACCESS_NETWORK_STATE" />
```

Those `<uses-permission>` tags are used to specify which permissions your app requires. The user will be prompted with them before they install your app. It's best to limit the list to only those permissions that you require, otherwise users can become suspicious. PhoneGap requires that you include the `READ_PHONE_STATE` and `INTERNET` permissions; all the others are optional, and fairly self-explanatory.

Find the `<activity>` tag, and make sure it has the following attribute: `android:configChanges="orientation|keyboardHidden"`. This tells the phone not to reload **index.html** when the phone is rotated or when the keyboard is hidden—PhoneGap takes care of this for us.

Now the moment you've been waiting for! Let's run it in the simulator. Right-click the project name in the left panel, find **Run As**, and click **Android App**. The emulator can take a moment to boot, so be patient.

BlackBerry

We don't need to use Eclipse for BlackBerry, as we can create a new project using an Ant build file. We'll go through importing the resulting project into Eclipse at the end.

Open up a console (**cmd.exe**), and navigate to the folder that was created when we unzipped the PhoneGap ZIP file:

```
cd C:\phonegap\BlackBerry\WebWorks
```

Next, use Ant to create the new project (this will create the project in **C:\Projects**):

```
mkdir c:\Projects
ant create -Dproject.path="C:\Projects\startracker"
```

You may need to update the path to the BlackBerry WebWorks Packager in **project.properties**. If the `ant` command to build your project fails, make sure it's pointing to the correct directory.

To build your project:

```
ant build
```

And to run it in the simulator:

```
ant load-simulator
```

Access Denied

If the simulator fails, citing an Access Denied error, try running **cmd.exe** as an administrator.

WebOS

The PhoneGap package we downloaded earlier has a **webOS** directory that includes a **Makefile**—this will compile and deploy a project for us. There's also a skeleton app that's ready to go, so we'll run that now to make sure everything is set up correctly.

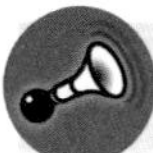

Windows

Windows users will need to slightly modify the **Makefile**, as batch files on Windows require a `.bat` extension. Open the **Makefile** in your favorite text editor, find all the instances of `palm-install`, `palm-launch`, and `palm-package`, and add `.bat` at the end. Also note that you will need to run the Cygwin shell to run `make`.

First, we need to run the emulator, so open a terminal and run:

```
palm-emulator
```

On Windows:

```
palm-emulator.bat
```

Again, in your terminal, navigate to the PhoneGap webOS directory and run `make` (change the directory depending on your setup):

```
cd ~/Downloads/phonegap/webOS
make
```

Review

As we've seen, using a system like PhoneGap is an easy way to convert your mobile web applications into real applications that you can sell in the app marketplace. If you're a web developer, leveraging PhoneGap means you can dive into developing native apps for mobile platforms without needing to learn any new programming languages. You can use all your existing knowledge of JavaScript and CSS and carry it over into the native world.

By now we should have our development environment set up, and we now know how to set up PhoneGap projects for a number of different platforms. Next, we'll look at what the PhoneGap API will allow us to do, and start taking the web app code and converting it into an installable application.

Chapter 8

Making Our Application Native

So, we've installed PhoneGap and all the development tools required to build native applications for our target platforms. Now it's time to actually take our web app—which up until now has been happily sitting on a web server—and set it loose in the native environment. We've written the app as a single HTML page that uses Ajax to talk to a server; this has allowed us to make smooth transitions between the pages. But building the app this way is also going to help us out as we move over to PhoneGap.

The Anatomy of a PhoneGap Application

As we saw in the last chapter, PhoneGap creates a skeleton native app for your platform of choice. Inside that app's folder structure is a **www** directory. PhoneGap will look for the **index.html** file in this directory, load it into the embedded browser, and render and display it on the screen—just like a regular HTML page.

Now is a good time to explain a fundamental difference between a real web server and what's happening in a PhoneGap application. Rather than making a request to an external web server, as is usually the case with web pages, the browser is loading the file from the local file system; in other words, it's the equivalent of double-clicking the HTML file from a folder on your desktop to open it in your browser. You'll have noticed when you do this that the URL starts with file:// rather than http://, which is how we know that we've loaded the file locally rather than from the server. This is exactly what PhoneGap does as well.

So, how does this affect us? Loading HTML files from the file system has some key pros and cons that you need to think about when using PhoneGap. Firstly, and most importantly, there are no server-side languages like PHP or Rails to talk to a database, or render header and footer templates, or any of what you might be accustomed to doing when building websites and web applications. The page that's displayed must be plain old static HTML. Of course, you can use JavaScript to perform any dynamic functions you require, and you can talk to your web server via Ajax if you need to retrieve information from a database.

This brings us to a fairly major advantage of loading files from the local file system, though: you're able to make Ajax requests to any server. Earlier in the book, we ran up against the cross-domain security problem that occurs when making Ajax requests from the file system on a desktop browser. However, this problem doesn't affect PhoneGap, so you can make Ajax calls to any domain to your heart's content.

Enough dillydallying, let's take our HTML files and drop them into our PhoneGap app. The first step is to create a new project for your desired hardware. If you followed along with the previous chapter, you'll already have done this. Next, we need to copy all the HTML, JavaScript, and CSS files that we created into the **www** directory of our project. Make sure the main HTML file is named **index.html**, and that you're using relative file paths for all the CSS and images; you can organize the files into folders if you like, as long as they sit below the **www** directory.

Relative versus Absolute

When you reference stylesheets, images, or JavaScript files from an HTML file in a website or web application, you refer to them either as relative to the root of the site (absolute paths), or as relative to the directory the HTML file sits in (relative paths). Because PhoneGap loads the HTML from the file system, there's no root directory, so you'll need to use relative paths; this means that URLs to your resources should not begin with a slash (/).

Now that your files have been copied over, fire up the simulator the same way we did when testing the empty app in the last chapter. If all goes well, you should see your application running in the simulator!

After you clean up the balloons and streamers, there are still a few bits and pieces we need to polish up before we can submit the app to the marketplaces, buy a Learjet, and wait for the royalty checks to flood in.

If you tested your app on an iOS emulator from Xcode, and were watching carefully as the app loaded, you'll have noticed that it flashed up a PhoneGap splash screen, which won't make our client too happy. The homescreen icon (on all platforms) is equally uninspiring, and the app name is barely user-friendly. Thankfully, we are just a couple of simple configuration-file tweaks away from dressing up our app to be indistinguishable from its native brethren.

Icons, Splash Screens, and Names

The base app that PhoneGap sets up for each platform has a few defaults, which are meant to be replaced before you launch your app. Let's go through the process of customizing our app, which differs slightly for each of the platforms we're targeting.

iOS

Splash screens and icons for iOS come in a variety of forms, for the iPhone 3, iPhone 4 (with the higher-resolution Retina display), and iPad. Hence, before diving in, you should decide whether you want to make your app available for the iPad. Our app certainly isn't optimized for a larger screen—it's just a single column list that we designed with small, handheld screens in mind. That said, we've been careful to use ems and percentages for the dimensions of our components, so the app is perfectly capable of stretching to iPad size. To better inform our decision, let's start by testing out our app in an iPad simulator to see how it holds up.

To simulate your app in an iPad, select **iPad simulator** from the menu in the top left of the Xcode window, as shown in Figure 8.1.

Figure 8.1. Pick the device you want to simulate

Now, click **Build and Run** to launch the iPad simulator. The results, shown in Figure 8.2, are less than inspiring.

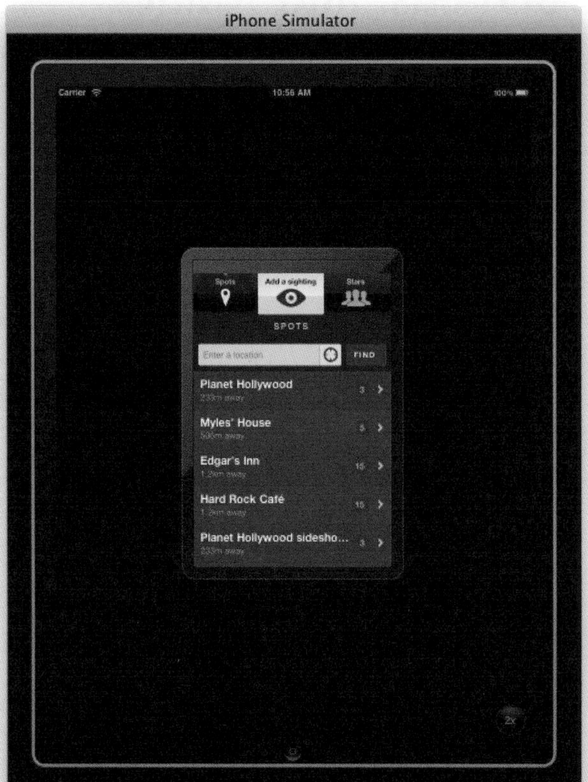

Figure 8.2. Uh-oh. Our app shows up in an iPhone-size window in the middle of the iPad's screen

What went wrong here? By default, the app created by PhoneGap is targeted specifically at the iPhone. In order to prevent apps from breaking that were never designed with the iPad in mind, the iPad runs iPhone apps in an iPhone-sized window in the middle of the screen. In our case, however, we've been careful to make our app stretchy, in order for it to work at any screen size. So, we want to see it behaving like a real iPad app.

To make this happen, choose **Edit Project Settings** from Xcode's **Project** menu. Select the **Build** tab, then under **Deployment**, find the entry for **Targeted Device Family**. **iPhone** will be selected by default, so change this to **iPhone/iPad**. Now when you relaunch your app in the iPad simulator, it will display in full screen, as shown in Figure 8.3.

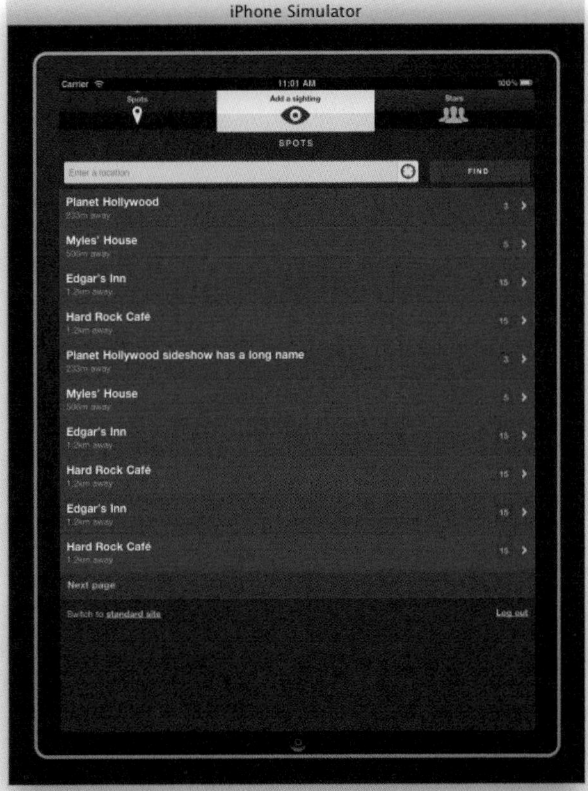

Figure 8.3. Our app is now running full screen on the iPad simulator

This may not be optimal, but it's certainly better looking than the puny little iPhone window we had before. If we really wanted to, we could design an iPad-specific version of our app that puts all that screen real estate to better use. But that's a project for another day.

Now that we've sorted out the iPad version, let's start working on our splash screens and icons. iPhone splash screens come in two different flavors, regular and double size—and the iPad has both portrait and landscape splash screens.

Application Screenshot

As we discussed in Chapter 3, iPhone splash screens were originally designed to have a screenshot of the application in an initial state. Unless there are specific branding requirements for the app, this is probably the best approach, as it makes the app appear to load more quickly.

Here are the file names and sizes that are required:

- **Default.png**, 320×480px, for the standard iPhone display

- **Default@2x.png**, 640×960, for the iPhone 4's Retina display
- **Default-Portrait.png**, 768×1004, for the iPad in portrait orientation
- **Default-Landscape.png**, 1024×748, for the iPad in landscape orientation

Next we should tackle the icon. The standard iPhone home screen icon needs to be 57×57, and Retina display icons 114×114. The iPad's icon, meanwhile, should be 72×72px. Lucky for us, we created icons matching these dimensions back in Chapter 2 when we created homescreen icons for our web app. Here are the filenames required:

- **icon.png**, 57×57px
- **icon-72.png**, 72×72px
- **icon@2x.png**, 114×114px

Once you've created these new graphics, you need to add them to the **Resources** section of Xcode. To do this, simply drag the new files from the Finder into the Resources directory of your projects in Xcode. You'll be asked how you'd like to copy the files; just click **Add** as the defaults are fine. At this point, if you fire up the simulator and return to the home screen, you'll see a nice, shiny icon for your app.

Troubleshooting

Xcode caches resources like icons to speed up the **Build and Run** operation. If, after changing your icon files, they're failing to show up in the simulator, try selecting **Clean All Targets** from the **Build** menu.

Finally, we need to tweak the app name that appears on the home screen. In the Resources section of the project, find the **PLIST file** for your app. It will be named after the app, so in our case it's **startrackr-Info.plist.** Click to open it, and scroll down until you find the **Bundle Display Name** setting. Change it to "StarTrackr!" (or whatever name you'd like your users to see). There is a limit to how many characters you can enter, although it's a soft limit; the font used on the home screen is a variable width, meaning that each letter has a different width. A general rule is 12 to 15 characters, but it will be trial and error.

To test your app on a Retina display, select **Hardware** > **Device** > **iPhone 4** from the simulator menu. You'll now see your higher resolution icon in action!

iPhone 4

For some reason, the Retina display simulator looks like an iPad. Don't ask us why.

Android

Android apps are without a default splash screen, so we'll ignore that issue for the moment, but we still need to sort out the icon and application name.

There are four screen densities that we need to consider when creating icons for Android devices: Low (ldpi), Medium (mdpi), High (hdpi), and Extra High Density (xhdpi), each requiring a different icon size.

When talking about screen resolutions, it isn't as simple as thinking about the number of pixels a screen has; you need to think about the physical dimensions of the screen as well. For example, you can have two devices that are both 480×800px, but one device might have a 3×5" display, and another might have 2×3.3" screen. Both devices display the same number of pixels, but the larger device's screen is 1.5 times the size of the other.

To make sure the icons and text are big enough to read, Android categorizes these two devices differently. The 3×5" device would be considered a medium density device, having 160 dots per inch, whereas the 2×3.3" device is a high density device, as it packs in 240 dots per inch.

So how does Android categorize all the different screen sizes and resolutions? Well, there's really no hard and fast set of rules, but the end result is that we need to make differently sized icons—four of them—based on the screen density:

- low density (120 dpi) 36x36
- medium density (160 dpi) 48x48
- high density (240 dpi) 72x72
- extra high density (320 dpi) 96x96

Each icon is stored in the **res** directory (for "resources") in another folder specific to the density: **drawable-ldpi**, **drawable-mdpi**, **drawable-hdpi**, or **drawable-xhdpi**.

To change the app's name, we simply tweak a value in an XML file. In the **res/values** directory, there's a file called **strings.xml**. Open up this file (just double-click it if you're using Eclipse), and look for the `app_name` key. Change the value to `StarTrackr!` (or whatever name you'd like your users to see for your app) and save the file.

BlackBerry

BlackBerry apps have both a splash screen and an icon—in fact, they have two icons, a regular and a highlighted version (like a mouseover hover state). If you thought having to do four different icon sizes for Android was bad enough, just about every BlackBerry device has a different screen size and icon size. And while it would have been easier had they given us the option to create multiple icons for different sizes, a BlackBerry app can only have one icon associated with it. The BlackBerry will analyse the image to work out the real height and width of it (after cropping out any transparent border). Developers have managed to come up with some numbers that, while seeming like voodoo, work in the widest range of cases.

For BlackBerry 6 devices, the most recent version, the magic number seems to be 68×68px, with most of the icon being inside a 49×49px box in the center of the image. You can have bits that protrude beyond that box, but not by more than 5px. The easiest way to do this in Photoshop is to create a 49×49px icon, and then increase the canvas size up to 68×68. In addition, make sure you save the image out as a PNG with transparency.

The loading screen uses a similar system. Thankfully, it's overlaid on a black background, so we can use transparencies for a decent result. The general rule here is a 200×200 full transparency PNG.

Both icons and the loading screen need to be saved in the **www/resources** directory of your project. PhoneGap will have put some default files in there for you, so if you see an **icon.png**, **icon_hover.png**, and **loading_foreground.png** file, you're in the right place.

To update the app name, open the **config.xml** that's in the **www** directory, and change the value associated with the `name` key.

WebOS

WebOS uses two icons—one for the home screen and one as part of the app loader splash screen. The home screen icon is 64×64, but like the BlackBerry requires a transparent border, so you have an effective working area of 56×56. The extra 4 pixels allows the phone to compensate for slightly different-sized screens. By default, this icon file lives in the **img** directory inside **www**, and is (once again) a transparent PNG.

PhoneGap applications don't reference the larger splash icon or custom splash image by default—but we're just one small configuration tweak away from sorting that out. First of all, generate a 256×256 version of your app icon, and save it in the **www/img** directory (let's call it **icon-256x256.png**). You might also want to create a separate background image that's 320×480px, and save it in the **www/img** directory as well (we'll call that one **splashscreen-background.png**).

Finally, open the **appinfo.json** file that's in the **www** directory and add these keys:

```
"splashicon": "img/icon-256x256.png",
"slashBackground": "img/splashscreen-background.png"
```

You can also change the name of your application here by changing the value associated with the `"title"` key.

Time to Tweak

So the app is finished, then? Well, almost. There are a few more steps we can take to minimize any snags during the app marketplace approval process. We want to disguise the fact that our app is really a web page as much as possible—as much for our own credibility than anything else—so we need to make some changes.

PhoneGap JavaScript Helpers

As we discussed in the last chapter, PhoneGap acts as a bridge, providing an API you can access via JavaScript to interface with the device's hardware. These JavaScript methods are made available by the **phonegap.js** file (or **phonegap-*version*.js**), which is also found in the **www** directory. In order to make use of this functionality in your app, you need to include this file in your HTML with a `<script>` tag:

```
<script src="phonegap.0.9.5.min.js"></script>
```

Are we ready?

Because it can take some time for an application to be completely initialized when it is first started, it's quite possible that our JavaScript code could try to access some hardware functionality before it's ready—at which point it falls in a heap. In the same way that we can wait for `window.onload` when dealing with a regular browser, PhoneGap gives us an an event called `deviceready`, which is fired when the app has finished its initialization sequence.

This event is accessed just like any other event in JavaScript. Let's move our app initialization code into a `deviceready` event handler:

```
function onDeviceReady() {
  loadPage("spots.html", "spots");
  $("#tab-bar a").click("click", function(e){
    e.preventDefault();
    var url = e.currentTarget;
    loadPage(url, $(this).attr("data-load"));
  });
  ⋮
}

document.addEventListener("deviceready", onDeviceReady, false);
```

We need to wait for this event to fire before we try to access any of the custom JavaScript functions that PhoneGap gives us. As such, you shouldn't consider your application loaded until this event has fired.

Alerts

Using JavaScript alert boxes is a really simple way to display messages or to get basic inputs from a user. On our devices they look fairly close to the message boxes you would see from a native app, except for a few small giveaways. On the iPhone, the file name of the web page you're looking at is displayed in the title, so in our case it would always say **index.html**. On Android, the title is simply "Alert." We're also stuck with the default **OK** button. Thankfully, PhoneGap exposes a JavaScript API that lets us create an alert with a custom title and button. The method is called `navigator.notification.alert()`, and takes up to four parameters:

```
navigator.notification.alert(message, alertCallback, [title], [button])
```

The first parameter, *`message`*, is the message we want to display to the user. The second is a function that will be called when the alert message is dismissed. This is a bit different from the standard `alert()` method from JavaScript, which stops execution of the code until the alert box is dismissed. It can be a bit of a trap if you're used to the way JavaScript usually deals with the alert box.

The third parameter is the title of the alert box, and the final parameter is the label on the button that the user clicks:

```
$("#tab-bar li").bind(touchEndEvent, function(){
  navigator.notification.alert("Coming soon!", function() {}, "Not ready yet…",
➥"No problem");
});
```

PhoneGap also provides three other methods on the `navigator.notification` object: `confirm()`, `beep()`, and `vibrate()`. `confirm()` works like the JavaScript equivalent: it provides a dialog box with two options. `beep()` and `vibrate()`. These allow you to cause the device to beep or vibrate respectively, which can be useful for apps that have the ability to check for incoming messages, for example. For a full breakdown of these methods and how to use them, have a look at the Notification section in the PhoneGap documentation.[1]

Network Checks

Because our app talks to our web server via Ajax, it requires a network connection to work. While we can deal with an intermittent or lost connection on a request-by-request basis, we won't make it that far if the user has turned off their device's networking capabilities. Most smartphones these days have both WiFi and cellular data connections, but that doesn't mean that all users will have them enabled. Some users will turn off WiFi to conserve battery power, while others may be without a data plan (or they might be using a device like an iPod Touch, which lacks cellular data capabilities altogether).

---

[1] http://docs.phonegap.com/phonegap_notification_notification.md.html

While often it's of little interest to us which network our users are connected to, some applications might want to force a WiFi connection if they're planning on downloading a lot of data. Others might require a 3G connection, so we need a way of checking whether each of these connection types is enabled. If they aren't, we should warn the user that they need to enable them to continue.

To do this, we can use the `navigator.network.isReachable()` function. The function takes three parameters: a URL to ping, a callback function, and, optionally, an options hash. Here's an example:

```
function checkNetwork(reachability) {

}
navigator.network.isReachable('http://www.sitepoint.com', checkNetwork);
```

The URL to ping is an easy one: simply put the URL of the website from which you intend to load data. This can either be an IP address or a hostname, although using a hostname is probably a better idea. If you do use an IP address, set the `isIpAddress` option in the options hash to true:

```
navigator.network.isReachable('http://184.73.225.31', checkNetwork,
➥{ isIpAddress: true });
```

The callback will be passed a single object; unfortunately, it's impossible to reliably predict what that object will look like. As such, you need to check it for a `code` property before doing anything else. Either the object itself or its code property will contain one of three constants:

- `NetworkStatus.NOT_REACHABLE`
- `NetworkStatus.REACHABLE_VIA_CARRIER_DATA_NETWORK`
- `NetworkStatus.REACHABLE_VIA_WIFI_NETWORK`

Here's how you'd use those constants in your code in order to react to the network state:

```
function checkNetwork(reachability) {
  var networkState = reachability.code || reachability;

  if networkState == NetworkStatus.NOT_REACHABLE {
    // no network
  }
  else if networkState == NetworkStatus.REACHABLE_VIA_CARRIER_DATA_NETWORK {
    // cellular data
  }
  else if networkState == NetworkStatus.REACHABLE_VIA_WIFI_NETWORK {
    // wifi data
  }
```

```
}

navigator.network.isReachable('phonegap.com', checkNetwork);
```

This should be one of the very first tasks we perform in our app (after checking that the device is ready), because we rely on network connectivity so heavily. If there's no connection, we can just pop up a notification warning the user that they won't be able to successfully track celebrities without turning on at least one of their network interfaces.

Geolocation, Storage, and Device Orientation

We've already seen that our app can use the browser's built-in Geolocation API, and we can store values in a database using Web SQL. On some supporting browsers, we're also able to access the phone's accelerometer to implement clever functionality, such as shake gestures. However, not all browsers on the phones and devices that PhoneGap supports implement these APIs. The good news is that PhoneGap is clever about this: on phones with supporting browsers, PhoneGap will use those built-in W3C APIs, while on phones that don't, it will fall back to the device's native interface.

The best part is that PhoneGap's APIs use the same syntax as the W3C ones, so if you've built your app to leverage these APIs in the browser, it's all ready to go with PhoneGap.

Hardware Buttons

While touch screens are extremely popular in the smartphone world, some manufacturers do add a couple of hardware buttons, like Menu and Back buttons, to their devices. For a real feeling of nativeness, we should capture the events that are fired by these buttons, and perform an appropriate function.

The iPhone and Palm Pre don't have any hardware buttons that we're allowed to do anything with, so you can safely ignore this section if you're only interested in targeting iOS or webOS. Android phones, however, do have a couple of hardware buttons—four of them, in fact: Home, Menu, Back, and Search. (In reality, this varies somewhat from one device manufacturer to another, but for the majority of Android devices, those four will be present).

The buttons are fairly self-explanatory. The home button takes you back to the phone's home screen, so don't mess with this one. The other three buttons are fair game, though, and if we want our users to feel comfortable using our app, we should probably make use of them.

Back

The Back button takes your application back a screen. When running our app in the browser, this behaves like a browser's Back button, which we've already set up our app to handle using the History API. However, in a native Android app, the Back button moves to the previous "activity." In our case, since our whole application is embedded in a single web view component, that's going to mean exiting the app—less than an ideal experience for our users!

PhoneGap provides a `backbutton` event that we can capture. We'll use it to trigger the `back()` method of the browser's history, which in turn will cause the `popstate` event to fire. Fortunately, our app has already been built to handle this gracefully:

```
document.addEventListener('backbutton', function(e) {
  window.history.back();
});
```

Because we've already done the work of wiring up the History API with our app's functionality (in Chapter 5), that's all we need to do to make the device's Back button working as intended.

PhoneGap on BlackBerry is yet to abstract the hardware Back button, but luckily the WebWorks SDK provides a JavaScript function that fires a callback when the Back button is pressed. To enable it, open up **config.xml** and add the following key:

```
<feature id="blackberry.system.event" version="1.0.0" />
```

In your application code, you'd then use the following:

```
blackberry.system.event.onHardwareKey(blackberry.system.event.KEY_BACK,
➥function() {
  window.history.back();
});
```

Menu

The Menu button is a bit like the right button on your mouse: it's used to open up a context menu relating to the screen you're currently on. It's a handy way of giving the user additional options without cluttering the user interface all the time. Listening for the Menu button click is just as simple as the Back button. You just drop in the following code:

```
document.addEventListener('menuKeyDown', function(e) {
  showMenu();
});
```

A really simple way to track menus on different screens is to include a hidden `div` on every screen, which you can find using a `class` name (say … `menu`); then, when you receive a `menuKeyDown` event, you can slide the `div` into view. On Android devices, menus are usually closed by pressing the Back button, so you should push another state onto the History stack when you display a menu—that way everything will work as the user expects.

Search

The Search button allows your users to search inside your app, but again, it tends to be context-specific. For example, if you're in the contacts app, it will search through your contacts. Handling the Search button is the same as the Menu button—you just have to listen for a different event:

```
document.addEventListener('searchKeyDown', function(e) {
  showSearch();
});
```

If your app has a search page or search screen, it's definitely worth hooking it up to the Search button when you're making an Android version. It's easy enough to do, and your users won't be frustrated by pressing the Back button in an app they *know* has search functionality, only to see nothing happen. Depending on the app you're building, you might have one search function for your entire app, or a search function specific to each screen.

Paparazzi—Accessing the Camera

So far, we've seen how to access an impressive range of device functionality from our web app—and, consequently, our PhoneGap apps. As we've already seen, PhoneGap is clever in its handling of HTML5 APIs: it will use the API if the browser supports it, but fall back to direct calls to the device's hardware if not. The magic doesn't stop there, however. PhoneGap has all the system access of any other native app, and can pass that access along to your app via a set of JavaScript APIs.

The hardware you can access via PhoneGap varies between platforms, and not all of it will be relevant to every app. We'll focus on one particularly useful example here, but the same concepts apply to any part of the API you want to use. For a full list of all the available APIs, and examples of how to use them, be sure to check out the PhoneGap documentation.[2]

The most relevant piece of hardware to our StarTrackr app, after the GPS of course, is the camera. The vast majority of smartphones come with built-in cameras. Wouldn't it be cool if users could snap pictures of stars when they catch a glimpse of them out on the street? They could then upload the photo and GPS coordinates straight to our servers, earning them valuable street cred. Lucky for us, PhoneGap has a very simple API that lets you talk to the camera from within your app.

File Input

You might be wondering why we aren't simply using the `file` input type? Most phones have some sort of photo gallery, so surely users could just select and upload a photo they've taken already? Nope! Well, not on iPhone at least—iOS lacks support for file inputs. Android 2.2 or greater fares a little better, bringing up a gallery dialog. But all told, support is flaky at best, so it's best to use the native APIs here.

---

[2] http://docs.phonegap.com/

The magic function we want is:

```
navigator.camera.getPicture(cameraSuccess, cameraError, { cameraOptions })
```

It's extremely simple to use: the first parameter is a callback function that will be called if the camera returns an image, or if users select an image from their gallery. The second parameter is another callback function that will be called if there's an error; and the final parameter is a set of options.

The options parameter is a JavaScript object, which can contain the following attributes: `quality`, `destinationType`, `sourceType`, and `allowEdit`.

Because we're taking photographs, the default image format is JPEG. When you create a JPEG, you can choose to set the quality of the image; the higher the number, the sharper the image, but the bigger the image file size becomes. The size of the image becomes important on mobile devices, as they can have both memory and bandwidth limitations, so it's well worth tweaking the quality. Quality can be a number between 0 and 100. The PhoneGap team recommends keeping the quality of iPhone photographs to less than 50, to avoid memory errors. It should be noted that webOS and BlackBerry both outright ignore the `quality` parameter, so if you're only targeting those devices, you can safely leave this option off.

There are two "places" you can put the resulting image, determined by the `destinationType`: the file system, or into a Base64 encoded string. Your choice depends on whether you need to save the image locally or not; if you're just going to display it, use a Base64 encoded string by setting `destinationType` to `Camera.DestinationType.DATA_URL`. If you plan on saving the file to the device's file system, use `Camera.DestinationType.FILE_URL`.

What is Base64?

Base64 encoding translates each byte of a file into one of 64 different ASCII characters (plain old text), which means we can store it and read it like any other string.

Generally, when dealing with the contents of files in PhoneGap, we have to deal with Base64 encoding. Why's that? Well, in HTML there are two ways to import an asset (like an image file): as a URL or as a Base64 encoded string. The former mode is what you're used to:

```
<img src="myimage.jpg" alt="an image from a URL" />
```

But you can also provide the image source in the form of a data: URL, in which you provide a Base64 encoded string:

```
<img src="data:image/jpeg;base64,AAABAYA=\n" alt="This is valid" />
```

The last important option is sourceType, which allows you to tell the device where to pull the photo from. There are three choices: the photo library, the camera, and the saved photo album. The first and last are libraries of existing photos, and are quite similar (so similar in fact, that on Android, they're actually the same thing). It should be noted that BlackBerrys and webOS ignore this setting completely.

The three constants you use to provide the value of sourceType are:

- Camera.PictureSourceType.PHOTOLIBRARY
- Camera.PictureSourceType.CAMERA
- Camera.PictureSourceType.SAVEDPHOTOALBUM

Let's look at the two callbacks, which are far less complex.

The *cameraError* callback simply returns an error message string, which you would more than likely display in an error dialog. The *cameraSuccess* callback will return your Base64-encoded string, or a file URL, depending on what you asked for as your destinationType.

Now that we're familiar with the API, let's see what it looks like when put into practice in an app:

ch8/www/javascripts/app.js *(excerpt)*

```
document.addEventListener("deviceready", function() {
  $('#photo a').click(function() {
    navigator.camera.getPicture(function(data) {
      console.log('Image saved');
      $('#photo-viewer').html('<img src="data:image/jpeg;base64,' + data
➥+ '" alt="">');
    }, function(str) {
      navigator.notifications.alert(str, 'Error');
    }, {
      destinationType: Camera.DestinationType.DATA_URL,
      allowEdit: false,
      quality: 50
    });
  });
}, false);
```

We've specified that we want our photo as a Base64 string, and set the quality to 50. The getPicture() method is attached to a link in our interface, and if the picture's returned successfully, we use our Base64 string in an <img> tag to display the image on the screen.

Running for Real

Right, now we're on the home stretch. Our application is finished and ready to roll on all our target platforms, and the client is happy with the result. At the end of this chapter, we'll be looking at how we can submit our app to the various app marketplaces. But before we do that, we should try running our application on a real device (assuming you have one handy). Simulators are great for fiddling with the app's functionality and interface, but there's no substitute for testing on real hardware. For instance, the iPhone simulator tends to run much faster than real iPhones, whereas the Android simulator is much slower than real Android phones.

For the most part, testing on a physical device isn't that much more difficult than testing on a simulator. Let's walk through the required steps for each platform.

iOS

On iOS, there are a few hoops that need to be jumped through before you can run your app on a physical device. All code that runs on an iPhone needs to be signed with a certificate first, and you have to be a paid up Apple developer to acquire a developer certificate. To register, go to https://developer.apple.com/programs/ios/ and follow the instructions.

Once you're enrolled, log in to the Apple Developer Center and click on **iOS Provisioning Portal**; then follow the step-by-step instructions. First of all, create and sign a developer certificate. Click on **Certificates**, and then the **How To** tab. Once you've created and uploaded your certificate, make sure you save it in a safe place; otherwise, you'll need to repeat the process, re-signing your apps in order to test them.

To stop developers from circumnavigating the App Store, Apple limits the number of devices that you can use for development to 100 per year—more than enough for most development purposes. As such, you need to register each device that you're going to test with. Click the **Devices** link and hit the **How To** for instructions.

Device Updates

Every time you install an iOS update on your iPhone or iPad via iTunes, you'll need to make sure you install the corresponding SDK from the Apple developer site. Thankfully, new SDKs are generally available before the release of a new version of iOS, so you can test your software before the rest of the world gets to play.

Next up, you need to create an App ID. This is a unique ID that Apple uses to identify your application. Once created, it's unable to be changed or deleted, so pick a name that's meaningful from the outset. The App ID is made up of two parts: the bundle seed and bundle identifier. Generally, you'll want to produce a new bundle seed for each application you create, unless you plan on building a suite of applications that can share keychain information. The recommended way to build the bundle identifier is to use a reverse domain, where the last element is your app name; so in our example, we would use com.sitepoint.startrackr.

Once you've submitted the App ID, Apple will generate a provisioning profile, which is what tells Xcode to allow you to have permissions to install the app on your device. Click the provisioning link, then click **New Profile**. Add a profile name (we can use startrackr), and select the following: the certificate you uploaded before (there should only be one at this stage anyway), the startrackr app, and all the devices you wish to test the app on. Once you submit and save the provisioning profile, you can download it. Double-click the downloaded file, and it should fire up the Xcode organizer. Include it in your list of provisioning profiles.

We're nearly there! Open up the startrackr app in Xcode, and find the **startrackr-Info.plist** configuration file that we edited earlier. You need to find the **Bundle identifier** key and enter the Identifier that you created earlier; so in our example, com.sitepoint.startrackr. Note that we don't need to include the bundle seed. Now plug your phone into your computer, select **Device** from the drop-down in the top-left of Xcode, and hit **Build and Run**. Your application will now be running on your phone.

Android

Running your app on an Android phone is much easier. First, you need to enable USB debugging on your phone. This can be found under **Settings** > **Applications** > **Development**. Once you've enabled USB debugging, plug in your phone, and open your project in Eclipse. Right-click on the project name in the project explorer, and select **Properties**. Find the **Run/Debug Setting** section, and select your project; then click **Edit**. Click on the **Target** tab and select **Manual**. This will force Eclipse to ask you what device to load when you run the project.

Next, run the app, and you should see a dialog asking you to choose a connected device or one of your AVD emulators, as shown in Figure 8.4. When your phone is plugged in, you should see it in the top panel. Select it and hit **OK**. After a couple of seconds, your app should be running on the phone.

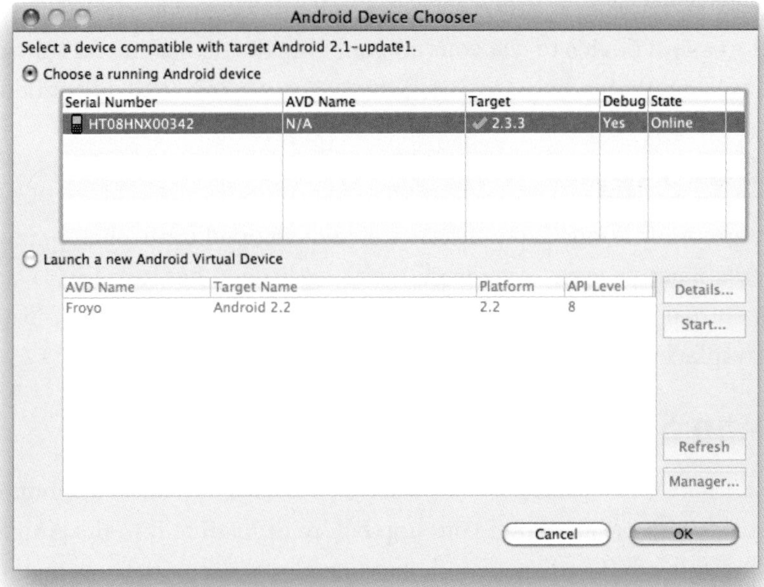

Figure 8.4. Choosing an Android device or emulator

BlackBerry

BlackBerry devices require code to be signed before you're able to load it up on real hardware. The process can take a couple of days, so don't leave it to the last moment before a deadline. Unlike the Apple process, registration is free; it does require a credit card to make sure you're a real person, but no charges will be made.

Go to https://www.blackberry.com/SignedKeys/ and fill in the form. Your keys will arrive in your email box with instructions on how to install them, so we'll skip covering that here.

Running the app on your phone is similar to running the app in the simulator, except that it's a slightly different command:

```
ant load-device
```

Now press the BlackBerry button on your phone and go to the downloads folder. You should see the app sitting there, itching to be run. Tap—and away she goes! After you enter your top secret, key-signing password, of course. If having to re-enter your password irritates you too much, you can save the key in the **project.properties** file by adding the following key:

```
sigtool.password=shhdonttellanyone
```

WebOS

WebOS is by far the easiest device to test your app on. Plug the device in and run `make`. If the phone is detected, it will run on that; otherwise, it will try to run on any available emulators.

Selling Your App

This is the final step in our PhoneGap journey: we've developed our web app, plugged it into the various SDKs to create native apps, enhanced it with additional hardware APIs, and tested it out on emulators and on real devices. Now it's time to show it to the world, by uploading it to the respective app marketplaces.

The Apple App Store

Just as you needed to create a developer certificate to test your app on your phone, you must have a distribution certificate in order to sign your app before uploading it to the App Store. Head over to http://developer.apple.com/ and log in with your developer account. Click on the **iOS Provisioning Portal**, find the **Distribution** section, and follow the how-to guide on **Obtaining Your iOS Distribution Certificate**.

Next, you need to create a provisioning profile, which is similar to the developer profile you created in Chapter 1. Click on the Provisioning link in the left menu; then click the Distribution tab. Select **App Store** as the distribution method, and give the profile a name. We recommend using the name of the app, as it makes it easy to identify down the track. Finally, select the application you wish to distribute from the drop-down menu. Hit the **Submit** button, and after a few moments, you should be able to download the new mobile profile. Once you've downloaded and installed it, jump back into Xcode, as we'll need to compile the code in a special way for distribution.

You may have noticed, while you were developing your application in Xcode, that there were two different build targets: Debug and Release. The Debug target includes a bunch of extra stuff that allows the remote debugger to work. Obviously this isn't required on a release version, so these extra bits are removed to make the app file a bit smaller. To publish our application, we need to clone the Release build target.

Open up the **Project** menu, and select **Edit Project Settings**, which should open up the project info screen. Select the **Configurations** tab, and choose **Release**. Click the **Duplicate** button, and call the new configuration "Distribution." You can now close this window.

Next, in the main project window, find the **Targets** group in the left-hand panel. Open it and double-click on the **startrackr** application. Select the **Build** tab, and choose **Distribution** from the **Configuration** drop-down menu. Find the **Code Signing** section, and select the correct distribution profile for this app in the **Any OS Device** menu (if everything was set up correctly, the right option should be in bold). Finally, open up the **Properties** tab and ensure that the **Identifier** field is set to the correct name (in our example, com.sitepoint.startrackr), and that a version number is set. The version number defaults to 1.0, which makes sense, but feel free to change it if it's unsuitable.

Now we just need to compile and package the code. In the main project window, select the distribution target from the drop-down menu, and then select **Build** from the **Build** menu. If all went well, your application is compiled and ready to be uploaded!

This is the point where you need to put on your marketing hat, and come up with some words and images that will be shown in iTunes. Go back to the developer portal, select the **iTunes Connect** link, and then click on **Manage Your Applications**. Click the **Add New App** button at the top of the screen and start filling in the application details.

First of all, you'll need to enter the full name of the application. This can be different from the name of the application that you're using on the home screen, and should be as descriptive as possible, as that's the first thing that potential customers will see. You'll be asked for the SKU number, which is a unique ID used to identify your application. Enter a unique number; for example, a shortened version of the app name, as that is the most obvious way of identifying it. Select the bundle ID that corresponds to the app you're submitting.

Next, you have to pick the all-important pricing point, and when you want the application to be released. Apple stops you from setting arbitrary prices; you'll have to pick one from the pricing matrix. Don't worry too much about getting the price point exactly right, as you can change it easily later on; you can even run sales to generate buzz. Remember that Apple takes 30% of the sale price, so if you're selling your app for 99¢, you'll only have 70¢ in your pocket.

Release Date

The release date is the date you request, or the date that the app is approved—whichever is later. So setting a release date for tomorrow won't result in a faster approval for your application!

Now it's time to channel your inner writer, and create a description for your application. You have 4,000 characters to tell customers why your app is awesome, and why they should buy it. Make the first sentence or two the most compelling, as that is what's displayed on the summary screen of iTunes (users have to click **more** to see the rest). Of course, you can tweak it later on, but try to create a bang for the release.

You need to select two categories that the app fits into, as well as a set of keywords that will help with search. Category selection is also very important, as many users will look for new apps using categories. Keyword selection is even more important, as they are unable to be changed without resubmitting your app and going through the approval process again.

The rest of the fields are straightforward, though you should pay special attention to the the reviewer notes field. You can leave additional notes for the reviewer here, including demo passwords or instructions on how to use the app. As a general rule, the easier it is for the reviewer to do their job, the more likely your app will be released in a timely manner.

Each app in iTunes has a content rating, ranging from 4—which means it's suitable for children and sensitive people who are easily offended—all the way up to 17+, which is only for adults. The rating is generated based on the options you select in the ratings matrix, although Apple will change it if they feel your rating is inappropriate.

The final piece of the marketing puzzle is your application icon and screenshots. You will need to create a 512×512px app icon that will be displayed in iTunes. Because you have a bit more space to play with, your images can have more detail that the home screen icon, so it's worthwhile designing an eye-catching image. You can also upload up to six screenshots of your app in action. The easiest way to do this is to load up your app on your phone, find the screen you want, and hit the Power and Home buttons at the same time. This will take a screenshot and save it in your photo gallery.

Once you've entered all the details, and you're happy with the preview, hit the **View Details** button, and the **Ready to Upload Binary** button to start the upload process. Xcode comes with a helper application called Application Loader, which is located at **/Developer/Applications/Utilities/Application Loader.app** (you should be able to find it using Spotlight). Open this up, enter your Apple developer username and password, and you should see your app in the drop-down list. Head over to Xcode, and select the **Products** folder in the left-hand panel. Control-click the **.app** file that was built, and select **Reveal in Finder**. Then control-click the **.app** file, and click **Compress**. Now drag the resulting **.zip** file onto the Application Loader icon. Hit the **Send** button, and it's all done! It's now in the hands of the Apple reviewers to approve the application for sale.

The Android Market

The Android Market requires the application to be signed using a certificate as well, although they'll happily accept a self-signed certificate. The details are on the Android website.[3]

Once your certificate is set up, you need to recompile your application for release. To do this, right-click on the application in the project explorer, and select **Export**. Pick **Android** > **Export Android Application.** If you haven't already created a keystore, you may need to create one now. The certificate requires an alias (simply, a short name), so use your company name. The Android Market requires that your certificate be valid for a long time—pick 100 years. Finish filling in the details, and save the **.apk** somewhere. It's this **.apk** file that you submit to the market.

Head over to http://market.android.com/publish and sign in with your Google account. You'll need to register as an Android developer, so fill in your details, and pay your registration fee. Once that's been approved (pretty much immediately), you're ready to upload your app.

---

[3] http://developer.android.com/guide/publishing/app-signing.html#cert

Select the release **.apk** file that you created, and add at least two screenshots of your application running. To take a screenshot in Android, you can either download a third-party app from the Android Market, or you can plug your device in via USB and then, in Eclipse, click **Window** > **Show View** > **Other**, and select **Android** > **Devices**. This will bring up a list of real devices and emulators that are currently running, and will allow you to take a screenshot (the icon looks like a little camera).

Now you need to upload a high-resolution application icon, 512×512px (coincidently the same size as the iOS version—convenient!). This will show up in the marketplace, so make it catchy! You can also upload two optional promotional graphics, and a video for publicity. We'd recommend you do this, as the more marketing material you can supply, the better chance you have of outshining the competition.

Next, you need to supply your 4,000-character description (again, it's the same as the iOS description, so feel free to cut and paste). You also have the opportunity to supply up to 80 characters of promotional text—so if you have a sharp, snappy strap line, drop it in here. Pick your application type (either game or application) and a category.

To sell your application, you need to click **Set up a Merchant Account at Google Checkout**. Select your content rating, and finally your price. Unlike the Apple store, you can pick an arbitrary price (between 99¢ and $200). What you *can't* do is change the price once you've selected it. If you do find you want to change the price later on, you have to upload a brand new **.apk** file.

The rest of the form is quite straightforward. Once you've filled it all in, hit **Publish** and you're all done!

BlackBerry App World

To submit an app to the BlackBerry store, you also need to become a BlackBerry vendor. This is separate from the developer licence that you already signed up for. Again, it can take a couple of days to be approved, and you'll need to prove your identity, either via a business registration certificate, or some personal ID. Once your application is approved, you can log in to https://appworld.blackberry.com/isvportal/.

To get started, click the **Manage Products** link, and then **Add Product**. Enter the name of the application, and give the application an SKU; for our example, let's give the application the name "Startrackr," and the SKU of "startrackr." Select a category and a licence type: you can choose from Free, Paid, or Try & Buy. Unlike some of the other app marketplaces, BlackBerry allows you to provide a trial version of your application that the user can upgrade if they like. If that sounds like the option for you, select Try & Buy.

Next, you can add the description of the application. The maximum for the BlackBerry App World is 4,000 characters. More cutting and pasting! At least the app marketplaces can agree on something.

Avoid becoming too blasé, though, as you'll have to do some image resizing; the large format icon in the Blackberry app marketplace is 480×480px, and the screenshots are 640×640px.

Just like many of the other app marketplaces, you can limit the distribution of your app to certain countries. Yet, what seems fairly unique to the BlackBerry is that you can choose which carriers you wish to limit your application to.

Once you've entered all the information, you're ready to prepare and upload your application for distribution. Click the plus symbol under the **Releases** column to add a binary. You'll need to tell BlackBerry if your application will support user-generated content, so that they can warn your users in case other users upload naughty pictures or rude words.

Next, fire up the command shell, change to your app's directory, and run:

```
ant build
```

This will create a a **build** directory that will house a ZIP file named after your application, as well as three directories: **OTAInstall**, **StandardInstall**, and **widget**. As we will be distributing this application via the marketplace, we'll use the **.cod** file in the **StandardInstall** directory.

Switch back to your web browser, and double-check the version number of the application. Add any release notes, and then hit **Add filebundle**. A new row will appear; fill in a name for this bundle. As an app release can contain different bundles for different devices, give each bundle a name that you'll be able to recognize easily later. Select your platform (in our case, **Smartphone**), and select the OS version we're targeting (remember that PhoneGap requires at least version 5). Next, select the devices you're targeting. This will depend on what you've tested your application on, and what screen sizes your app will work on. Finally, hit the **Add File** link, and select the **.cod** file in the **StandardInstall** directory. Once the file has uploaded and you have confirmed the upload, hit the **Next** button, and then the **Save** button.

Now the moment of truth. On the final screen, you can hit the **Submit Release for Approval** button, and your app will be presented to RIM for approval.

Palm App Catalog

To submit your apps to the webOS App Catalog, you'll need to create a webOS developer account (this one is free). Head over to https://developer.palm.com/ and click the **Sign Up** button; complete the registration. HP—which acquired Palm in 2010—pays developer commissions using PayPal, so make sure you have a PayPal account set up as well.

We need to package our app into an **.ipk** file, which is what we'll upload to HP. Your first task is to open up the **appinfo.json** file that is in the root of your application directory, and modify the details in there to match your application. You need to give the application a unique ID. HP recommends using a reverse domain (similar to bundle identifiers on iOS); for example, com.sitepoint.startrackr.

As this is the first time we've published this app, we can leave the version number as 1.0.0. Enter your company name in the vendor attribute, and enter the app name in the title attribute. For our Startrackr app, it might look similar to this:

```
{
  "id": "com.sitepoint.startrackr",
  "version": "1.0.01",
  "vendor": "Sitepoint",
  "type": "web",
  "main": "root.html",
  "title": "StarTrackr",
  "icon": "img/icon.png"
}
```

Next, in the command line, from the root of your application directory, run:

```
palm-package ./
```

This should create a filename that looks a little like this: **com.sitepoint.startrackr_1.0.0_all.ipk**. Your name might differ, depending on the options you set in **appinfo.json**.

Once that's all set up, click on the **My Apps** link at the top of the page, and click the **Upload** button. Select the **.ipk** you just created and hit **Next**. You now need to upload a small (48×48) and large (64×64) application logo, as well as a company logo that will be used for marketing purposes.

Select the minimum OS version the app can run on; for most apps, 1.0.0 should be fine. Then pick your distribution method. Palm offers a beta mode, which can be useful if you want to have users try out your software before releasing it. If you're happy with the state of your app, select **App Catalog**.

Next, you need to pick if the app is free or paid. HP allows you to set an arbitrary price; you set it in US dollars, and it will automatically convert it to other currencies for you. Put your desired price in the **Set the Price** section, and hit **Generate Prices**.

Now you can enter your marketing spiel. This time you only have 2,000 characters to play with for your description, so you may have to edit down the description you used for iOS or Android. You can also enter much shorter strap lines of 50 and 25 characters, for that extra bit of high-impact punch. HP requires at least three screenshots, and will allow you to upload a YouTube video also. To take a screenshot on a webOS device, hit the Orange, Sym, and P keys together—the screenshot will appear in the Photos application under **screencaptures**.

Enter in your support details. If any of your users experience any problems, this is how they'll reach you.

The last three screens of the wizard are fairly straightforward: select your tax category, enter any legal details, double-check your app against the supplied checklist, and add any notes that might be important to the reviewer (like demo logins). Once you're happy, hit the **Submit** button and you're all done!

Time for Celebration

We've just turned our humble little web app into a real native app! As you've seen, PhoneGap provides a simple way to deploy a single codebase across all the major mobile platforms, and gives you access to the marketplaces and a potential extra source of revenue. PhoneGap won't be the appropriate tool for every project—sometimes a mobile website is all you need, and sometimes a web app can better serve your ends—but it's good to have the option.

Throughout this book, we've gone from learning the concepts of designing for mobile devices, adapting our traditional websites to look and perform better, adding application-like functionality, and finally bundling it up as a real deal native app. While the exact choices you make will depend on the specifics of the project, we hope we've provided you with the tools to enter this new era of web design with a competitive edge. Go on now, build something cool!

Appendix A: Running a Server for Testing

We've spoken about how you can test your mobile site in a normal desktop browser without a server, by loading your HTML using the file:// protocol. Sometimes, however, it can be quicker—and in the case of Ajax, essential—to test a site on a real device via a server. Of course, this requires a server.

If you've been developing for the Web for some time, you may already have access to a development server, in which case just throw your files on that as you would for any other website. Don't worry if you have no development server, though, as there are a number of simple ways to serve up the files from your local machine to your device, as long as they're on the same WiFi network.

But before you can do that, you'll need to find your IP address. In Linux and OS X, open up a terminal, and type:

```
ifconfig
```

Your network device will probably be called something like `eth0` on Linux, or `iw0` on OS X—take note of the IP address allocated to it.

On Windows, open up **cmd.exe** and type:

```
ipconfig
```

Find your network card, and note down the IP address. In the following examples, we'll assume that your IP address is 192.168.0.1. Just replace that number with your own IP address when accessing the server.

Using Python

Both OS X and Ubuntu come with Python installed by default, and include a super-simple web server module called SimpleHTTPServer, which you can call from the command line. To run it, change into the directory that has your website's **index.html**, and run:

```
python -m SimpleHTTPServer
```

The server will start on port 8000, so you can access it at http://*192.168.0.1*:8000. Just point your phone's browser to that address, and *voilà*, your site is there!

Using Ruby

If you have Ruby installed, you can install the adsf (A Dead Simple Fileserver) gem, by running:

```
gem install adsf
```

Then, in the directory that houses **index.html**, run:

```
adsf
```

This server runs on port 3000, so point your browser to http://192.168.0.1:3000.

Built-in Servers

While the Python and Ruby methods are the quickest way to serve up your site, they do rely on having Ruby or Python installed (which you may be without, especially if you're a Windows user), so you may need to use a "real" web server.

Built-in Servers: IIS on Windows

Windows Vista and Windows 7 can both run versions of the IIS web server. To install it, open the Control Panel and choose **Programs and Features**; then select **Turn Windows features on or off** from the left column. Next, select **Internet Information Services**, and click **OK**. This will install IIS. After that, you need to set up a site.

Again from the Control Panel, select **Administrative Tools**, then **Internet Information Services (IIS) Manager**. The easiest way to get things running is to create a project directory inside **C:\Inetpub\wwwroot**, and then point your browser at that directory: http://192.168.0.1/*startrackr*.

Built-in Servers: Apache on Linux

Apache is arguably the most popular web server for Linux, so we'll set that up. Under Ubuntu, run:

```
sudo apt-get install apache
```

Start the server up by typing:

```
sudo apachectl start
```

It will automatically start when you first install it, so you'll only need to do it after you reboot your computer.

Again, to keep it simple, we'll create a directory inside **/var/www**. First, add yourself to the `www-data` group, so that you can edit files in the **/var/www** directory:

```
sudo gpasswd -a username www-data
```

Then create and set the permissions of the directory:

```
sudo mkdir /var/www/startrackr
sudo chgrp www-data /var/www/startrackr
sudo chmod g+w /var/www/startrackr
```

Copy your project files over, and point your browser at http://192.168.0.1/startrackr.

Now you're all ready to test your mobile app to your heart's content!

Index

Symbols

A

B

C

D

E

F

I

J

K

L

M

N

O

P

Q

R

S

T

U

V

W

X

Z